ORGANISE, EDUCATE, CONTROL

About the Editors

Andrew Reeves is currently a Professorial Fellow at Charles Darwin University and Deakin University where he works on collaborative research and cultural projects. A historian by training, he worked for many years in Australian museums and more recently as a senior advisor to Senator Kim Carr, then Minister for Innovation, Industry, Science and Research. He has published widely in the fields of labour and industrial history and material culture studies. Co-author, with Anne Stephen, of *Badges of Labour, Banner of Pride*, a pioneering study of the place of banners and celebration in the Australian labour movement, his most recent book is a history of the mineworkers in Victoria's black coal industry, *Up from the Underworld: Mineworkers and Community in Wonthaggi, 1909–1968*.

Andrew Dettmer is National President of the AMWU. He has held that position since mid 2012. Prior to this he was Queensland and Northern Territory State Secretary of the union from 2003 and was a Federal Industrial Officer of ADSTE from 1988. He has been involved in the labour movement and the Australian Labor Party for over 30 years. Originally from Victoria, he has recently moved back there from Queensland to undertake his duties as National President. Andrew has a lifelong interest in labour and trade union history, and holds an Honours degree in history from Monash University.

ORGANISE

EDUCATE

CONTROL

The AMWU in Australia 1852-2012

EDITED BY ANDREW REEVES AND ANDREW DETTMER

MONASH University
Publishing

Monash University Publishing
Building 4, Monash University
Clayton, Victoria 3800, Australia

www.publishing.monash.edu

Monash University Publishing brings to the world publications which advance the best traditions of humane and enlightened thought.

Monash University Publishing titles pass through a rigorous process of independent peer review.

National Library of Australia Cataloguing-in-Publication entry:

Authors: Reeves, Andrew, editor; Dettmer, Andrew, editor.

Title: Organise, educate, control : the AMWU in Australia, 1852-2012 / edited by Andrew Reeves and Andrew Dettmer.

ISBN: 9781922235008 (paperback)

Subjects: Australian Manufacturing Workers Union--History; Labor unions--Australia--History; Labor--History; Australia--Social conditions.

Dewey Number: 331.880994

www.publishing.monash.edu/books/oec-9781922235008.html

Series: Australian History

Design: Les Thomas

Printed in Australia by Griffin Press an Accredited ISO AS/NZS 14001:2004 Environmental Management System printer.

The paper this book is printed on is certified against the Forest Stewardship Council ® Standards. Griffin Press holds FSC chain of custody certification SGS-COC-005088. FSC promotes environmentally responsible, socially beneficial and economically viable management of the world's forests.

Contents

Part 1: AMWU Politics

Part 2: AMWU People

Foreword

I have been a proud member of the Australian Manufacturing Workers Union since 1959, when, at the time, my application was witnessed by the General Secretary of the Sheet Metal Working, Agricultural Implement and Stovemaking Industrial Union of Australia, Albert McNaulty.

My joining of the union arose from the fact that as the new advocate of the ACTU about to argue national wage cases based on the Metal Trades Award, I did not have to seek leave to appear before the Arbitration Tribunal if I was a member of the union party to that award. On receiving this advice, I joined the Sheeties, with gusto, as a research officer.

Out of respect for and involvement in the union movement, I have kept my membership ever since. I was particularly proud when, at the 2010 AMWU National Conference, I was honoured with the conferring of Honorary Life Membership, reflecting my 50 year plus membership.

The AMWU has been prosecuting the interests of its members for the past 160 years. Its longevity and many achievements are due to successive strong leadership over this period and to the fighting spirit and dedication of its membership committed to lifting the standard of working conditions for all workers of our nation.

Our union has a glorious history, and may it extend into the future.

I send best wishes to all members.

— Bob Hawke

The Honourable RJ Hawke, AC, was Prime Minister of Australia from 1983 to 1991, having previously served as President of the Australian Council of Trade Unions from 1970 to 1980.

Preface

The AMWU in all its previous manifestations has a diverse, vibrant and rich history. As the name suggests, since our formation from 1852 we are an amalgamation of many unions such as the Typewriter Mechanics Union, the Female Confectioners Union (referred to in these pages) and the Shipwrights, my original union. However it is the more recent amalgamations, commencing with the amalgamation of the Amalgamated Metal Workers Union and the Association of Draughting, Supervisory and Technical Employees in 1991 through to the PKIU in 1995, which created today's AMWU, covering workers across the whole spectrum of manufacturing.

The common thread that runs through our history of amalgamations was the recognition by members and leaders of the need to build a stronger and more effective voice for working people.

Over our 160 year history our union has faced many challenges and threats. As this book goes to print, our members, the current custodians of this great union, must confront the challenges of our time.

Manufacturing in Australia is under stress as never before. Our union needs to rise to the challenge. The high Australian dollar, the introduction of free trade agreements which neither benefit Australian workers nor lift the rights of workers in developing countries, the mediocrity of many Australian managers, continuing attacks by conservative politicians on our right to organise. All of these challenges must be met if we are to succeed in our historic mission of representing the manufacturing workers of Australia.

But it is from our great history that we can draw our strength. It is a history that reminds us all of the struggles and sacrifices of the past, the courage and the innovative ways by which members of the AMWU have contributed to the development not just of their own lot but of Australian society.

I congratulate all those associated with this project, particularly those who have written from the aspect of the shop floor.

— Paul Bastian

Paul Bastian is the National Secretary of the Australian Manufacturing Workers Union, having previously served as National President from 2009 to 2012 and NSW State Secretary from 1997 to 2009.

Introduction

The Australian Manufacturing Workers Union, or AMWU, can trace its origins back to the earliest years of Australian trade unionism. Many date its establishment to the first meeting of the Sydney branch of the Amalgamated Society of Engineers, held on the immigrant vessel *Frances Walker* in Sydney Harbour in October 1852. Although we do know of even earlier efforts at union organisation, most notably in the printing industry, these attempts collapsed amid the economic dislocation that followed the discovery of gold in New South Wales and Victoria after 1851. As a consequence, 1852 is the year from which we date an uninterrupted presence of AMWU unions in Australia.

The AMWU is a large and complex organisation. Over the past century and a half, it has incorporated more than 40 unions, welding them today into a national union of more than 100,000 members.

This history reflects the achievements of the union since the 1850s, and it does not shy away from the challenges and controversies of these years, including references to activities during peace and war, to the role and place of women in the labour movement, and the many industrial campaigns and strikes the union has led to further the wellbeing of working Australians. This book does not attempt a comprehensive history of the AMWU, but rather it is a set of essays, stories and interviews that seek to reflect the diversity of the union and its members.

In the first essay, Nikki Balnave and Greg Patmore detail the industrial influence of the AMWU since the middle of the nineteenth century. They argue that there has been a continuity of militancy and political sophistication in the way the union has acted in the workplace and the community. Amid a number of themes, they demonstrate that the scepticism about politics and politicians held by modern workers is nothing new.

Others provide more detailed case studies that reflect this line of argument. Andrew Dettmer analyses the process by which the first of the 1990s amalgamations, that between the Amalgamated Metal Workers Union and Association of Draughting, Supervisory and Technical Employees, took place in 1991, while Bobbie Oliver evaluates the impact of an earlier phase of union amalgamation in Western Australia (WA). Keir Reeves writes about the young engineers movement that flourished in Melbourne in the 1930s and 1940s, while Cathy Brigden deals with an exceptional union experiment in Australia – the all-women Female Confectioners Union. Andrew Reeves, in a change of pace, discusses the importance and role of the banners of the union and their place in its industrial and political campaigning. Andrew Scott, a former AMWU research officer now at Deakin University, writes about one of the most important (and neglected) union documents of the late twentieth century: *Australia Reconstructed.*

In a rare interview, Laurie Carmichael reflects on his nearly 70 years as an AMWU member, activist and leader, focusing principally on the shorter hours campaigns of the late 1970s and early 1980s. Robyn McQueeney has interviewed three current AMWU women activists in Tasmania and demonstrates the continuing pressures on women as union delegates and leaders. Cora Trevarthen uses the reminiscences of a legendary AMWU organiser, Fred Thompson, to tell something of his story and his influence on Australian unionism in Far North Queensland and the Northern Territory to the time of his death in 2011. Glenys Lindner concentrates on the experiences of an AMWU union family at the Risdon zinc refinery in Hobart, while Ric McCracken has provided us with an account of the rich working culture of metalworkers at the Midland Railway Workshops in Perth. John Hempseed and Chris Harper, the president and secretary respectively of the Queensland Coal Shop Stewards (QCSS), have contributed a detailed account of the QCSS since its formation in 1974. They stress the challenges the union has faced in the coal industry since that time.

As said previously, the histories of the union contained in this volume do not claim to be comprehensive. What they do succeed in doing is to demonstrate the close links with and the enduring influence of the union on the development of the society in which it has existed for more than 160 years.

The editors hope that this volume can serve as a spur to action, encouraging you as readers to be as active as those many members, past and present, described in these pages. These episodes of the union's history did not happen by accident. Instead, they occurred in the context of collective action and a shared understanding of the nature of the relationship between labour and capital; in other words, the only way forward for working people is through the exercise of their collective strength and their ability to influence and assert the rights of labour.

We wish to thank all the contributors to this book. A large number of suggestions and contributions were received, but unfortunately not all could be fitted into this volume. We do, though, wish to thank all who have given generously in both time and effort, as well as the many officials and staff of the union who have assisted with the realisation of this project, particularly: John Short, Secretary of the Tasmanian Branch; Peter Cozens, National Executive Officer; Alison Chalk, Executive Assistant to the National President; and the staff of the Rockhampton office of the union.

— Andrew Reeves and Andrew Dettmer, Melbourne, January 2013.

List of Abbreviations

Amalgamated Engineering Union (AEU)

Amalgamated Metal Workers and Shipwrights Union (AMWSU)

Amalgamated Metal Workers Union (AMWU)

Amalgamated Metals, Foundry and Shipwrights Union (AMFSU)

Amalgamated Society of Engineers (ASE)

Association of Architects, Engineers, Surveyors and Draughtsmen of Australia (AAESDA)

Association of Draughting, Supervisory and Technical Employees (ADSTE)

Australian Association of Draughtsmen (AAD)

Australasian Council of Trade Unions, later Australian Council of Trade Unions (ACTU)

Australasian Society of Engineers, Moulders & Foundry Workers Union (ASEM&FWU)

Australian Council of Salaried and Professional Associations (ACSPA)

Australian Industrial Relations Commission (AIRC)

Australian Labor Party (ALP)

Australian Manufacturing Workers Union (AMWU)

Australian Workers Union (AWU)

Australian Workplace Agreements (AWAs)

Boilermakers and Blacksmiths Society (BBS)

Carlton Apprentices Committee (CAC)

Communist Party of Australia (CPA)

Construction, Forestry & Mining Employees Union (CFMEU)

Electrical Trades Union (ETU)

Electrolytic Zinc Company (EZ)

Eureka Youth League (EYL)

Federated Engine Drivers and Firemen's Association (FEDFA)

Industrial Commission (IC)

League of Young Democrats (LYD)

Maritime Union of Australia (MUA)

Maritime Workers Union of WA (MWU)

Melbourne Trades and Labour Council (MTLC)

Melbourne Typographical Society (MTS)

Metal Trades Employers Association (MTEA)

Metal Trades Federation of Unions (MTFU)
Printing and Kindred Industries Union (PKIU)
Queensland Coal Shop Stewards (QCSS)
Queensland Colliery Employees Union (Miners Federation, Queensland
    Branch) (QCEU)
Queensland Trades and Labour Council (QTLC)
Sheet Metal Workers Union (the SMWU)
Trade Development Council (TDC)
Trades Hall Council (THC)
United Mineworkers Federation of Australia (UMFA)
Vehicle Builders Employees Federation (VBEF)
Victorian Manufacturing Confectioners Association (VMCA)
Waterside Workers Federation (WWF)
Western Australian Government Railways (WAGR)
Women's Employment Board (WEB)

PART 1
AMWU POLITICS

Chapter 1

The AMWU

Politics and Industrial Relations, 1852–2012[1]

Nikki Balnave and Greg Patmore

This chapter explores the political and industrial relations strategies of the AMWU from its Australian origins in 1852 until the present. It will primarily focus on the history of the Amalgamated Society of Engineers (ASE), later the Amalgamated Engineering Union (AEU), prior to its amalgamation with other metal industry unions to form the AMWU in 1973.

We focus on three periods: first, 1852 to 1891, before the establishment of the Labor Party and the compulsory arbitration system; second, we examine the strategies of the union from 1891 to 1973, when 'labourism' dominated the Australian labour movement, emphasising compulsory arbitration, political action through the Labor Party, tariffs and the White Australia Policy; third, we conclude with an overview of developments since 1973, which have seen the dismantling of many traditional tenets of labourism, particularly compulsory arbitration and tariff protection.

1852–1891

The early years of the unions that later merged to form the AMWU occurred against the background of rapid growth in Australia's white population and cities. The gold rushes of the 1850s trebled Australia's population. By 1860 there were 1,145,585 whites in Australia, and this figure trebled again over the next three decades to 3,022,000 by 1891. A substantial proportion of Australians lived in cities and towns. In 1851 the population of Melbourne and Sydney was 29,000 and 54,000, respectively. By 1891 these figures were 473,000 and 400,000. Forty-one per cent of Victorians and 35 per cent of

---

[1] Our thanks to Andrew Dettmer for reading the draft and providing welcome comments.

the residents of New South Wales (NSW) lived in their capital cities by 1891.[2]

The Australian economy expanded. The wealth generated by the gold rushes laid the foundations of a 'long boom' from 1860 to 1890. Gross Domestic Product (GDP) increased from £53.4 million in 1861 to £211.6 million in 1891 (1911 constant prices). Economic growth did slacken in the 1880s, and there were minor recessions in 1863, 1871, 1879 and 1886. Economic conditions also varied between the colonies. While Victoria experienced a recession from 1863 to 1866, there was an economic boom in Queensland. In South Australia (SA) the 'long boom' ended in 1882, with emigration exceeding immigration continuously from 1885 to 1889.[3]

Manufacturing expanded rapidly during this period, but continued to serve the needs of a growing domestic economy rather than export markets. It is estimated that between 1861 and 1890 this sector more than doubled its share of GDP. The colony of Victoria was the largest manufacturer. Victorian factory employment increased from 5340 in 1861 to 58,639 in 1890–91. Overall, Australian factory employment grew from 10,800 in 1851 to 149,200 in 1890–91.

The important industries that dominated manufacturing were: metal-working and engineering; clothing and footwear; building materials; and food, drink and tobacco processing. Factories were unsophisticated and small. However, the average size of the workforce per factory increased during this period – in Victoria from 10.8 persons in 1871 to 17.6 persons in 1891. There were some large-scale enterprises. In Sydney, the engineering firm P.N. Russell employed 300 to 400 workers by the late 1860s, while Morts Dock employed 1000 workers in March 1886. By April 1891 Australian manufacturing employed 16.5 per cent of the workforce.

But in the metal trades, employment was unstable. The availability of work depended upon the season and the winning of short-term government and private contracts. The failure of imported parts and machinery to arrive at crucial points in the production process could severely disrupt output. An important source of labour for the metal trades was immigration.[4]

Immigrants on the *Francis Walker* bound for Sydney from Britain in 1852 would form the first Australian branch of the ASE. An estimated 40 per cent of the members of the Australian branches of the ASE between

2   Patmore, G 1991, *Australian Labour History*, Longman Cheshire, Melbourne, p. 42.

3   Patmore, G 1991, *Australian Labour History*, p. 42.

4   Patmore, G 1991, *Australian Labour History*, pp. 46–8, 53–4.

1856 and 1889 received their initial union experience in Britain. The ASE, which covered fitters, turners, patternmakers and smiths in the metal trades, had its headquarters in London. The union unilaterally set wages and conditions, and withdrew its members from establishments where employers refused to comply. It controlled labour supply by insisting on an indentured apprenticeship of between five and seven years, and maintained a strict ratio of apprentices to journeymen (qualified tradespeople). Australian employers found it very difficult to substitute cheaper labour for these trades because of the skills involved.

The union provided significant benefits for illness, unemployment, retirement and funerals. These benefits were attractive in a society where there was no welfare state. However, it required members to pay high subscription rates. These benefits also played an important industrial role. The union could deny them to members who did not observe union policy. Unemployment benefits discouraged distressed members from seeking work at less than union rates. By 1891 the union had branches in every colony except WA and comprised 2515 members.[5]

Another significant union that was to play an important role in the history of the AMWU was the Boilermakers. The United Society of Boilermakers and Iron Shipbuilders of New South Wales were formed in 1873 and JT McGowen, later to become the first Labor Premier of NSW, was its secretary intermittently from 1874 to 1890. A branch of the Boilermakers Society was formed in Newcastle in 1877. Like the ASE the Boilermakers were concerned with enforcing a standard pay rate, and the union tried to ensure that there was a closed shop with all boilermakers being members of the union.[6]

There were problems for the ASE and the Boilermakers in ensuring complete control of the trades they covered. The differential between the wages of the skilled and the unskilled was more compressed than in Britain. Australian skilled workers did not enforce the indentured apprenticeship as rigidly as their British counterparts. But at the same time the opportunities for upward social mobility were declining. During the 1870s and 1880s

[5] Patmore, G 1991, *Australian Labour History*, pp. 56–57; Shields, J 1995, 'Deskilling Revisited: Continuity and Change in Craft Work and Apprenticeship in Late Nineteenth Century New South Wales', *Labour History* 68, p. 19.

[6] Nairn, B 'McGowen, James Sinclair (1855–1922)', *Australian Dictionary of Biography*, National Centre of Biography, Australian National University, available at http://adb. anu.edu.au/biography/mcgowen-james-sinclair-7360/text12785, accessed 12 September 2012; Robinson, G 1977, *One Hundred Years History. A History of the Newcastle Branch of the Boilermakers Society of Australia 1877–1977*, Sydney, AMWSU, pp. 2–3.

technological change and productive reorganisation challenged existing work practices. It has been estimated that the ASE never enrolled more than half its potential membership until the 1880s. Similarly, the Boilermakers could not always obtain a closed shop; in May 1882, in the Redfern locomotive workshops in Sydney, they were unsuccessful after management threatened to dismiss and blacklist all boilermakers who went on strike over the issue.[7]

The ASE and the Boilermakers also showed a strong interest in broadening the labour movement. The ASE provided donations to other unions that were on strike, and affiliated to local trades and labour councils. The Sydney and Adelaide branches of the ASE affiliated to their local trades and labour councils, when they were established in 1871 and 1884 respectively. The Boilermakers undertook similar actions, with their Newcastle branch donating £10 to support fellow workers during the 1890 maritime strike and imposing a levy on its members to support the strike fund. It also participated in a demonstration to support the strikers.[8]

1891–1973

The Australian economy performed badly during the 1890s and the early years of the twentieth century. There was a severe depression in the 1890s; unemployment reached an estimated peak of 28.3 per cent in Victoria in 1893. Unions tried to defend their position in a series of unsuccessful strikes, and tensions heightened between capital and labour. While there was a brief return to prosperity in 1900 to 1901, drought prolonged the stagnation of the economy until 1906. After this there was strong economic growth, which culminated in a boom between 1909 and 1913. There was a continuing trend towards market concentration and large-scale production in particular industries. While there were 12,000 establishments in manufacturing employing less than 20 persons each by 1913, there were 580 that employed more than 100. These larger enterprises employed 41 per cent of the manufacturing workforce.[9]

---

[7] Patmore, G 1985, *A History of Industrial Relations in the NSW Government Railways*, PhD thesis, The University of Sydney, pp. 415–417; Patmore, G 1991, *Australian Labour History*, p. 67.

[8] Buckley, K 1970, *The Amalgamated Engineers in Australia, 1852–1920*, Australian National University, Canberra, pp. 104–105; Markey, R *In Case of Oppression. The Life and Times of the Labour Council of New South Wales*, Pluto Press, Sydney, p. 16; Robinson, G 1977, *One Hundred Years History*, p. 5.

[9] Patmore, G 1991, *Australian Labour History*, pp. 141–142.

State intervention increased during this period. SA and Victoria had tariffs before federation in 1901, while NSW gave preference to local industry in government contracts. Federation established a unified national market, with uniform tariff protection against overseas competition effectively beginning with the 'Lyne Tariff' of 1908.[10] Historian Ray Markey argues that 'Australian employers favoured tariff protection rather than modernisation as a means of off-setting relatively high labour costs'.[11]

The state regulation of industrial relations also spread through compulsory arbitration and wages boards prior to the First World War. The 1890s depression and the employers' victories in the major strikes between 1890 and 1894 forced the weakened unions to drop their hostility to the state and support arbitration legislation. While Ray Markey has highlighted the opposition of socialists and some unions, and the continued suspicion of the class origins of lawyers and judges within the labour movement, the majority of trade unions in NSW did opt for state arbitration by 1900. The Labor Party became an important instrument for the unions to shape the form and content of compulsory arbitration and other industrial legislation.[12]

State intervention in Australian industrial relations finally took two forms: the compulsory conciliation and arbitration system, and the wages boards system. Compulsory arbitration involved permanent state tribunals with the power to settle disputes and enforce their decisions. There were provisions for the registration of unions, which brought grievances to the tribunals on behalf of workers. Both unions and employers could unilaterally bring the other party before the tribunal. Wages boards consisted of an equal number of employer and employee representatives and a chairman. There was usually no system of registration and a wages board could periodically review the minimum wages and conditions without a dispute. Despite these differences, the chairman could compulsorily determine the outcome if the board was deadlocked. There were industrial jurisdictions at both federal and state government levels.[13]

Australian workers formed a Labor Party in the 1890s. Prior to the 1890 maritime strike many unionists were reluctant to support the direct representation of labour in parliament. Victorian unionists supported the

---

[10]   Patmore, G 1991, p. 142.

[11]   Markey, R 1988, 'The Aristocracy of Labour and Productive Reorganisation in NSW, c. 1880–1900', *Australian Economic History Review*, vol. xxviii, no. 1, p. 54.

[12]   Markey, R 1988, *The Making of the Labor Party in NSW 1880–1900*, University of NSW Press, Sydney, pp. 268–281; Patmore, G 1991, *Australian Labour History*, p. 102.

[13]   Patmore, G 1991, *Australian Labour History*, p. 104.

liberal protectionists, and the non-payment of parliamentarians was an impediment during most of the period. Many unionists accepted the idea that parliaments were independent and not subject to any interests. They believed that political discussions would weaken industrial action by dividing unionists. There was also the orthodox economic doctrine, which held that the laws of supply and demand rather than parliamentary action determined wages and conditions. The unsuccessful experiment by the NSW Trade and Labour Council with political representation during the mid 1870s reinforced these views.[14]

These views were challenged in the 1880s. The reorganisation of work fuelled discontent against employers. There were new ideas questioning capitalism that came from the United Kingdom (UK) and United States (US). Henry George, Edward Bellamy, Karl Marx, William Morris and Laurence Gronlund inspired locals to form groups to debate radical ideas.[15]

In 1889 and 1890 trade unions moved to form a Labor Party. The Intercolonial Trades Union Congress at Hobart in 1889 unanimously called for the direct representation of the working classes in parliament. In January 1890 the NSW Trades and Labour Council endorsed a plan for candidates to stand at the next general election. It approved an election platform in 1890. There were several factors that prompted the council's action – the introduction of the payment of parliamentarians in 1889, the end of classless legislature through divisions over protection and free trade, the growth of affiliation to the Labour Council, and the failure of trade unions to achieve several major legislative goals through traditional means. While most affiliates were unenthusiastic, the first steps towards a Labor Party had been taken before the commencement of the maritime strike in August 1890.[16]

The defeat of the unions in the maritime strike and subsequent strikes during the 1890s reinforced the push towards the formation of a Labor Party. The aggressive actions of colonial governments in trying to break the 1890 maritime strike highlighted the need to ensure that sympathetic governments were elected to parliament. Unionists accused the various governments of assisting the maritime employers by providing police, special constables and even the military to protect strike breakers. Labor representatives had to win seats to counter the employers' influence in parliament.

---

[14] Patmore, G 1991, *Australian Labour History*, p. 64.

[15] Patmore, G 1991, *Australian Labour History*.

[16] Patmore, G 1991, *Australian Labour History*, pp. 64–65.

The fortunes of the early Labor Parties varied across Australia. The Labor Party in NSW held the balance of power in the Legislative Assembly between July 1895 and August 1904, while Queensland briefly saw the formation of the world's first ever Labor government in 1899. By contrast, while the Melbourne Trades Hall Council formed a Labor Party in May 1891, it had to revive it four more times over the next 11 years. The Labor Party won majority government in the Commonwealth, NSW and SA parliaments for the first time in 1910.[17]

In general, the ASE was reluctant at first to support either state intervention into industrial relations or the Labor Party. Its skilled workers saw little need for a Labor Party, and some saw their interests more closely aligned with liberal middle-class reformers such as CC Kingston in SA. An ASE member was elected to the Victorian Parliament in 1900 as a Liberal, and yet received financial support from the Melbourne District of the ASE. There were ASE members active in the early Labor Party such as DM Charleston, who successfully stood as United Labor Party candidate for the SA Legislative Council in 1891. Ken Buckley notes that from 1903 there was a 'decided movement of opinion' towards the Labor Party in Australia. R Howe, the Secretary of the Sydney District Committee of the ASE, won the Sydney seat of Dalley in NSW in 1910; he was funded by an ASE levy.[18]

The ASE, due to its industrial strength, also showed a limited interest in taking advantage of conciliation and arbitration. It did register under the NSW Industrial Arbitration Act of 1901 and the WA legislation in 1902. There was also recognition of the value of registering collective bargaining agreements with the arbitration court, as happened when the Fremantle and Perth branches of the union entered into an agreement with the WA Railway Commissioners in 1904. The ASE in NSW obtained its first award in 1908. The compulsory arbitration system proved to have benefits for the ASE and other metalworkers unions. It stimulated the growth of union membership particularly if the award was made a 'common rule', so that it covered all workers in the industry. It provided a means of removing substandard conditions in certain firms. One negative for the ASE and other skilled labour was that arbitration narrowed the differential between skilled and unskilled workers. This was compensated to some degree by obtaining

---

[17] Patmore, G 1991, *Australian Labour History*, pp. 65, 74–81
[18] Buckley, K 1970, *The Amalgamated Engineers*, pp. 142–147.

over-award wages through bargaining directly with the employer at the workplace, which depended on the industrial strength of the union.[19]

From 1914 onwards ASE members grew increasingly militant against the background of the First World War, which saw a serious dislocation of the Australian economy. Inflation undermined real wages, and unemployment among trade unionists almost doubled during 1914. In the early months of the war industrial tribunals exacerbated the decline in real wages by refusing to hear claims or calling for wages to be held at pre-war levels due to the national emergency. While unions did not initially oppose the war and many unionists enlisted, there was growing discontent over inflation. Unionists believed that producers were profiteering from the war. There was a growing influence of socialists within the ASE, with WP Earsman, a member of the Melbourne District Committee and later foundation secretary of the Communist Party of Australia, advocating syndicalism, with its belief in the General Strike. Readers of the union's *Monthly Report* also began to see the language of class-struggle enter the journal's pages.[20]

Employers fuelled this discontent by trying to weaken the control of the ASE and other skilled workers over the production process, both before and during the First World War, by implementing new production techniques and technology, such as high-speed steel and semi-automatic machines. A small number of firms also showed an interest in implementing elements of scientific management, or 'Taylorism'. At the newly established Commonwealth Small Arms Factory in Lithgow, opened in 1912, the union fought a continual battle with management to stop semi-skilled machine operators being introduced into the tool room. Early in 1914, ASE members stopped John Danks & Son, a brass manufacturer in Melbourne, timing jobs after the union threatened to strike.

As early as 1915, the NSW Government Railways management began timing jobs in the railway workshops. Management also experimented with card systems, which involved the transference of the work recording function from the individual worker to the supervisor. A major strike commenced on 2 August 1917 against the introduction of a card system into the railway and tramway workshops. The ASE strongly opposed the card

---

19   Buckley, K 1970, pp. 148–152, 168–169, 173.
20   Buckley, K 1970, *The Amalgamated Engineers*, pp. 219–220, 224; Patmore, G 1991, *Australian Labour History*, p. 83; Turner, A 'Earsman, William Paisley (1884–1965)', Australian Dictionary of Biography, National Centre of Biography, Australian National University, available at http://adb.anu.edu.au/biography/earsman-william-paisley-6079/text10411, accessed 26 November 2012.

system, considering it to be a 'speed up' method and claiming that it broke a promise that working conditions would not be altered while the Empire was at war. Other railway and tramway workers such as engine drivers and guards supported the workshop employees, and the strike went beyond the railways and tramways. It involved 76,000 NSW workers or one-third of all NSW unionists. The strike ended in a defeat after several weeks, with all ASE branch officials and shop stewards, who joined the strike, with the exception of one, being dismissed.[21]

The defeat of the 1917 General Strike, combined with the split in the Labor Party over the issue of conscription, and broader international events such as the Russian Revolution, encouraged Australian trade unions to examine their political and industrial role. The ASE began to strengthen its national organisation and move towards autonomy from its UK parent. The Commonwealth Council (CC), a full-time executive, succeeded the part-time Australasian Council in January 1917. Following a series of mergers in the UK the ASE became the AEU on 1 July 1920. In Australia the AEU had 16,562 members, seven full-time organisers and 98 branches. The AEU secured its first federal award in May 1921, which included a 44-hour week and fixed a ratio of one apprentice for each three tradesmen. There was a push for the AEU to gain autonomy from the British parent union with a vote of Australian members in 1922 supporting the proposition by 3912 votes to 3809. While the CC supported the ballot result, it was overturned when the London-based AEU Final Appeal Court upheld an appeal against apprentices participating in the ballot. The failure to obtain autonomy limited the possibility of mergers with other unions such as the Boilermakers, as they would be required to surrender their identity in any amalgamation. Such amalgamations, as existed, were limited to small unions such as the Melbourne Cycle Trades Union in 1923.[22]

One of the major issues confronting the AEU during the 1920s was the 44-hour week. Employers successfully appealed against this provision in the federal award, and the 48-hour week was restored in September 1922. The union turned to state Labor governments for assistance. The Queensland

[21] Buckley, K 1970, *The Amalgamated Engineers*, p. 271; Patmore, G 1994, 'American Hustling Methods – The Lithgow Small Arms Factory 1912–1922', *Labour History*, no. 67, pp. 42–56; Patmore, G 1991, *Australian Labour History*, pp. 144, 148; Patmore, G 1985, 'A History of Industrial Relations', pp. 342–350.

[22] Amalgamated Engineering Union (AEU) 1946, *Souvenir. 25th Anniversary History*, AEU, Sydney, 1946, pp. 28, 89; Sheridan, T. 1975, *Mindful Militants. The Amalgamated Engineering Union in Australia 1920–1972*, Cambridge University Press, Cambridge, pp. 44–48.

Labor government passed legislation in 1924 that provided a 44-hour week for all workers. In NSW, metalworkers had gained a 44-hour week against the background of skill shortages in May 1921, but lost it in September 1922 following the election of a non-Labor government. Following its election in 1926, the Lang Labor government legislated for a 44-hour week for all workers from 4 January 1926. The 44-hour week was again repealed twice and reintroduced, depending upon the character of the government in power in NSW until June 1933, when the NSW Industrial Commission settled the issue with a judgement in favour of the retention of the 44-hour week, citing the potential for greater unemployment with longer hours.[23]

The working hours issue highlighted the major problem of overlapping jurisdictions between the federal and state industrial arbitration systems. The Commonwealth Court only influenced 6.7 per cent of wages in 1913. During the 1920s it grew from 22 per cent of all wage changes in 1921 to 61 per cent in 1929. Unions became convinced they could obtain better results from the Federal Court than state industrial tribunals. The AEU played an important role in the extension of the Federal Court's jurisdiction through the Privy Council decision in the Engineers Case, which allowed the Federal Court to obtain jurisdiction over state instrumentalities such as railways, where the AEU had large numbers of members employed in railway workshops.

In 1926 another important extension of the Federal Court power occurred in the *Cowburn Case*, when the High Court held that through Section 109 of the Australian Constitution the Commonwealth law was paramount over the state award. Therefore the federal award, which prescribed a 48-hour week, prevailed over the more favourable NSW legislation for a 44-hour week. This sparked a protest by metalworkers, including AEU members, and a subsequent lockout by the Metal Trades Employers Association (MTEA) in May 1926. There was an agreement with the MTEA and the NSW government that affected employees would be able to work on the basis of 44 hours' work for 44 hours' pay. BHP, however, demanded that engineers must agree to a condition that they work on this basis only if they agreed to forfeit the federal award and accept the inferior conditions of other employees. When the engineers refused to accept these conditions, BHP and the associated firm of Rylands dismissed over 400 members on 25 May,

---

23 AEU 1946, *Souvenir*, p. 101; Patmore, G. 'Industrial Conciliation and Arbitration in NSW before 1998', in Patmore, G. (ed.), *Laying the Foundations of Industrial Justice. The Presidents of the Industrial Relations Commission of NSW 1902–1998*, Federation Press, Sydney, 2003, pp. 19–26; Sheridan, T. 1975, *Mindful Militants*, pp. 92–93.

and the subsequent dispute continued for 15 months. The AEU eventually regained the 44-hour work in its federal award in February 1927.[24]

Concerns about uncertainty and the potential for industrial conflict led the federal non-Labor Bruce-Page government to unsuccessfully initiate a referendum that allowed the Commonwealth to take over state industrial jurisdiction in 1926. It also made an unsuccessful attempt to abolish federal arbitration with the exception of the maritime industry through legislation in 1929 after the states refused to hand over their industrial powers.[25] While the AEU criticised the Bruce-Page government for its class bias in proposing these reforms, it remained committed to arbitration and rejected calls for deregistration from the federal system in protest against the Bruce-Page government's legislative reforms.[26]

The debates about Commonwealth versus state industrial powers were soon overshadowed by the Great Depression. The first signs of a major downturn appeared in 1927 as the supply of overseas capital began to dry up. Unemployment rose from 10 per cent in 1928 to 28 per cent by 1932. The percentage of AEU members unemployed increased from 2.5 per cent in 1927 to a peak of 25.5 per cent in 1932. Union activists were particularly vulnerable to retrenchment, with half the members of the AEU Melbourne District Committee being unemployed in May 1930. Other metalworkers also faced increased levels of unemployment. The Newcastle branch of the Boilermakers had 53 per cent of its 560 members unemployed in April 1931.[27]

While the Labor Party led by James Scullin won a landslide victory in the October 1929 federal elections the party began to splinter over how to deal with the economic slump. There was a hostile Senate, a ministry with no previous federal cabinet experience, and within the NSW branch of the party there were divisions between Federal Treasurer Ted Theodore and Jack Lang, leader of the state Parliamentary Labor Party. Joseph Lyons, a former Labor Premier of Tasmania, and five others left the Labor Party, concerned about its expansionary policies, which Lyons believed would destroy the economy. This group merged with the Nationalists to form the United Australia Party (UAP) in May 1931, with Lyons as leader. Scullin rejected

---

[24] AEU 1946, *Souvenir*, p. 125; Patmore, G 2003, 'Industrial Conciliation and Arbitration in NSW', p. 26; Sheridan, T 1975, *Mindful Militants*, pp. 93–4.

[25] Patmore, G 2003, 'Industrial Conciliation and Arbitration in NSW', p. 26.

[26] Sheridan, T 1975, *Mindful Militants*, pp. 100–101.

[27] Patmore, G 1991, *Australian Labour History*, p. 145; Robinson, G 1977, *One Hundred Years*, p. 19; Sheridan, T 1975, *Mindful Militants*, pp. 106, 113.

Lang's call for the repudiation of interest payments on overseas debts. Seven of Lang's supporters left caucus in March 1931, and Scullin lost his majority in the House of Representatives. His government survived until November 1931, when the UAP and the Langites combined to defeat Labor in the House. In the ensuing elections on 19 December the UAP won a landslide victory.[28]

AEU members and other unionists faced wage cuts and the deterioration of their conditions as the Depression continued. The Full Bench of the Commonwealth Arbitration Court cut the basic wage by 10 per cent in January 1931, concluding that the existing wage level was above 'marketable productivity'. This decision was followed by state jurisdictions over the following 18 months. AEU members could also find themselves subject to work rationing, with approximately 4300 metalworkers employed by MTEA members working an average of 26 hours per week between May 1931 and May 1932.[29]

The AEU took a number of steps to minimise the impact of unemployment. In a period of limited state assistance, the AEU provided various benefits to members of approximately £360,000 from 1926 to 1932, which helped sustain unemployed members. The AEU supported work rationing schemes as a way of spreading the work to avoid unemployment. The union also focused on increasing the level of work available by calling for increased tariff protection, a 30-hour five-day week (endorsed by the 1932 ACTU Congress), subsidies for local industry and preference for goods manufactured in Australia. While there was disillusionment with the shift of the Scullin Labor government towards deflationary economic policies, the union continued to support the Labor Party and called for party unity in the wake of the Labor Party fragmentation during the Depression.[30]

While the 1930s Great Depression was more severe than the one of the 1890s, recovery was faster. The repeated droughts of the 1890s did not occur in the 1930s, and the federal government, through tariffs and devaluation, stimulated recovery. Unemployment among AEU members fell from 20.2 per cent in 1933 to 3.3 per cent in 1939. As the economy recovered, the union campaigned to improve the conditions of it members.

---

[28] Patmore, G 1991, *Australian Labour History*, pp. 85–88.

[29] Patmore, G 1991, *Australian Labour History*, p. 86; Sheridan, T 1975, *Mindful Militants*, pp. 109, 113.

[30] AEU 1946, *Souvenir*, p. 150; Sheridan, T 1975, *Mindful Militants*, pp. 110–113, 116–117.

The union was federally deregistered in February 1938 after members at Morts Dock and Cockatoo Island in Sydney went on strike over the decision of Judge Beeby of the Commonwealth Arbitration Commission to exclude them from an extra three shillings for work done on shore due to the different nature of ship repair work. While the union's executive initially took the view that members had sufficient strength to obtain wage increases despite deregistration through over-award negotiations, they decided to hold a ballot for re-registration, citing concerns that other unions may take advantage of the union's deregistered status to expand their coverage at the expense of the AEU. Union members voted 5659 to 1621 for re-registration, and the union's application was successful on 8 November 1938. The union also continued its campaign against the introduction of scientific management. It opposed the use of a stopwatch and the introduction of a bonus scheme in Sydney at Waygood Otis, the lift manufacturer, in March 1936. The campaign, however, failed because neither AEU members nor those of the rival Australasian Society of Engineers (ASE) supported the position.[31]

The union also faced internal divisions over the conflict within the NSW Branch of the Labor Party, which saw the expulsion in 1936 of three members of the union who attended a conference organised by the anti-Lang NSW Labor Council to reform the NSW ALP. In 1938–39 the union threw its support behind the anti-Lang forces. Joseph Cranwell, Chair of the AEU Commonwealth Council, was elected president of the NSW Branch of the Labor Party in August 1939 and played a critical role in stabilising the party at a unity conference in Sydney. Although not a Member of Parliament, he chaired a Parliamentary Labor Party meeting on 5 September at which William McKell, later Labor Premier of NSW and Governor-General, defeated Lang in a leadership ballot.[32]

The internal fighting in the NSW Labor Party was overshadowed by the outbreak of the Second World War in September 1939. Unlike the First World War, the Second World War encouraged economic expansion. Enlistment absorbed existing unemployment and did not significantly disrupt the economy. The substitution of unavailable imports and the close proximity of the fighting (after Japan entered the war) helped sustain growth.

[31] AEU 1946, *Souvenir*, pp. 194, 225–228; Patmore, G 1991, *Australian Labour History*, pp. 145, 148; Sheridan, T 1975, *Mindful Militants*, pp. 134–140.

[32] Patmore, G 'Cranwell, Joseph Archibald (1889–1965)', Australian Dictionary of Biography, National Centre of Biography, Australian National University, available at http://adb.anu.edu.au/biography/cranwell-joseph-archibald-9857/text17439, accessed 8 October 2012; Sheridan, T 1975, *Mindful Militants*, pp. 119–120.

Unemployment fell from 9 per cent in 1939 to 1 per cent in 1945, the year the war ended. During the war, munitions production boosted the size and scale of manufacturing and helped employers realise the benefits of specialisation, planned production and product standardisation. At its peak in 1942–43, 61.23 per cent of the manufacturing workforce worked in factories with more than 100 workers. The average factory employed 28.98 workers. The metal trades workforce practically doubled between 1938–39 and 1943–44 from 177,000 to 341,000.[33]

While there were changing attitudes to the war by trade unions depending on the government in power, the AEU worked with both non-Labor and Labor federal governments. The Menzies and Fadden non-Labor governments, which depended upon the support of two independents after the 1940 general elections, received limited support from trade unions for the remote European conflict. There was considerable industrial unrest in 1940–41, especially in coal mining. The conservative federal governments threatened to break strikes with non-union labour and repressive legislation. They also cracked down on dissident opinion. Menzies banned the Communist Party, which opposed the war, in June 1940.

Although the communists reversed their position following the German invasion of the Soviet Union in June 1941, the party remained illegal until December 1942. While the AEU and the Australian Workers Union (AWU) agreed to join a union advisory committee established by Menzies, and chaired by Cranwell, the ACTU boycotted it due to the government's attitudes towards strikes and civil liberties. Independents withdrew their support from the Fadden government in October 1941, and John Curtin, the leader of the Labor Party, became prime minister. The Labor Party won a majority of seats in the 1943 and 1946 elections. The Curtin government initiated regular meetings with ACTU officers and gained union support for the war effort. While the ACTU advised on manpower and industrial issues, Curtin would not allow union representation on the Economic Planning Committee, which planned essential war production. Cranwell questioned the ability of the ACTU to represent AEU members, and in a deputation to Curtin in March 1942 AEU representatives criticised the government for meeting ACTU representatives rather than them to discuss issues relating to female labour.[34]

---

[33] Patmore, G 1991, *Australian Labour History*, pp. 150–151; Sheridan, T 1975, *Mindful Militants*, pp. 144–145.

[34] AEU 1946, *Souvenir*, pp. 272–273; Patmore, G 1991, *Australian Labour History*, p. 88; Patmore, G 'Cranwell'.

Two major issues facing the AEU during the Second World War were the dilution of skilled labour and female employment. The Menzies government proposed to increase the output of munitions by allowing men who had not been apprenticed or trained in any way to enter the metal trades. While the ACTU opposed dilution on the grounds that it would undermine living standards, the AEU entered into an agreement with the government in May 1940 to provide for dilution under the joint supervision of the union, employers and the Department of Supply. The AEU saw the influx of new entrants into the metal trades as inevitable with the wartime demand, and were concerned about the experience in the UK during the First World War when unions lost control over the process. With the recovery of manufacturing after the Depression, the AEU's growing membership and strategic importance in the production process placed it in a strong position to gain a favourable deal from the government and defy the ACTU. Despite a condemnation of the AEU at the April 1940 ACTU Congress, other metal trade unions – including the ASE, the Boilermakers, the Blacksmiths, the Moulders and the Sheet Metal Workers – followed the AEU and entered into similar agreements by October 1941. Overall, a total of 34,472 male dilutees entered the occupations covered by the AEU.[35]

Despite processes such as dilution, during the Second World War labour shortages occurred in male occupations. Federal governments and women's magazines such as the *Woman's Weekly* encouraged women to enter industry and contribute to the war effort. The number of women working in paid employment increased from 678,000 in July 1939 to 811,000 by June 1945. Participation rates of single and married women increased from 55 and 5 per cent in 1933 to 65 and 11 per cent in 1943. The percentage of female employees in the metal trades grew from 5.8 per cent in 1939–40 to a peak of 16.2 per cent in 1943–44. Women left domestic service, retailing, clerical occupations and the clothing industry to take advantage of lucrative 'war loadings' in munitions and related industries.[36]

Despite the expansion of female employment opportunities, women remained disadvantaged. Employers, unions, governments and industrial tribunals made it clear that women employed in 'men's' work would be replaced as soon as the war ended, and would return to the home, especially

---

[35] AEU 1946, *Souvenir,* p. 252; Hagan, J 1981, *The History of the A.C.T.U.,* Longman Cheshire, Melbourne, pp. 109–111; Sheridan, T 1975, *Mindful Militants,* pp. 153–156.

[36] Patmore, G 1991, *Australian Labour History,* pp. 172–173; Sheridan, T 1975, *Mindful Militants,* p. 161; *The Australian Woman's Weekly,* 31 May 1941, p. 9.

if they were married. Long hours, the refusal of employers to pay male rates to women in many traditional male jobs, the pay differences between traditional female occupations and war work, work intensification and inadequate childcare fuelled industrial unrest among women employees. There were strikes by female workers in the munitions factories.[37]

Within the metal trades there were longstanding concerns about the threat of cheaper female labour to male jobs. To remove this incentive to employ female workers the AEU and other metal trades unions supported equal pay for equal work. Prior to the war, women had gained employment on light repetitive work such as nut and bolt making and drilling. The wartime dilution agreements between unions and the federal governments reduced the traditional barriers to women employed on tasks controlled by male craftsmen. The AEU and other unions tried to protect traditional male jobs by, for example in May 1942, attempting unsuccessfully to persuade the Commonwealth Arbitration Court to stop women doing certain types of core making. The influx of women into the metal trades, however, prompted the AEU, following a postal vote of Australian members of 13,726 votes to 8257 in favour, to admit women for the first time on 1 April 1943, when a women's section was founded. As part of the process of organising women in the industry, the first annual conference of AEU women shop stewards was held in Sydney on 10 November 1943.[38]

A major question with the influx of female workers was their relative pay rates to male workers. In March 1942 the federal Curtin Labor government, which wanted to increase female wage rates to attract women into industry and protect existing male wage rates, established the Women's Employment Board (WEB) to determine rates for industries where there were no awards for women. Employers objected to the Board's independence from the federal arbitration system and were concerned with the long-term consequences of any departure from the traditional 54 per cent level of relativity. Although they could pass on increased costs through war contracts to the government, employers argued before the WEB against wage rises for women on the grounds that female employees were not as productive as men. Despite employer opposition, the Board set rates ranging from 75 to 100 per cent of the male rate, with 90 per cent being the most common. It justified the lower

---

37 Patmore, G 1991, *Australian Labour History*, p. 173.

38 Heagney, M 'Women in the Engineering Industry' in AEU 1946, *Souvenir*, pp. 51–55; Ryan, E and Conlon, A 1989, *Gentle Invaders. Australian Women at Work*, 2nd edn, Penguin, Melbourne, p. 134; Sheridan, T 1975, *Mindful Militants*, pp. 159–162.

rates on the basis of the lesser physical strength of women and their higher levels of absenteeism and labour turnover. There was a lack of statistical evidence to support the Board's conclusions concerning absenteeism and little consideration given to extra unpaid labour performed by women in the home. By the time the government scrapped the Board in October 1944, its decisions only affected 9 per cent of the female workforce.[39]

The Commonwealth Arbitration Court was reluctant to increase the award wages of the women not covered by the WEB. Here the AEU became involved in several stoppages to increase the relative rate of women's wages. AEU members at ACI Engineering in Sydney ceased work in December 1942 over the employment of females at rates lower than the rates for males doing a similar class of work. Conferences with government representatives that followed this dispute led to the AEU accepting proposals in regulations gazetted in May 1943 that provided equal pay for women for second-class machinist rates and for preference for males over their female equivalents.[40] As Sheridan notes the AEU saw such 'stoppages as the best means of bringing pressure on the government to guarantee the post-war rights of male engineers'.[41]

Despite fears within the AEU that the Australian economy would slide into depression following the Second World War, the economy boomed in the immediate postwar period, with a pent-up consumer demand for durables, increased foreign investment and increased tariff protection. Immigration was a major feature of this period, net migration constituting one-third of Australia's population gain between 1947 and 1966. Many of these migrants were not from the UK, the traditional source. There was unprecedented economic growth in the 1950s and 1960s with Gross National Product (GNP) averaging between 4 and 5 per cent per year. Unemployment remained minimal, despite minor recessions in 1952, 1956, 1961 and 1966, and labour turnover was high. An important contributor to this growth was the continued modernisation and expansion of manufacturing. The average annual rate of growth for manufacturing output, employment and productivity between 1949–50 and 1967–68 was 6.1 per cent, 2 per cent and 4.1 per cent. There was also a growth in manufacturing exports, which grew from 6 per cent of the total value of Australian exports in 1953 to 21 per cent

[39]   Patmore, G 1991, *Australian Labour History*, p. 173.

[40]   AEU 1946, *Souvenir*, pp. 283–284; Sheridan, T 1975, *Mindful Militants*, pp. 162–163.

[41]   Sheridan, T 1975, *Mindful Militants*, p. 162.

in 1971. Total employment within the metal trades sector of manufacturing grew between 1953–54 and 1967–68 by 58 per cent to 628,953.

The economic and industrial significance of the metal trades is highlighted by the role of the Metal Trades Award as the focus of most major federal arbitration cases such as the basic wage and wage margins for skill. Although small enterprises continued to employ a significant number of Australian workers, large-scale corporations became more common. With the decline of munitions work and the proliferation of small businesses, especially garages, to take advantage of the postwar consumer boom, the percentage of employees in small enterprises increased again. Despite this, in 1963–64, 52.21 per cent of manufacturing employees still worked in factories with more than 100 workers. Both migrant and native-born workers needed regular incomes to meet greater consumer expectations and finance hire purchase payments.[42]

Economic prosperity and the conservative approach of the Commonwealth Arbitration Court towards wages fixation fuelled industrial militancy and over-award bargaining. Despite the existence of wage-pegging regulations until 1946, metal trades employers offered illegal over-award payments to attract labour. Federal Conciliation Commissioner Galvin's decision to abolish a war loading in the Metal Trades Awards in 1952, the abandonment of basic wage indexation in 1953, and the federal arbitration tribunal's policy of restraint from 1956 to 1959 all exacerbated over-award bargaining. Between 1954 and 1964 the over-award for the average AEU tradesperson increased from £2 to £4 and 10 shillings.[43]

During the 1960s there was concern over the contribution of over-awards to wages drift, which economists argued could increase inflation and decrease economic growth. From 1959 the Commonwealth Arbitration Commission hinted that employers could reduce over-awards through absorption into the existing awards. In the 1967 Metal Trades Work Value Case, the commission explicitly encouraged employers to absorb over-awards. This prompted the 'absorption battle' of January and February 1968, which involved 400 stoppages of work and a total 24-hour stoppage in the metal trades. The

---

42 Patmore, G 1991, *Australian Labour History*, pp. 150–151; Sheridan, T. *Mindful Militants*, pp. 266, 276; Wright, C 1995, *The Management of Labour. A History of Australian Employers*, Oxford University Press, Oxford, pp. 38–42.

43 Hutson, J 1983, *Penal Colony to Penal Powers*, AMFSU, Sydney, Revised edn, p. 206; Isaac, J 1967, *Wages and Productivity*, F.W. Cheshire, Melbourne, p. 118; Quinlan, M 1982 'Immigrant Workers, Trade Union Organisation and Industrial Strategy', PhD Thesis, University of Sydney, vol. 2, p. 557.

issue was referred back to the commission, which decided that 60 per cent of metalworkers awarded a $1.60 increase or less could keep the increase without any absorption. Labour-market pressures again fuelled increases in over-awards from 1969 to 1971. Negotiations between employers and unions and the higher level of consent clauses in awards led to a decline in the contribution of over-awards to total pay increases before the end of 1972.[44]

Workplace-initiated industrial action was common in this period. There was a spread of shop committees with AEU representatives forming a 'ginger group' on the committees pressing for an aggressive approach to industrial issues. In some plants, such as Malleys in Sydney, shop committees were an extension of the bargaining power of shop stewards. In the metal trades some shop committees formed area committees, which conducted multi-plant and even multi-industry negotiations with management in a specific neighbourhood or region. Shop stewards and shop committees played a crucial role in increasing wage rates in the metal trades by winning increases at plants that were well organised. The unions generalised those increases through the whole of the metal industry by a mixture of bargaining and arbitration. Moderate unions and employers regarded the shop committees with suspicion as vehicles for communist influence and for exposing unions to sanctions by industrial tribunals through wildcat or unofficial strikes. Despite efforts by the ACTU to limit the role of shop committees through a charter in 1961, they continued to grow.[45]

The AEU faced legal restrictions on its members taking industrial action. In the federal jurisdiction, employers invoked penal sections against unions with members involved in workplace disputes. As a consequence of the 1968 'absorption battle' the Commonwealth Industrial Court fined the AEU $23,192 during the first seven months of the year, which compared to $33,050 for the previous 18 years. The Clarrie O'Shea Case, which concerned the jailing of the Victorian secretary of the Australian Tramways and Motor Omnibus Employees Association for contempt by the Commonwealth

---

[44] Brown, W 1984, 'Wage Drift in Australian Metal Industries Revisited', in Howard, WA (ed.), *Perspectives on Australian Industrial Relations*, Longman Cheshire, Melbourne, p. 146; Hutson, J 1983, *Penal Colony to Penal Powers*, pp. 206–208; Patmore, G 1988, *The Arid Terrain? A Historical Survey of the Workplace in Australia*, Working Paper No. 6, Centre for Industrial Relations Research, University of Sydney and Labour Studies Programme, The University of Melbourne, p, 12; Sheridan, T 1975, *Mindful Militants*, pp. 278–279.

[45] Patmore, G 1988, *The Arid Terrain?*, pp. 13–15; Rimmer, M 1983, 'Union Shopfloor Organisation', in B Ford and D Plowman (eds), *Australian Unions. An Industrial Relations Perspective*, Macmillan, p. 133; Sheridan, T 1975, *Mindful Militants*, pp. 279–280.

Industrial Court in May 1969, led to a 24-hour strike by unionists in the metal trades and transport sector. An anonymous benefactor paid O'Shea's fine and penal provisions were more or less abandoned at the federal level. In the state jurisdictions the AEU could still pay a high price for rank and file–initiated action. In 1971 the WA Industrial Commission deregistered the AEU and two other unions after 'guerrilla warfare' in the steel fabrication industry.[46]

The immediate postwar period did see an increase in employer interest in scientific management and new technology. By the late 1940s simple and cheap electronic and electro-mechanical devices that modified existing machinery and eliminated and simplified labour were widespread in Australian industry. In the metal trades the AEU and the Boilermakers were successful in their opposition to time and motion payments. The AEU fought a major battle with the Commonwealth Department of Supply over this issue and held stoppages in Melbourne in 1963 and Lithgow in 1964. At Lithgow 112 members at the Small Arms Factory tool room refused to work under a form of time and motion study.[47]

While the AEU took advantage of the favourable climate to defend and enhance its members' interests, the union operated in a political environment of conflict between communists and anti-communists in the Australian labour movement. The first communist AEU official was JF Newman, who was elected Perth organiser in September 1942. EJ Rowe and A Wilson, both communists, won positions on the Commonwealth Council of the AEU in June 1943 and September 1947 respectively. The movement, anti-communist industrial groups and later the National Civic Council were also active in the union.[48] While according to Tom Sheridan their efforts within the AEU were not as successful as in other unions such as the Federated Clerks, 'the struggle was none the less fierce for that'.[49] In 1952 JE Burke, with the support of the Industrial Groups, was successful in defeating Rowe.

---

[46] Hagan, J 1981, *The History of the A.C.T.U.*, pp. 269–270; Patmore, G 1988, *The Arid Terrain?*, p. 13; Harley, B 2004, 'Managing Industrial Conflict', in J Isaac and S Macintyre (eds), *The New Province for Law and Order. 100 years of Conciliation and Arbitration*, Cambridge University Press, Cambridge, pp. 335–356; Sheridan, T 1975, *Mindful Militants*, pp. 281–282.

[47] AEU 1967, *50 Years Commonwealth Council*, Amalgamated Engineering Union, Commonwealth Council, Sydney, pp. 22–23; Patmore, G 1991, *Australian Labour History*, pp. 152–153.

[48] Sheridan, T 1975, *Mindful Militants*, pp. 205–205; Wilson, A 1976, *The Unseen Hand*, AMWU, Sydney, pp. 6–7.

[49] Sheridan, T 1975, *Mindful Militants*, p. 200.

However, by the end of the year another communist, CG Hennessy, won a vacancy on the Commonwealth Council.[50] The Industrial Groups called for the supervision by the Commonwealth Arbitration Court of the 1953 Council ballots by petition on the grounds of communist malpractices in the ballot, which Sheridan argues was based on 'no firm evidence'.[51] While the petition attracted 1816 signatures, the Commonwealth Council, District Committees and many branches condemned the petition and organised a counter-petition of over 38,000 signatures. The union had to proceed with the ballot after a Full High Court on 11 September 1954 dismissed an application by the AEU to restrain the Commonwealth Arbitration Court from doing so. While there were gains by the groupers in the subsequent election, it did not have any impact on AEU industrial policies. After some further turmoil that reflected the 1955 split in the ALP, the tactic of the right wing of tendering petitions in union elections had ceased by 1966. Communists, such as Laurie Carmichael and John Halfpenny, continued to play an important role in the development of the union over the next few decades.[52]

During the next six years the AEU gained autonomy from its UK parent and amalgamated with two other metal trades unions. After protracted negotiations over the financial details of separation, the AEU gained autonomy and had new rules successfully registered in September 1968, dropping 'Australian Section' from its title in February 1969. The old Commonwealth Councilmen became the national organisers, with the council being extended to include directly elected state representatives. The Boilermakers and Blacksmiths Society of Australia (BBSA) had undertaken the first postwar amalgamation in the metal trades in 1965. In 1967 the AEU and BBSA set up a joint research department. The Sheet Metal Workers Union in 1970 also joined discussions with the AEU and the BBSA about amalgamation. Members of the three unions endorsed the amalgamation in a ballot in April 1971. Despite attempts by the Democratic Labor Party and Liberal Party backbenchers to have the McMahon Liberal-Country Party federal government block the amalgamation, and legal action by right-wing members of the merging

---

[50] Wilson, A 1976, *The Unseen Hand*, p. 7.

[51] Sheridan, T 1975, *Mindful Militants*, p. 214.

[52] AEU 1967, *50 Years Commonwealth Council*, p. 16; 'John Halfpenny dies aged 68', *The Age*, 20 December 2003, available at http://www.theage.com.au/articles/2003/12/20/1071868698880.html, accessed 26 November 2012; Sheridan, T 1975, *Mindful Militants*, pp. 205–265; Wilson, A 1976, *The Unseen Hand*, p. 21.

unions, the Amalgamated Metal Workers Union (AMWU) came into being on 2 April 1973 with over 160,000 members. As will be seen, the union faced major challenges over the next few decades with longstanding practices such as industry protection and compulsory arbitration coming under challenge.[53]

1973–2012

The beginning of the 1970s saw the end of the postwar boom in Australia, evidenced by rapid increases in unemployment and inflation. The Whitlam Labor government, which held power federally from 1972 to 1975, significantly expanded public sector expenditure, although it became more fiscally conservative as unemployment and inflation rose. Despite its social radicalism, the government shifted towards market liberalisation in the area of trade policy as it sought to create a more competitive market economy. An Industries Assistance Commission was established to review industry protection, slash tariffs and move against restrictive trade practices. These developments occurred within a context of limited dialogue between the government and unions.[54]

Following the dismissal of the Whitlam government in 1975, the newly elected Liberal-Country Party coalition Fraser government adopted a 'fight-inflation-first' policy to deal with the economic problems gripping Australia. This policy involved restricting the growth of the money supply, cutting government expenditure to reduce the budget deficit, and an incomes policy aimed at minimising or reversing the effects of cost-push inflation by reducing real wages. The strategy also involved an acceptance by the government that a sustained high level of unemployment was necessary to deter unions from pushing for excessive wage increases outside the centralised wage-fixing system. Unemployment increased from 4.7 per cent in 1976 to 9.9 per cent in March 1983. The government also amended the Trade Practices Act to prohibit secondary boycotts and established the Industrial Relations Bureau, set up to supposedly 'protect' the rights of workers who refused to strike. Nevertheless, high levels of inflation persisted, and the 1970s and early 1980s saw growing industrial unrest and conflict as unions attempted to make up for losses in real wages under

---

53 Robinson, G 1977, *One Hundred Years*, pp. 28–9; Sheridan, *Mindful Militants*, pp. 293–304.

54 Patmore, G and Coates, D 2005, 'Labour Parties and the State in Australia and the UK', *Labour History*, no. 88, 2005, p. 126.

the Fraser government.[55] While the ACTU endorsed the reintroduction of centralised wage fixing in 1974, the shift from full to partial wage indexation, and the failure of the government to provide compensatory tax relief meant that 'Unions would try within the constraints imposed by economic circumstances to negotiate with employers to have the difference made up by way of direct bargaining'.[56]

The AMWU's initial response during the 1970s was to use industrial action and the arbitration system to protect real wages and living standards. The union focused on over-award payments so that it could remain within the existing wage-indexation guidelines and hence also benefit from national wage increases. It also embarked on a campaign for a 35-hour week to save jobs. As in previous years, gains made by the metal trades unions generally flowed on to other unions in order to maintain wage relativities. A major factor in the 1981–82 wages breakout was the achievement of a 38-hour week and a $39 per week increase in wages by the metal industry unions. However, this outcome was closely followed by a rapid rise in unemployment, particularly in the metal industry. While still concerned with the industrial wage, the AMWU began to give more priority to the social wage and taxation as a way of addressing the issues faced by workers. As Gwynneth Singleton notes, 'An incomes policy that was based on the interaction of the industrial and social wage and taxation required a comprehensive strategy utilizing both the industrial and the political process. The AMWU had not previously ignored the political alternative. It just had not been given priority.'[57]

The shift in AMWU strategy also saw an increased role for the union's 'combined research department', which increased in both size and influence over the 1970s. As Scalmer and Irving note, the researchers employed by the AMWU were 'better resourced and more assertive than those in other Australian unions', and were 'regarded by both other unions and the Department of Labour as a model for others in the middle 1970s, praised for the broad scope of their work and the specific nature of their output'.[58] The research and reports generated by the research department strongly influenced union policy formation on issues such as tariff protection

[55] Singleton, G 1990, *The Accord and the Australian Labour Movement*, Melbourne University Press, Carlton, Victoria, p. 52–54.

[56] Singleton, G 1990, *The Accord*, p. 55.

[57] Singleton, G 1990, *The Accord*, p. 66.

[58] Scalmer, S and Irving, T 1999, 'The Rise of the Modern Labour Technocrat: Intellectual Labour and the Transformation of the Amalgamated Metal Workers Union, 1973–85', *Labour History*, no. 77, p. 66.

and incomes policy, and formed the basis of submissions to government inquiries. The research also supported an active rank and file, mobilising members around specific issues and empowering them to shape union policy at conferences. During the 1970s, the union's research staff 'functioned like a cadre within the union – bringing theoretical insights down to members and inciting them to new forms of industrial and political action'.[59]

In the late 1970s and early 1980s, the research department began to collectively produce pamphlets, which provided analysis and solutions to Australia's economic problems, including *Australia Uprooted, Australia Ripped Off,* and *Australia on the Rack* (1982). The latter was a precursor to the Accord, and promoted the idea of a social contract based on a social wage, interventionist industry policy and tripartite industry planning. In a draft document entitled *A Strategy for the 1980s in the Metal Industry*, the AMWU also welcomed the prospect of an accord with a future Labor government involving a prices and incomes policy to control inflation, and a stimulatory Keynesian fiscal policy to counter the impact of the Fraser government's policies on real living standards and to generate employment.[60]

Laurie Carmichael, then assistant national secretary of the AMWU, was one of the architects of the Accord through his position on the ACTU Executive. As early as 1975, against the background of the challenges facing the reformist Whitlam Labor government, Carmichael was advocating the development of a special relationship between the federal Labor government and the unions to buy time for major social and economic reforms. Key elements of the Accord included: a commitment to a centralised wage system with wage indexation; provisions to prevent non-wage outcomes rising faster than wages; price surveillance; tax reform; intervention in industry to improve performance and create jobs; a universal health insurance scheme; and the repeal of anti-union legislation. In return, unions were not to submit 'extra claims' outside the wage principles set by the Australian Industrial Relations Commission (AIRC), the renamed federal arbitration tribunal. While the Accord was a bipartite agreement between the ACTU and the Australian Labor Party (ALP), employers sat on tripartite committees overseeing industry policy.[61]

---

59 Scalmer, S and Irving, T 1999, *The Rise of Modern Labour*, p. 68.

60 Scalmer, S and Irving, T 1999, *The Rise of Modern Labour* pp. 73–74; Stillwell, F 1986, *The Accord and Beyond*, Pluto Press, Leichardt, p. 8.

61 Stillwell, F 1986, *The Accord and Beyond*, pp. 10–11; interview with Bill Kelty by Andrew Dettmer, 13 September 2011, Melbourne; Patmore, G and Coates, D 2005, 'Labour Parties and the State', p. 133.

The inclusion of an industry policy component was essential to guarantee AMWU support for the prices and incomes Accord. The original Accord document ruled out further tariff cuts in the midst of high unemployment, and planned a review of the Industries Assistance Commission, which held an anti-tariff line. In 1984, the AMWU produced a document entitled *Policy for Industry Development and More Jobs*. The union was also represented by Laurie Carmichael in the ACTU/Trade Development Council (TDC) Mission to Western Europe in 1986. This initiative produced the 1987 *Australia Reconstructed (AR)* report, which advocated strong state intervention across a range of policy areas such as trade, wages, prices, industry development and the labour market. As an extension of the Accord, *AR* sought to cement the role of unions at all levels of economic and industrial policy decision-making.[62]

Elements of *AR* such as superannuation, education and training, and union amalgamations did have an impact on government and union policy.[63] However, in general, the policy agenda set out in the report did not receive the support of the Labor government. The centre-left faction, consisting of middle-class professionals with few links to trade unions, held the balance of power in the Parliamentary Labor Party. These parliamentarians were strong supporters of the free market, modernisation and efficiency. The government's first efforts towards deregulation and microeconomic reform involved the 1983 decision to float the Australian dollar and abolish exchange controls. The Labor government increasingly adopted economic rationalist strategies in response to deteriorating terms of trade, exploding foreign debt and inflation during the mid 1980s.[64]

---

[62] Jones, E 1997, 'The Background to Australia Reconstructed', *Journal of Australian Political Economy*, no. 39, pp. 20–22; Scalmer, S and Irving, T 1999, 'The Rise of the Modern Labour Technocrat', pp. 74–75.

[63] The AMWU embraced the process of amalgamation over the following years. Having initially merged with the Federated Shipwrights in 1976, forming the Amalgamated Metal Workers and Shipwrights Union (AMWSU), the union in 1983 merged with the Federated Moulders (Metals) Union, changing its name to the Amalgamated Metals Foundry and Shipwrights Union. It returned to the name Amalgamated Metal Workers Union in 1985. A series of further amalgamations from 1991 has seen the name of the union change a number of times; first, to the Metals and Engineering Workers Union (1991–1993); second, the Automotive Metals & Engineering Union (1993–1994); third, the Automotive Food Metals & Engineering Union (1994–1995); and finally, to the Automotive Food Metals Engineering Printing & Kindred Industries Union. Nevertheless, the union is still known as the AMWU or by some as 'the metalworkers'.

[64] Patmore, G and Coates, D 2005, 'Labour Parties and the State', p. 133; Jones, E 1997, 'The Background to Australia Reconstructed', p. 36.

The Accord also underwent several revisions over the mid to late 1980s to early 1990s that saw a shift away from centralised wage determination to enterprise bargaining overseen by the AIRC, often referred to as a process of 'managed decentralism'. The economic downturn led the Accord partners to focus on wage restraint and improving productivity through microeconomic reform. The Commonwealth Commission abandoned wage indexation in December 1986. In March 1987 the commission introduced the two-tier wages system, which combined elements of centralisation and decentralisation. The second tier required unions and management to enter into negotiations to improve productivity at the workplace through 'restructuring and efficiency exercises' that included an examination of restrictive work practices, multi-skilling, retraining and the reduction of demarcation barriers.[65]

The AMWU was 'one of the few apparently consistent supporters'[66] of the new wage system. As Margaret Gardner outlined:

> The Metal industry is regulated by a complex minimum rates award, in an industry with a variety of the 'inflexible' work practices that tend to be associated with skilled work. The AMWU is a large, well-organized union with significant resources. The two new principles [restructuring and efficiency, and supplementary payments] are ideally suited to a union with expertise about its industry and room for trade-offs that may in some cases improve and preserve jobs.[67]

In the August 1988 and August 1989 National Wage Cases, the AIRC adopted the principle of 'structural efficiency'. This principle allowed employers and unions to facilitate award restructuring, where awards with obsolete job classifications systems and frustrating 'dead-end' jobs would be replaced by awards that provided for multi-skilling and career paths.[68] The Metal Industry Award was the first restructured award approved by the commission, and took force from March 1990. The award 'formalized the link between award restructuring and training at an industry level and was a landmark in the evolution of the training reform agenda'.[69]

---

65 Patmore, G 2003, 'Industrial Conciliation and Arbitration in NSW', p. 41.

66 Gardner, M 1988, 'Australian Trade Unionism in 1987', *Journal of Industrial Relations*, 30(1), p. 151.

67 Gardner, M 1988, 'Australian Trade Unionism', p. 151.

68 Patmore, 'Industrial Conciliation and Arbitration in NSW', p. 51.

69 Brown, T 2006, 'From Union Inspired to Industry Led: How Australian Labour's Training Reform Experiment Turned Sour', *Journal of Industrial Relations*, 48(4), p. 496.

Accord Mark 6, which was negotiated before Labor's victory in the March 1990 federal election, included a continued commitment to the award restructuring process, the consideration by the national wage case of the principles upon which enterprise agreements should be determined, increased superannuation and greater access to childcare. However, the AIRC in the National Wage Case of April 1991 rejected several key features of the previous Accord, arguing for example that the relationship between unions and employers was not 'mature' enough to proceed further down the path towards enterprise bargaining. In October 1991 the commission reversed its earlier decision concerning enterprise bargaining, and allowed unions and employers to negotiate wage/productivity agreements at the enterprise level. The emphasis on enterprise bargaining remained a feature of the Accord until its demise in 1996, and was legislatively reinforced by the Labor federal government with the *Industrial Relations Reform Act 1993*.[70]

The AMWU supported the decentralisation of bargaining. As Chris Briggs notes, skilled workers were able to negotiate real wage increases, and 'the AMWU was important in rebuffing pressure from quarters of the union movement for a recentralization of bargaining during 1993/94'.[71] However, as the shift towards enterprise bargaining gained momentum, unions lost control over key elements of economic, industry and social policy. According to some critics, including Tony Brown, the union-inspired competency-based training system of the late 1980s was 'killed' by Labor's acceptance of enterprise bargaining 'as it uncoupled awards and training', and 'employer associations and state education bureaucracies re-asserted control and established a new training market'.[72] However, the same competency-based system continues to deliver consistent training outcomes to manufacturing workers today.

While several industry plans were established in the early years of the Accord, these were short-lived and undermined the government's desire for a general reduction in tariffs. The May 1988 economic statement announced a tariff reduction program that would cut average industry protection levels from 13 per cent to 8 per cent over a period of four years. This was followed in 1991 with a program to reduce average tariffs to 3 per cent by 2000 and to

---

[70] Patmore, G 2003, 'Industrial Conciliation and Arbitration in NSW', p. 51.

[71] Briggs, C 2001, 'Australian Exceptionalism: The Role of Trade Unions in the Emergence of Enterprise Bargaining', *Journal of Industrial Relations*, 43(1), p. 39.

[72] Brown, T 2006, 'From Union Inspired to Industry Led', pp. 503, 491.

abolish quotas on imports of textile, clothing and footwear by 1993. These moves placed increasing pressure on Australian import-competing industries to reduce their prices and increase efficiency. For the manufacturing sector to be competitive in a low-tariff regime, it required other sectors on which it was reliant such as transport, freight, power, telecommunications and the labour market, to also increase their level of efficiency. This brought forth a range of related policies, including privatisation and microeconomic reform.[73]

The election of the Howard government in 1996 marked the end of the Accord. This government's policies reflected the neoliberal philosophies of the 1990s and 2000s, which placed ultimate faith in the market and included a strong anti-union agenda. In contrast to the previous regime under Labor, unions were largely excluded from political decision-making. The federal *Workplace Relations Act 1996* introduced individual contracts in the form of Australian Workplace Agreements (AWAs), reduced arbitrated awards to 20 allowable matters, and limited the power of the AIRC to intervene in industrial disputes. It also effectively denied workers the right to strike, especially when negotiating multi-employer, industry-wide agreements.[74]

The AMWU was at the forefront in lobbying the Senate to reject the anti–industry level bargaining legislation of the Howard government.[75] In 1999 it was central to establishing Campaign 2000, in which it, along with other key unions such as the Electrical Trades Union (ETU) and the AWU, sought to secure a common expiry date in many enterprise agreements in Victoria and therefore gain bargaining power in the next round of negotiations at which point they would present a separate but identical log of claims to each employer. While benchmark agreements were swiftly secured with one group of employers, the unions ultimately settled for a number of agreements with smaller pay increases. Some employers adopted a tough stance in negotiations or refused to negotiate union agreements, while others

---

[73] Patmore, G and Coates, D 2005, 'Labour Parties and the State', p. 133; Willis, R 2003, 'The Economy: A Perspective from the Inside', in Ryan, S and Bramston, T (eds), *The Hawke Government: A Critical Perspective*, Pluto Press, North Melbourne, p. 153.

[74] Balnave, N, Brown, J, Maconachie, G and Stone, R 2009, *Employment Relations in Australia*, John Wiley & Sons, Milton, Qld, 2nd edn, p. 468; White, C 2009 'Firewalling the Right to Strike in Australia?', available at http://chriswhiteonline.org/2009/09/firewalling-the-right-to-strike-1/, accessed 29 April 2013.

[75] Australian Trade Union Archives, available at http://www.atua.org.au/biogs/ALE0977b.htm, accessed 7 October 2012.

chose to lock out their workers.[76] Employers also used the detailed clauses in the Act 'to stall the union and to keep the issue of the legitimacy of pattern bargaining very much before the Commission and the public'.[77]

The 1996 Act, however, was a diluted version of the Howard government's vision of industrial relations. After gaining control of the Senate in 2004, the government secured the passage of the federal *Workplace Relations Amendment (Work Choices) Act 2005*, the main thrust of which was to individualise employment relations and marginalise the role of third parties such as industrial tribunals and trade unions. Among its most controversial elements were the avid promotion of AWAs and the removal of protection from unfair dismissal for the majority of working Australians.[78]

In response, the Your Rights at Work (YRAW) campaign, spearheaded by the ACTU and state labour councils, was launched. This campaign helped to personalise the negative impact of Work Choices on workers. One key case receiving media attention in 2006 was that of a Radio Rentals store that dismissed three union activists and demanded that staff sign AWAs with reduced wages and working conditions. When AMWU members refused to accept the AWAs and voted in favour of industrial action, the company locked them out. There followed a three-week standoff, after which the company finally agreed to enter into a collective agreement. As Alison Barnes notes, the case demonstrates the 'unintended consequences of Work Choices' in that it created a 'rapprochement between the leadership of the left-wing AMWU and the right-wing shop, Distributive and Allied Employees Association (SDA). The SDA donated a significant sum to the AMWU-administered Radio Rentals Dispute Fund.[79]

The AMWU was also involved in the YRAW campaign on a more general level. In 2005, focus groups involving a mix of voters and AMWU members were held across four states to test the campaign strategy and advertising methods. The union and the ACTU also 'ran tracking polls to chart shifts in knowledge and opinion' against the focus group findings.[80] The AMWU, along with four other unions, sponsored the 'Light the

[76] Ellem, B 2000, 'Trade Unionism in 1999', *Journal of Industrial Relations*, 41(1), pp. 74–75; Ellem, B 2001, 'Trade Unionism in 2000', *Journal of Industrial Relations*, 42(2), pp. 210–211.

[77] Ellem, B 2000, 'Trade Unionism in 2000', p. 211.

[78] Balnave et al. 2009, *Employment Relations in Australia*, pp. 468–470.

[79] Barnes, A 2007, 'Australian Unions in 2006', *Journal of Industrial Relations*, 49(3), p. 383.

[80] Muir, K 2008, *Worth Fighting For: Inside the Your rights at Work Campaign*, U NSW Press, Sydney, p. 56.

Fuse' tour in March–April 2006 with the purpose of 'lighting the fuse of discontent throughout regional Queensland'.[81] Indeed, the AMWU was a big supporter of the various mass rallies aimed at mobilising and activating workers and communities. The union was a significant contributor to the YRAW advertising campaign, and assisted the marginal seats campaign through funding and other forms of support.[82]

The activism of the YRAW campaign significantly contributed to the downfall of the Howard government in the November 2007 elections. The new federal Labor government rolled back some of the more objectionable features of the Work Choices legislation, but continued the push towards a national system of Australian industrial relations. The *Workplace Relations Amendment (Transition to Forward with Fairness) Act 2008* prohibited the making of new AWAs and restored the no-disadvantage test for collective agreements. Its *Fair Work Act 2009* created a new one-stop agency called Fair Work Australia to replace the Australian Industrial Relations Commission and the Fair Pay Commission. There were still aspects of the Howard government's reforms retained, such as restrictions on industrial action and union rights of entry. The idea that unions were no longer the exclusive representatives of workers in negotiating collective agreements was also reinforced by this legislation. The federal Labor government also embraced the idea of a single national system of regulation, at least for the private sector, through the use of the corporations' power and even extended it to the idea of harmonising the legislation in regard to Occupational Health and Safety laws.[83]

During the Howard government years, a number of 'free trade' agreements were signed and implemented as part of a strategy to expand bilateral free trade relationships. Within this context of a more open economy, the AMWU continued to fight to protect manufacturing jobs in Australia. The union in October 2012 conducted a campaign across Australia to urge industry and government to buy Australian.[84] Paul Bastian, AMWU national secretary, noted that 'Currently less than 10 per cent of steel being sourced for the resources sector is Australian-made, while steel fabrication at Kwinana (WA) sits idle and youth unemployment is 26.4 per cent'.[85]

---

[81] Williams, D 2008, ETU, Qld Branch, cited in Muir, *Worth Fighting For*, p. 113.

[82] Muir, K 2008, *Worth Fighting For*, p. 165.

[83] Patmore, G 2012, 'Industrial Relations', in Clune, D and Smith, R (eds), *From Carr to Keneally. Labor in Office 1995–2011*, Allen & Unwin, Sydney, p. 178.

[84] AMWU 2012, http://www.amwu.asn.au/read-article/news-detail/1032/Jobs-campaign-goes-coast-to-coast/ accessed 31 October 2012.

[85] AMWU 2012.

Conclusion

From its beginnings on a ship travelling from Britain to Australia in 1852, the AMWU has grown to become a crucial player in Australian industrial relations and politics. The ASE, later the AEU, represented a strategic group of workers at the centre of Australian manufacturing. While, because of its industrial strength, it was slow to endorse the new Labor Party and embrace conciliation and arbitration, it became committed to both these crucial aspects of Australian labourism. Its industrial strength allowed it to be flexible during the Second World War in regard to dilution of work during the war and the 1980s in regard to award restructuring. It also has remained an important force in promoting and defending Australian jobs, particularly in the manufacturing industry. One of the benefits of the 1973 amalgamation was the development of a research department, which had a strong influence within the union and beyond on issues such as tariff protection and incomes policy during the late 1970s and early 1980s. While in recent years the AMWU continues to face challenges in terms of cheap imports undermining Australian manufacturing, as was shown in the YRAW campaign, the AMWU can still fight the forces undermining trade unionism and assist in bringing about political change.

Chapter 2

The Hope of the World

The Amalgamation of ADSTE and the AMWU

Andrew Dettmer

The AMWU of 2012 is a strong independent union of 100,000 workers. These days, any collective organisation finds it tough to survive. The fact that in 2012 we celebrated 160 years of the AMWU[86] and its predecessors is a major achievement in itself.

The AMWU's origins can be found in the five unions that amalgamated in the 1990s – the Amalgamated Metal Workers Union; the Association of Draughting, Supervisory and Technical Employees (ADSTE); the Vehicle Builders Employers' Federation (VBEF), the Confectionery and Food Preservers Workers Union (CFPWU) and the Printing and Kindred Industries Union (PKIU).

This is the story of the first of these amalgamations, between the Amalgamated Metal Workers Union (AMWU) and ADSTE, which took place officially on 1 April 1991. The two unions came together after a long period of consideration, characterised at times by procrastination, dissension and even outright hostility. Twenty-one years later, the soul of ADSTE (and many members and officials) continues in the Technical, Supervisory and Administrative Division of the AMWU. It is a tribute to the far-sightedness of those activists and officials who supported the amalgamation and guided it through to completion.

ADSTE was predominantly a white-collar union. It comprised draughts-persons, technical officers, production planners, foremen and women, supervisors, surveyors, laboratory technicians, experimental officers and (in the Australian public service) tradespeople of various sorts. However, unlike

---

86 In this chapter, to distinguish between the present Australian Manufacturing Workers Union, and the Amalgamated Metal Workers Union, the latter will be referred to as the Metal Workers Union.

many traditional white-collar unions, it did not include administrative personnel or managers, with the exception of Chief Draughting Officers and similar classifications. A further distinguishing feature was that most ADSTE members came off the shop floor. Many of them boasted a trade qualification – at amalgamation, around 60 per cent of ADSTE's 20,000 members were trade qualified. This meant that ADSTE had a greater proportion of tradespeople than its amalgamation partner, the AMWU, in which approximately 55 per cent of its 160,000 members held a trade.

Amalgamation has been a fact of life throughout the history of unions. It was generally seen as a way of building strength. It is celebrated in the names of many unions, including the Amalgamated Society of Engineers (ASE).

When the 26 original Australian members of the ASE formed the Sydney branch in 1852, they did so hoping to transfer the aims of the ASE to the antipodes, and to 'guarantee … to every man the full enjoyment of the produce of his labour'. The ASE (from 1920, the Amalgamated Engineering Union [AEU]) comprised smiths, fitters, turners, mechanics and other tradespeople. As a condition of membership, all had to be trade qualified through an apprenticeship that generally lasted seven years.

The division of labour of the nineteenth century would be unrecognisable to modern eyes, based as it was on high levels of craftsmanship and individual workshops. Before mass production, individual artisans were responsible for the production of finished items. At the conclusion of his apprenticeship (apprentices were all men – no women were allowed to undertake indentures in the metal trades), but prior to being considered a tradesman, the worker was considered to be a 'journeyman'. This often involved an actual journey from place to place in search of work (literally, 'on the journey'). It was only at the conclusion of this 'journey', sometimes lasting years, that a worker would be considered a craftsman.

The ASE was jealous of its rights and prerogatives as a union of tradesmen, and refused to admit into membership those who could not present proof of the successful completion of their indenture. This 'craft consciousness' led to members of the ASE being described as 'labour aristocracy' – or more commonly, as the 'Gentleman Jims'. The image of the fitter or mechanic with his leather apron over a shirt and tie was not far off the mark.

The artisanal mode of production often meant that these craftsmen developed, drew and fabricated the required object, be it a metal wheel or an entire (steam) engine. It's no accident that the original and celebrated engineers such as James Watt built upon the ingenuity of tradesmen (in Watt's case, a blacksmith named Thomas Newcomen) to develop their concepts.

Modern forms of production began with the assembly line, fundamentally developed by Henry Ford. He required a detailed division of labour, and automated many tasks previously performed by hand. Through this, specialised roles were developed for draughtsmen, production planners, foremen and supervisors, and became common throughout engineering plants around the world.

Commonly, the more capable tradespeople would develop the capacity to undertake technical drawing, plan the production process, schedule production materials, undertake quality control, and test finished products. It was from these ranks that the union, which ultimately became ADSTE, was formed.

The height of technological advancement in the late nineteenth century was the steam locomotive. Railways were a crucial part of the economic development of Australia. They required significant investment, mainly by the government of the Australian colonies. Likewise, iron shipbuilding, motor vehicle and aircraft production, introduced as the twentieth century progressed, also evolved increasingly specialised skills at greater levels of complexity, often completely divorced from the application of manual skills on the factory floor. The sociologist C. Wright Mills described the consequences of modern production methods for the worker thus: 'as a proportion of the labour force, fewer individuals manipulate *things*, more handle *people* and *symbols*'. Workers carrying out these more specialised functions and skills, previously unknown to Australian manufacturing and engineering, formed the Association of Architects, Engineers, Surveyors and Draughtsmen of Australia (AAESDA) in August 1915.

AAESDA was first registered in Queensland on 11 April 1917 at the height of the First World War. Being registered meant that the union had to subject itself to the laws and regulations of the Queensland industrial system, and as a result could then have awards made to cover the work carried out by its members. The original registered name was 'the Australian Union of Architects, Engineers and Surveyors, Union of Employees, Queensland'. E Harvey Gibbon is recorded as the first president and CB da Costa as the first secretary. The full name of AAESDA was finally registered on 30 March 1928.

AAESDA grew up in the workshops of the Queensland Railways, and soon spread to the Queensland public service and local government. AAESDA was a significant force in the departments of the Queensland public service, especially in engineering offices. Some of the first members of AAESDA were professional engineers, although in those days actual

Figure 2.1 Poster for a 'Yes' vote, ADSTE/AMWU amalgamation campaign.

AMWU national office

university-qualified engineers were relatively rare. In addition, architects in the Public Works Department, responsible for the design of public buildings, and surveyors in the Department of Public Lands were organised through AAESDA.

AAESDA continued into the 1920s and Great Depression of the 1930s. Annual returns showed membership of 108 at the union's inception; it rose to 243 by 1933.

Originally, all of the office holders were honorary, although they were able to obtain limited leave for union purposes, e.g. representing the union under the Queensland Industrial Arbitration Act. Hendy Caldwell had originally joined in 1916. He became part-time secretary of the union in 1933 and held the position until 1947.

Despite its title, AAESDA was registered, and only had members, in the state of Queensland. It was one of many small unions registered in the unionisation boom that occurred in the early years of the twentieth century. Many gave up the ghost under the pressures of the Great Depression but AAESDA continued to expand. At the outbreak of war in 1939 it boasted 528 members. That doesn't necessarily mean that members retained their employment throughout. Many no doubt kept their union ticket despite periods of unemployment, lay-off and short-time arrangements that were common during the Great Depression in both the private and public sectors.

AAESDA was very active through the arbitration processes available to unions. Awards in railways, water and sewerage, and the public service, showed a pretty good strike rate, with increases in pay, allowances, leave and other conditions. Some of these conditions were foreign to modern conditions; for instance, in local government under the then terms of the Award, engineers had to provide their 'own buggies and instruments'. No doubt this rankled with many – it was still noted by the union's advocate, JH Burgess, when writing in the 50th Anniversary edition of the union's journal *Blueprint* in 1967.

AAESDA had its origins during the First World War. It was in the Second World War, during another round of union organising, that AAESDA began to expand across borders, primarily into NSW. At the same time, the Australian Association of Draughtsmen (AAD) also came into being. Like the AAESDA, AAD had its origins in large factories; in this case, the aircraft factories and dockyards that became massive employers of skilled workers between 1939 and 1945.

AAD's original office bearers included Philip Lowe, a 25-year-old draughtsman from Cockatoo Dockyards, who became the first honorary

ADSTE — AMWU AMALGAMATION VOTE NO	ADSTE — AMWU AMALGAMATION VOTE NO

ADSTE — AMWU

AMALGAMATION

WHY YOU SHOULD VOTE

NO ☒

Amalgamation between ADSTE & the AMWU will result in:

- loss of a union identity for technical, draughting and supervisory employees;
- loss of control of union resources and decision-making;
- a takeover of ADSTE by the AMWU;
- less service to members in both unions;
- the establishment of a union that is so large that realistic involvement in decision-making would be virtually impossible;
- no elections for any union positions for four years;
- involvement of ADSTE & AMWU members in demarcation disputes which have nothing to do with them.

ADSTE — AMWU AMALGAMATION VOTE NO	ADSTE — AMWU AMALGAMATION VOTE NO

ASSOCIATION OF DRAUGHTING SUPERVISORY & TECHNICAL EMPLOYEES

MEMBERS ASKED TO
SUPPORT AMALGAMATION

Our union has been built on the vision and achievements of its founding members. We have a proud record of achievements, often setting new standards for the union movement. In the past, members have not been afraid to pursue the amalgamation and affiliations that have advanced the interests of all current day ADSTE members.

Since 1988 members representatives to Branch Councils and Federal Conference have had the courage and vision to secure a place for technical and supervisory employees within a dramatically changing trade union movement. The past several years have been a turning point for ADSTE. The change has not been without some pain and much soul searching for ADSTE.

Clearly members are aware of the need to change and have declared their support at Annual General Meetings of members and in the plebiscite for amalgamation.

An important objective of ADSTE's amalgamation has been to achieve a strong voice for technical and supervisory employees as part of a stronger and more relevant trade union movement.

DEMOCRACY, AUTONOMY HALLMARKS FOR NEW UNION

The new union produced by the amalgamation of ADSTE and the AMWU would continue the democratic traditions of both organisations, according to the memorandum of understanding signed by both unions in June this year.

The amalgamated union would allow for a large degree of autonomy, diversity and responsibility at the local level.

The memorandum states that while seeking to build greater solidarity and collective strength through amalgamation, members locally will continue to decide the best form of organisation.

"Thus at present, in some cases, action over issues and decisions may be taken by one group of members within a plant but not by others," the memorandum states "In other cases there may be plant-wide action and decision-making (for example, through joint site committees)."

The new union will continue and extend the tradition of the AMWU and ADSTE of providing adequate training and resources to rank and file activists.

SUPPORT AMALGAMATION   **VOTE YES**

Figures 2.2 and 2.3
Campaign circulars
and advertisements.

AMWU national office

IN OPPOSITION TO THE PROPOSED AMALGAMATION WITH ADSTE

Q. HAVE ALL MEMBERS HAD TIME TO CONSIDER THIS AMALGAMATION?

A. NO

AMWU members only know what the national leadership wants them to know. The **Metal Worker** hasn't published any alternatives on amalgamation except with ADSTE.

ADSTE members have only heard pro-AMWU amalgamation from their Federal Office and any opposition has been squashed. Even when a national plebiscite vote was held the membership was denied any information against amalgamation by the Federal Executive.

Q. WILL AMALGAMATION MEAN BETTER SERVICES?

A. NO

ADSTE is based on autonomous Branch structures which collect and control the members' fees. This means that generally there is one industrial official for every 800 – 1000 members. The AMWU is based on centralised control of funding. The collection and control of members' fees is done by the National Office. Currently there is one organiser or official for every 2000 – 3000 members. ADSTE members will get less service after amalgamation. AMWU members won't get any more.

Q. WILL AMALGAMATION LEAD TO LESS DEMARCATION DISPUTES?

A. NO

ADSTE rarely has demarcation disputes with the AMWU. They are generally with other technical, professional and supervisory unions. AMWU demarcation disputes are generally with other trades and non-trades unions. Amalgamation will mean that members will be involved in more, not less, disputes.

Q. IS THIS A TRUE AMALGAMATION?

A. NO

ADSTE will disappear and be absorbed by the AMWU.

Q. WILL AMALGAMATION MEAN GREATER PARTICIPATION IN DECISION MAKING?

A. NO

ADSTE members are involved in decision-making through annually elected Branch Councils, composed of the Executive and delegates, which can determine all matters related to the operation of the union in that Branch including how resources are used, how many industrial officials are employed and so on. Branch Council meets every month at a minimum. The Branch is the front-line for the members and they make the decisions. Branches are directly run by and for the membership. The AMWU is centrally controlled and resources are allocated by the Central National Council. Branches are given enough to provide a basic service to members and members involvement is limited to State Conference, which meets once every two years, and State Council. Representation is strictly limited. Amalgamation will mean that ADSTE members will lose their current high level of involvement. AMWU members won't get any better involvement.

Q. WILL AMALGAMATION GIVE MEMBERS GREATER CONTROL OF THEIR UNION?

A. NO

The new union will have over 200,000 members, will be run from the Sydney National Office and decision-making will be centralised and strictly limited.

Q. AMALGAMATION IS MEANT TO MAKE UNIONS BETTER AND STRONGER ORGANISATIONS FOR UNION MEMBERS.

WILL THIS AMALGAMATION ACHIEVE THIS?

A. NO

The results of this amalgamation are clear. The AMWU should be talking to other trade unions. ADSTE should amalgamate with other technical, professional and supervisory unions.

Above and opposite:

Figures 2.4, 2.5 and 2.6
Campaign circulars and advertisements

AMWU national office

AMALGAMATION NEWSLETTER

adste WORKING TOGETHER

September 1990

Democracy, autonomy will be hallmarks of combined union

THE new union produced by an amalgamation of ADSTE and the AMWU would continue the democratic traditions of both organisations, according to the memorandum of understanding signed by both unions in June this year.

The amalgamated union would allow for a large degree of autonomy, diversity and responsibility at the local level.

The memorandum states that while seeking to build greater solidarity and collective strength through amalgamation, members locally will continued to decide the best form of organisation.

"Thus at present, in some cases, action over issues and decisions may be taken by one group of members within a plant but not by others," the memorandum states. "In other cases there may be plant-wide action and decision-making (for example, through joint site committees)."

Areas of conflict between policies of the two unions will be resolved first by reference to the National Council of the amalgamated union, and then, if necessary, to the first national conference of the amalgamated union. Thereafter all decisions of national and state conferences would be binding on all members of the amalgamated union.

The new union will continue and extend the tradition of the AMWU and ADSTE of providing adequate training and resources to rank and file activists.

This will involve developing delegates networks in industry areas; training; secondment off the job and between the general and the technical and supervisory divisions; development of shop stewards' and delegates' rights as an "industrial issue; and protecting the job and career rights of delegates.

Continued over page

Rank and file meet on amalgamation

ADSTE area representatives and AMWU
in Spring

AMWU and ADSTE are now the MEWU

The METAL WORKER

Volume 12   Number 4   April 1991

Incorporating Blueprint

The AMWU and ADSTE were officially amalgamated on April 1 to form the Metals and Engineering Workers' Union (MEWU).

The new union will have a membership close to 200,000 and be the principal union in the metals industry.

National Secretary George Campbell said the MEWU would provide a better service for members across the industry and, under award restructuring, a career path that could lead all the way to engineer.

Assistant National Secretary Graham Harris (formerly ADSTE Federal Secretary) said: "We now have a union with the collective strengths to look after the members. An informed, active and committed delegate structure will ensure the success of the MEWU.

GEORGE CAMPBELL, MEWU National Secretary

GRAHAM HARRIS, Assistant National Secretary

Carrington closes, 380 jobs lost

ATTEMPTS by unions and both local and federal governments to keep Carrington Slipways shipyard in Newcastle, NSW, open have failed and the company will close its gates this month at the cost of 380 jobs. The Federal Government has

made a commitment to the MEWU, however, that it will assist anyone who may reopen the shipbuilding facility when the Industry recovers from a slump that is also threatening Queensland's biggest shipyard.

Full story page 2

Industry statement frees up business...

NOW IT'S UP TO THE BOSS

DESPITE the accelerated slashing of tariffs in the Prime Minister's statement on industry policy last month and the potential negative impact this may have on employment opportunities there are sufficient incentives for business in the statement for them to now get on with the job of re-investing in our manufacturing and service sectors and delivering their contribution to our economic recovery.

It is time for industry to stop expecting the government to solve all their problems and to start working on improving the manufacturing and service industry in this country.

SUPPORT

With award restructuring, and the flexibility/productivity improvements that are part of the 4.5 per cent wage rise now being negotiated, the 4.5 per cent wage rise now being negotiated, the opportunity is there for smart companies to become more efficient and lead the way to economic recovery.

The tariff cuts in the industry statement went far beyond what was

By National Secretary GEORGE CAMPBELL

advocated by the MEWU and the ACTU.

However, tariffs are only part of the industry policy debate, and at least that part of the arguments is now behind us. The question now is how the other aspects of the statement offset the tariff cuts and give business the support required.

"It is time for industry to stop expecting the government to solve all their problems."

The cuts in wholesale tax announced are worth hundreds of millions of dollars to business and will have an offset effect on the tariff cuts as well as reducing the cost of goods produced.

Another major initiative is the extension of tax concessions for research and development. This write-off of 125 per cent was due to be phased out but is now to be maintained. This is a particularly welcome decision and should play a significant role in increasing the export of quality manufactures.

The government has also pledged $25 million over two years in support the unions' workplace reform, campaigns and award

Continued p2

INSIDE

Telecom picket to save jobs — P3

White asbestos cancer threat — P7

Price 40¢ ISSN 0727-1115 Published by the Amalgamated Metal Workers' Union, 136 Chalmers St, Surry Hills, NSW 2010 secretary. Lowe had brought together draughtsmen of Cockatoo in an informal committee, and later made contact with others at Babcock & Wilcox. These delegates met on 12 June 1942 in Adyar Hall, which then stood on Bligh Street in Sydney.

AAD soon made constructive contact with AAESDA in Brisbane. Draughtsmen were also becoming active in SA and WA. A meeting of 140 draughtsmen took place in Melbourne on 21 December 1942. The AAD grew quickly, so much so that a full-time secretary, Herbert Nicholson, was appointed in April 1943, and paid a respectable (for the time) £9 per week. The AAD was registered as a federal union in October 1943.

It was formed with the knowledge that if it wanted to be viable over the longer term it would need to amalgamate. The AAD formed eight committees, most of which met weekly or fortnightly, after hours. One of the committees was the 'General Business, Correspondence, Executive Affiliation and Amalgamation Committee'. It met every Friday at 7:30 pm. Given the long hours most workers had to put in during the war, this is a neat illustration of the dedication that those AAD pioneers showed in getting their union off the ground (and this committee had as a member 'Degerman, J (Miss)' who appears to be the first female representative of the union). While the AEU in Australia had some female members, at this time the British AEU prohibited women from joining until 1943.

The AAD and AAESDA worked closely together, and it was their clear intention to amalgamate. They did so, with the newly amalgamated AAESDA finally registered under the (Commonwealth) Conciliation and Arbitration Act at the end of 1947. (AAESDA had been granted federal registration on 11 October 1944.) The new *AAESDA Bulletin* appeared monthly from June 1948. Its masthead described it as the periodical of AAESDA 'with which is amalgamated the Australian Association of Draughtsmen'.

AAESDA was a union, or association, which prided itself on its advocacy for members before the arbitral tribunals of the day, whether it was the Commonwealth Court of Conciliation and Arbitration, the Public Service Arbitrator or the many parallel tribunals at the state level.

At the same time the AEU was beginning to shed its image as the 'Gentlemen Jims', especially after its prolonged strike in the metal trades in Victoria in 1946–47. Described as the most popular issue in the history of the AEU in Victoria, the resolution of the dispute in May 1947 resulted in a uniform 40-hour week across the metal industry and an increase in the fitters' margin (the level above the basic wage) of 23 shillings per week.

AAESDA had not participated in the strike; nevertheless, like other metal trades unions, they benefited from the improvements to pay and conditions. However, AAESDA members did find themselves in stop work action from time to time. In the July 1948 edition of the AAESDA *Bulletin*, the story was told of the members at Olympic Cables in Melbourne who had walked off the job, along with members of all other unions, after delegate RJ Graham was sacked on suspicion of being a member of the Communist Party. The story was recounted by Ted Deverall, Victorian divisional secretary, and son of GW Deverall, AEU Commonwealth councillor.

Even though AAESDA relied heavily on arbitration to advance members' interests, this was not a substitute for membership activity, which was as regular and intense as experienced in (say) the AEU. However, the tendency was to seek to make claims and litigate them, without being accompanied by industrial action. The claims were endorsed by members and they were the subject of regular reports back to meetings.

Employers often opposed arbitration; AAESDA's first Federal Log of Claims was served in 1946. Under the Conciliation and Arbitration Act, the service of a log of claims was usually followed by the finding of a dispute by the commission, and then by the making of an award. This process had been occurring almost as a matter of course since 1904. However, it didn't happen in AAESDA's case. Instead, employers took every objection possible and, despite AAESDA taking the matter to the High Court – and winning, ultimately AAESDA withdrew the log in 1954 and decided to pursue claims in the various state jurisdictions. As the 1967 anniversary edition of *Blueprint* stated, after 'we spent thousands of pounds ... we became the fairy godmother of the legal profession'.

AAESDA gained membership and coverage in the metal, vehicle, aircraft, chemical, local government and space-tracking industries, as well as in various other sectors. Overseeing much of this, as federal president, was Paul Allsop. Allsop had been a key part of creating AAESDA in NSW, representing it at the inaugural AAESDA Federal Council in December 1945, and then helping to bring AAESDA and AAD together in 1948. He was an engineer by profession and became honorary federal president the same year. He held that position until 1973, when he was appointed a Commissioner of the Australian Conciliation and Arbitration Commission.

Amalgamation between AAESDA and AAD was the key to AAESDA's success, allowing the union to build its membership and influence. However, other amalgamations and incorporations also helped strengthen the union. In the 1940s, the Commonwealth Public Service Temporary Technical

Officers Association was absorbed; in the 1950s the Federation of Scientific and Technical Workers likewise came into the fold.

In its fiftieth year, AAESDA could boast 12,738 members, situated in every state and territory. It had award coverage in both the public and private sectors, with slightly more (7322) in the private sector than in the combined (federal, state and local government) public sector. However, the membership was gradually changing. Until the 1950s and the amalgamation with the AAD, members had been predominantly professional engineers and architects. But with the rise of the Association of Professional Engineers of Australia (APEA, now APESMA [Association of Professional Engineers, Scientists and Managers Australia]) and its success in gaining award coverage for professional engineers in the Metal Industry Award in 1957, many professional engineers preferred to join the APEA. While AAESDA was the prime mover in that case, the APEA was able to take greater advantage of the success.

According to its rules, AAESDA was an apolitical association. Those rules prevented AAESDA from affiliating to political parties, and even extended to preventing political discussion. These prohibitions were honoured more in the breach – the Graham dismissal referred to above was no isolated example. In 1950 a new rule 67A was inserted by majority at the Federal Conference. The rule prevented members of 'extremist organisations' – a label applied to members of the Communist Party of Australia (CPA) – from being eligible for membership of AAESDA. The rule was rejected by the Industrial Registrar as 'tyrannical and oppressive'. In the *AAESDA Bulletin* of February 1951, the author described the discredited rule as 'a bid by Political Conservatives to control the Association' and the rejection by the Registrar as 'a humiliation to this Association'.

Formal political affiliations were generally left unstated in the publications and activities of the union. Many leading honorary and full-time officials were members of the ALP and some of the CPA. Some activists – generally divisional councillors – had connections to the Liberal Party of Robert Menzies. In addition, there was a distinct Masonic flavour to some of AAESDA's activities. The symbol of the union, of a pair of compasses, no doubt was designed to be reminiscent of the same Masonic symbol. For instance, the *AAD Bulletin* of April – May 1944 referred to the need for all members to 'humble ourselves to the Great Architect of the Universe', a term for God typically used by Freemasons.

AAESDA's Victorian administrative officer, and later branch secretary, Arthur Greig, was a member of the CPA. Graham Walker, federal secretary from 1961, was an ALP member, as was George Butcher, assistant federal secretary. At the same time, members of the National Civic Council and the Industrial Groups were also active in AAESDA, including John Forrester in Queensland and John Beedham in WA. Political matters were often battled out intensely, but the absence of formal affiliation of the union to the Australian Labor Party meant that the prize of votes at ALP state and national conferences, which made the internecine fights in the AEU, the Boilermakers and Blacksmiths Society, and other prominent metal industry unions, so bloody was lacking.

AAESDA, like most white-collar unions of the postwar era, was not affiliated to the Australian Council of Trade Unions (ACTU). AAESDA's officials and activists nevertheless saw the need for greater cooperation and solidarity between unions. AAESDA was a key mover in the formation of the Australian Council of Salaried and Professional Associations (ACSPA). AAESDA had commenced its attempts to set up a federation of associations in 1945. This had folded in 1947, but revived in the early 1950s. ACSPA finally came into being in October 1956, with approximately 200,000 union members represented. AAESDA Federal President Paul Allsop was also ACSPA's first federal president.

AAESDA expanded significantly in the 1970s and 1980s. Industrial action, previously only taken in extremis, was planned and executed. The first such campaign of programmed industrial action took place at International Harvester at Geelong in 1968. In the big campaigns of the period, such as the 1972–73 and 1979–81 wages and hours campaigns, AAESDA members joined in the industrial action, stop work meetings, and bans and limitations.

Amalgamation with the AEU was first contemplated in the 1960s. The AEU had long been in favour of amalgamation of all unions within the metals and engineering industry. Commencing in 1912, when the ASE originated discussions with the Australasian Society of Engineers about amalgamation, various schemes had been proposed: in 1931, with the Federated Ironworkers Association; and again during the Second World War with the Australasian Society of Engineers. Most attempts at amalgamation with the AEU foundered because of indifference or interference from the AEU's parent body in the UK, which the (Australian) AEU was part of until 1968.

One element that did improve cooperation between the unions was the Metals Trades Federation (later the Metal Trades Federation of Unions, or MTFU). The MTFU was sponsored by the AEU and had as one of its objectives the creation of a single union for the metal industry.

Once the AEU had finally separated from its parent body it was freed up to vigorously pursue amalgamation within the metal industry. In 1966 the Commonwealth Councils of the AEU and Boilermakers and Blacksmiths Society (BBS) had formed a joint research office. This cooperation between the AEU, BBS and eventually the Sheet Metal Workers Union (the SMWU) led to a successful amalgamation ballot in 1972, and the AMWU was registered on 2 April 1973.

The 1970s were not just a time of bad fashion and disco music. Union strength was at a peak and organised workers were able to make demands for a greater share in national prosperity. However, these campaigns came at a cost; the wages breakouts in 1972–73 and 1979–81 made the Australian economy very brittle. The election of the Whitlam Labor government in December 1972 was an opportunity for the labour and progressive movements to blossom. But the inflation and industrial stagnation that ensued, arising from the first 'oil shock' in 1973 (when OPEC decided to restrict oil production), meant the end of the period of full employment and economic growth that followed the Second World War. As the boom came to an end, so too did the Whitlam government, despite its early promise and delivery of many long-awaited reforms.

There was recognition by many that the labour movement and the Labor Party needed to do better. AMWU Assistant National Secretary Laurie Carmichael and ACTU Research Officer Bill Kelty (later the secretary) believed that Whitlam, and reformist governments generally, 'need more time'. That is, if a reformist social democratic government is to be successful it needs to have a program that can derive its success from an expanding rather than a contracting economy, meaning in turn that when the economy does contract, as it so clearly did from 1973, the reform program slows.

The thinking within the labour movement was led by the likes of Kelty and Carmichael, as well as Bob Hawke (while still ACTU president) and other leaders such as the Waterside Workers Federation Charlie Fitzgibbon and Ray Gietzelt of the Miscellaneous Workers. It was from this process that the social and political agreement ultimately called the Accord began in 1977.

In this period, the AMWU and AAESDA took a major role: the AMWU through the ACTU and AAESDA through ACSPA. Leaders of the two unions believed that the movement needed to act in a unified manner. The common thinking and activity meant that it was logical that the two peak bodies would come together. Inevitably, AAESDA's leaders started to think about themselves as being part of a union rather than a white-collar association.

The leadership also thought that a more representative name for the union would be required. This was especially so as Architects and Engineers became less prominent in the membership, and supervisors and technical officers became more so. In 1980, proposals were circulated to alter the name and image of AAESDA to reflect these changes.

In 1981, the union's name was changed to the Association of Draughting, Supervisory Technical Employees (ADSTE). At the same time, a distinctive 'adste' logo was designed and implemented. Little else changed. However, it gave rise to a split between the federally registered body, and the state registered body in Queensland. Under the leadership of Branch Secretary John Forrester, AAESDA maintained its separate registration, and following a period of around three years of attempted coexistence, the two organisations split, with money, membership and rules completely separated.

There was also a fairly nasty election for the position of federal secretary. Ted Benjamin had replaced Graham Walker on his appointment to the Arbitration Commission. With Benjamin's resignation, George Butcher became federal secretary, leaving his position of federal assistant secretary vacant. Both Victorian Branch Secretary Arthur Greig and ACT Branch Secretary Donna Valentine nominated. In the election that followed, a major split developed in the Federal Office, with some supporting Valentine and others supporting Greig. Despite the stiff contest, and a number of legal challenges, Arthur Greig was elected. On George Butcher's retirement a short time later, Arthur was elected unopposed as federal secretary.

Arthur was a small and wiry man, almost always clad in a skivvy and (in those days before smoking was banned in the workplace) with an inevitable 'racehorse', a skinny-roll-your-own cigarette, pursed between his lips. Arthur could be irascible, but he was also a person capable of eloquent and persuasive argument. One person who saw that irascibility first-hand was Des Heaney, who on first meeting Arthur was accused of being 'a stooge for the NSW Right' (which was news to an abashed Heaney, given that at the time he had been with ADSTE for three weeks).

Arthur was a thinker of great depth and saw the need for ADSTE to change. He was not confident about the outcome. As a long time AAESDA/ADSTE activist and official, he had been part of the Victorian branch since the 1950s. He was appointed as administrative officer in 1959 under John Pomeroy and was elected branch secretary in 1972. After winning the position of federal secretary, ADSTE's federal office staff was built up with additional industrial officers, including Ted Oliver (uncle of ACTU Secretary Dave Oliver), Mike Nicolaides, Julius Roe, Martin Schutz, Joe Nieuwenhuysen and Sandra Jones. Geoff Whitehead, who had replaced Greig as Victorian branch secretary, eventually stepped up to assistant federal secretary to Arthur. Whitehead was replaced as branch secretary by Judith Bornstein.

These significant changes were preceded by the demise of ACSPA. ADSTE had precipitated this by resigning from ACSPA and joining the ACTU in 1979. ACSPA then decided to fold its tent, and this precipitated a wholesale influx of white-collar unions into the ACTU.

This assisted in the thinking and discussion occurring around the Accord. By the end of 1982 a document was ready to be approved by the ACTU and the ALP, and it committed the parties to cooperative relations, a minimisation of disputation and moderation of wage demands. In return, various social policies such as Medicare and industry superannuation were to be implemented, as well as cooperative economic and industry plans. The Metal Workers Union, unique among unions, took the Accord to the membership for endorsement.

In the words of Bill Kelty, the Accord 'was to do some big things, not the little things. Sometimes you have to pay a big price to get some big things'. With the election of the Hawke Labor government in March 1983, the price was about to be paid.

The Australia of 1983 was vastly different to today. The Australian dollar was still fixed by government, many industries enjoyed high tariff barriers, and there was significant regulation protecting industry. For trade unions, membership was 58 per cent of the working population – and overwhelmingly male. In 1986, 63 per cent of male workers were union members compared to 44 per cent of female workers. Women comprised only 40 per cent of the workforce.

Following the principle that trade unions need to give reformist social democratic governments more time, the Accord committed unions to wage restraint. Unlike the wages freeze, implemented by the Fraser government in 1982, the national wage case of 1983 did award pay rises – but they were wage rises that protected worker's pay rates relative to inflation and didn't provide any growth in real wages.

The Accord also introduced tripartite processes between government, employers and unions. These specifically involved manufacturing; under Industry Minister Senator John Button, a number of plans were negotiated and implemented, including the car and steel plans. At the same time the

Australian Manufacturing Council was set up. ADSTE and the AMWU were heavily involved in all of these initiatives, which dealt with the significant restructuring of industries subject to 'structural adjustment', in the language of the time. These tripartite processes led to the economic and tax summits of 1983 and 1984. Under the Accord, unions had a place at the table.

A further element of the Accord process was the recognition that, to cope with more rapidly evolving industries, workers would need to be more highly skilled. As the 1980s progressed, higher skills levels for manufacturing workers were established, with the Metal Workers Union creating a special class tradesperson, and ADSTE, likewise, a principal technical officer, in 1985. These were brought to a successful conclusion in 1986. However, it was realised that the only way of ensuring that members could enjoy proper career progression would be through a single career path, incorporating semi-skilled, skilled trades, technical/draughting and professional engineer/ scientist classifications.

This was a particularly tall order given that the *Metal Industry Award 1984* Part 1 (there were six parts in all) contained 638 classifications, sometimes separated by as little as 20 cents per week. The reasons for many of these minor differences were lost in the mists of time.

The only way for such a career path to be created would be by maximum cooperation between all metal unions, but especially so between the Metal Workers Union and ADSTE. Demarcation disputes were a fact of life in many manufacturing workplaces. Probably the worst were at Williamstown Naval Dockyards near Melbourne. At 'Willy Dock', as it was known, some 27 unions were present; a tradesperson could not pick up a tool without first going to the tool store. As ACTU Secretary Bill Kelty described it, 'you couldn't have a modern workplace dealing with a modern economy on 1930s lines'.

Demarcation disputes did occur at times between the AMWU and ADSTE, especially in testing and commissioning work. For example, at the Commonwealth Aircraft Corporation, newly rebuilt engines were tested by highly skilled tradespeople; at the Government Aircraft Factory, literally over the fence, the same testing work was undertaken by technical officers. Yet the skills required were virtually identical and reflected the relative strengths of each union on site.

These tendencies and pressure points were recognised by most trade union leaders, especially in ADSTE and the Metal Workers Union. In 1987, the ACTU produced the document *Future Strategies for the Australian Trade*

Union Movement.[87] *Future Strategies*, as it was known, was the distillation of many years of thinking and discussion within the movement. While its key author was ACTU Secretary Bill Kelty, many others, especially Laurie Carmichael, influenced its content.

Future Strategies detailed the malaise of the Australian trade union movement. The significant percentage of Australian workers in trade unions masked the disorganisation inherent within narrowly based craft unions. So while nearly half of all union members belonged to those 16 unions with more than 50,000 members, less than 2 per cent belonged to those 155 unions with less than 1000 members. And for ACTU Secretary Bill Kelty, the validity of even these figures was doubtful; levels of financial membership – paying members – could be as low as one-third of the 'headline' membership.

Future Strategies defined the most pertinent question for the movement as not whether it 'can adapt and respond but whether it can adapt at sufficient rate not just to ensure its survival but to promote further growth'. It answered this question by proposing the formation of 18 unions from all existing trade unions. These quickly became known as the proposed 'super unions'. However, for Kelty and others, the suggested 18 unions were strategic unions, not dependent upon numbers to prove the validity of their existence, but their ability to promote the interests of working people and to do the 'big things'.

Of the proposed 18 unions, the key for the AMWU and ADSTE was the 'Metal Industry – Vehicle Industry – Oil' union. This was more or less in accord with the views of the leadership of the two unions at the time.

In ADSTE, the mid 1980s were equally momentous. On the resignation of Geoff Whitehead as assistant federal secretary in 1984, Graham Harris stepped up. Unlike many of the other new federal industrial officers recruited from public service backgrounds or from other unions, Harris was a long-term ADSTE member. He had been trained as a fitter at Holden's Elizabeth (SA) plant, and so had originally been in the AEU. After spending some time in the drawing office, he was then selected as a draughtsman in 1962, and joined AAESDA. As a job delegate or 'area representative', he took a key role in organising the AAESDA membership at Holden. He and the other delegates recruited all of the drawing office into AAESDA and so, without any agreement with their employer, they created a closed shop. (The high level of membership achieved by Graham and his comrades continues to this day.)

---

87 Australian Council of Trade Unions 1987, *Future strategies for the trade union movement*, Rev. [ed.], ACTU, Melbourne.

Graham had been voted on to the AAESDA SA Divisional Council in 1972, and from there became a federal conference delegate and federal vice-president. When recruited by Arthur, Graham left Holden's and shifted his family to Melbourne in 1983.

For Graham, amalgamation was, if not a necessity, nevertheless the only way that ADSTE would continue to grow in power and influence. In his experience, the previously well-defined demarcation between tradespeople on the shop floors and draughting and technical personnel in their offices was breaking down. With the introduction of Computer Numeric Controlled (CNC) machinery, Computer Aided Draughting (CAD) and Computer Aided Manufacturing (CAM), jobs that had previously been the exclusive purview of a tradesperson or draughting officer or production planner could be allocated to an office or production environment almost at will. Or at least that seemed to be the promise of the new technologies that were appearing.

To Graham, Arthur Greig was a fine union leader, but approached the question of amalgamation with trepidation (in my discussions with Arthur, he believed a split of ADSTE between the private and public sectors, and therefore into the AMWU and the then PSU, was inevitable). Graham had been contemplating the issue for some years. He believed that ADSTE should take advantage of the environment that was making amalgamation more attractive, and determine on an amalgamation that would protect ADSTE members' conditions and grow the union.

When the ACTU published 'Future Strategies', it was for Graham 'enormously influential. Without it, a lot of the amalgamations would never have come about. It was about generating an atmosphere in which almost the need to amalgamate was pre-determined ... all you had to figure out was where you were going ... Bill Kelty and co. were extremely pragmatic about where you were going after that, but the pressure and momentum for amalgamation was pretty irresistible'.

Tragically, as this momentum was growing, Arthur Greig was struck down by cancer. Despite being diagnosed as terminally ill, Arthur continued at work through most of 1987. He died, having willed his body to science in January 1988.

On Arthur's passing, Graham became federal secretary, with Mike Nicolaides as assistant federal secretary. The determination to amalgamate with another union had been discussed extensively and endorsed at the 1987 Federal Conference; the ADSTE *National News* of June 1987 decided on three alternatives: to either, '(a) Successfully amalgamate with most of the small unions, (b) Amalgamate with some of the smaller unions and a larger union, or (c) Amalgamate with a large union'. The small unions referred to include the Commonwealth Foremens Association, the Professional Radio and Electronics Institute of Australasia, and various CSIRO in-house unions, many of which had initials to challenge AAESDA's former nickname of the 'Alphabeticals'.

The 1988 Federal Conference decided that (c) – the 'big union' option – would be pursued. As the June 1988 *National News* described it, 'after a year of intense debate and education within ADSTE, conference decided on amalgamation with a large union as a priority ... The three main candidates are the Electrical Trades Union, the AMWU, and the Municipal Officers Association'.

With its reputation for deep thinking, the amalgamation was to be pursued in accordance with the 'ADSTE Amalgamation Charter', and this was duly printed in the July 1988 edition.

Consequently, the potential amalgamation partners made presentations to the Federal Executive Committee (the president, two vice-presidents, federal secretary and assistant federal secretary) of ADSTE. From this, and after significant discussion, debate and disputation, the Metal Workers Union was the choice of the December Federal Executive. This decision was to be reviewed by the Annual General Meetings (AGMs) that were a feature of ADSTE's governance. The AGMs had to be scheduled under rule in the first quarter of each year. The stage was set for conflict between the pro- and anti-amalgamation forces.

For ACT Branch Secretary Des Heaney, the only viable amalgamation was with the 'small unions', option (a) of the 1987 Federal Conference resolution. Heaney, who had replaced Donna Valentine as secretary in 1982, became the unofficial head of the anti-amalgamation group within ADSTE. Going into 1989, this group comprised the ACT, WA and Tasmanian branches and some others. NSW was ambivalent about amalgamation; Branch Secretary Bill Leslie supported amalgamation, but this was not a unanimous view on his executive.

Heaney had been recruited as an organiser by Donna Valentine in 1981. A former nurse, he became an honorary sub-branch secretary of the Health and Research Employees Association, and was then briefly employed by the theatrical union as an organiser. In Heaney's view, ACT branch councillors were 'public servants or university based ... some of them were doing extremely high-level technical and engineering work. They just couldn't comprehend the connection ... There was open hostility between the techs and the trades'.

Predictably, with a majority of the AGMs set to approve the in-principle decision to amalgamate with the AMWU, the battle commenced in earnest. A series of special general meetings in ACT, WA and Tasmania were purportedly called in December 1988, i.e. immediately after the Federal Executive decision and to pre-empt the AGMs. Unfortunately, as the federal court found later in 1989 (in *Heaney v Harris*), these meetings were not properly convened (as any union official knows, getting members to respond to union issues after the middle of December is well-nigh impossible); the demand to hold a plebiscite of members to confirm or condemn the decision of the Federal Executive was not validly made.

Notwithstanding this, the ADSTE Federal Executive determined to hold a plebiscite on amalgamation – in effect, determining to hold a vote about whether or not a vote should be held. In Graham Harris's recollection a plebiscite was 'always going to be held'; and from 29 November to 13 December 1989 the plebiscite vote took place. In the lead up, the contending forces argued vociferously for their positions – in the words of the anti-amalgamation forces to 'stop the takeover' and to vote against the '19th Century Union', which would result in ADSTE being 'submerged' into a 'centrally controlled ... predominantly, non technical' union that would be 'so large' as to make 'participation by rank and file technical workers ... impossible'. It urged those opposed to amalgamation to call the number of the ADSTE ACT Office.

The Yes case simply stated that the amalgamation process must be allowed to take its course; and that amalgamation would address concerns about skills, training and career paths, as well as strengthening each union.

The result of the plebiscite was, of 7326 votes cast, 4092 or 58 per cent were in favour of the vote for amalgamation to proceed. Negotiations on the scheme of amalgamation then proceeded to finality.

However, this was not the only notable result. The ACT branch remained obdurate in its opposition, but both the WA branch under Acting Secretary Peter Cox and the Tasmanian branch led by Phil Baker subsequently decided to support amalgamation with the AMWU. While this may have had an element of necessity about it, these decisions meant that the final run-up to the actual amalgamation ballot was relatively trouble free in ADSTE.

At the same time, amalgamation discussions in the Metal Workers Union were continuing. ADSTE, it was hoped, would be the first of many to form the metal–vehicle–oil union envisaged in 'Future Strategies'. However, the political nature of the union movement made this problematic – the left/right split between (on the left) the Metal Workers, ADSTE and its other amalgamation partners, and the Federated Ironworkers Association (FIA) and the Australasian Society of Engineers (ASE) on the right was looking like it would prevent a proper amalgamated union being created for the industry.

In this environment, the ADSTE/AMWU amalgamation came to be seen as possibly more important than it actually was – it provided a 'proof of concept' to the 'Future Strategies' grand plan, and also a test for the newly liberalised amalgamation regime under the *Industrial Relations Act 1988* (which had replaced the Conciliation and Arbitration Act). A situation where a large and overwhelmingly blue-collar trade union was amalgamating with a relatively small white-collar union, which contained supervisors, may have been unthinkable in the then recent past. However, in the environment that prevailed, plus the renowned discipline of the Metal Workers Union, the amalgamation vote was considered to be more or less a formality.

In ADSTE, on the other hand, the controversy around amalgamation with the Metal Workers Union was clear. Paradoxically, the plebiscite campaign, which was simply to determine the legitimacy of the decision-making process, led those who had opposed the amalgamation to realise that it was almost inevitable. And for Des Heaney and his colleagues, the alternative may have been too horrible to contemplate – that a failure to amalgamate may have led to the demise of ADSTE, because the union would not have any 'friends', and that between the ACTU and pro-amalgamation unions, that ADSTE would be 'wiped out'.

For those of us who actively believed in the benefits of amalgamation between ADSTE and the Metal Workers Union – the Victorian, NSW, SA and Queensland branches, as well as the federal office – the plebiscite cleared the decks. It meant that pro-amalgamation forces grouped around the 'Campaign for Amalgamation and Democracy' – or CAD – had a huge and positive affirmation by the members of the union. It also meant that previously standoffish officials and delegates of the Metal Workers Union realised the seriousness of the campaign. It was real.

The logistics surrounding the amalgamation proceeded. One issue that particularly exercised the interest and activities of ADSTE officials was the 'ADSTE Action Plan for Women'. This document had been negotiated by the female officials and organisers, and endorsed by the ADSTE Federal Conference. It reflected the concerns that ADSTE officials had expressed about the male-dominated nature of the Metal Workers Union. Both unions were male dominated. This reflected the gender segmentation of the industry organised by each union. The metal industry in Australia has always been significantly male dominated. In 1990 the Metal Workers Union had approximately 6 per cent female membership – the majority of these women were employed as process workers. ADSTE had approximately 11 per cent female membership. At the same time, a significant number of female officials and organisers had been recruited by ADSTE.

The first female full-time official of ADSTE was Judith Bornstein. She had worked in laboratories, and was a political activist in the ALP. Recruited as an organiser by Arthur Greig, Bornstein replaced Geoff Whitehead as Victorian branch secretary. Bornstein strongly supported Arthur Greig in his campaign for federal secretary against Donna Valentine, proving that politics could trump gender. Bornstein had been the first woman vice-president of the Victorian Trades Hall Council and a representative of women trade unionists on the ACTU Executive. She was appointed a commissioner of the Victorian Industrial Relation Commission in 1987. She left a legacy that gave importance to issues surrounding, and of importance to, women unionists.

The ADSTE Action Plan for Women built upon the work of early pioneers of the 'second wave' of feminism. Mary Owen, a standout among trade union women of the 1960s and 1970s, was originally employed in AAESDA's federal office in an administrative capacity before taking up a position with the ACTU. With the support of Graham Harris and Mike Nicolaides, the work of officials such as Judith Klepner and Deb Vallance (Victoria), Max Adlam and Anne Donnellan (SA), Robyn Fortescue (NSW), and Santina Bertone and Martina Nightingale (federal office), as well as rank-and-file delegates like Tracy Davis and Trudy Scott (who became federal vice-president), the endorsement of the Action Plan was a major achievement.

The ADSTE Action Plan for Women was an important document, less for what it contained than what it represented as an attempt by a major union involved in manufacturing to address gender segmentation in the workforce and the under-representation of women in the hierarchy of the union.

In the negotiations between the two unions, ADSTE representatives were adamant that the Action Plan for Women be adopted by the amalgamated union. This was agreed. ADSTE had formulated an Amalgamation Charter. This had then informed 23 clauses of a Memorandum of Understanding (MoU), negotiated between the two unions. The most innovative element of the Memorandum was the agreement to create a Technical and Supervisory Division of the amalgamated union. But despite all of this, it was never the intention of the two unions that this be a 'union within a union'.

The formalities continued to be negotiated to agreement in a reasonably amicable manner. On 7 June 1990, Moore DP of the Australian Industrial Relations Commission issued his decision approving the submission of the scheme to a ballot. It is relevant to note that no objections were made to the proposal to seek a ballot to approve the amalgamation.

Although the formal opposition of the ACT branch continued, the amalgamation ballot proceeded in an orderly fashion. The ballot papers were distributed to members of each union. Those to ADSTE members were distributed with both the pro- and anti-amalgamation arguments included. For Metal Workers Union members, there was simply the ballot paper.

Significant effort was put in to make sure there was a good ballot outcome. With the wisdom of hindsight, it appears the ADSTE/AMWU amalgamation may have been a 'lay down misère'. However, it didn't feel that way from the inside.

The amalgamation vote duly passed and the newly formed Metals and Engineering Workers Union came into existence officially on 1 April 1991.

Whether or not the amalgamation worked will be a judgement of history. In the words of Graham Harris, 'it's not something which will be undone'. Despite the downturn in manufacturing and the attacks on workers' rights exemplified by John Howard's Work Choices laws, we go on, thus giving life to the saying that 'The unity of labour is the hope of the world'. In the 160 years since its inception, the union has met all of the challenges thrown at it. In 2012, we had 100,000 members across diverse industries. In what is now the Technical, Supervisory and Administrative Division, the rules and the spirit of ADSTE continues to exist.

And many former ADSTE officials and activists continue to make a major contribution to the union.

Dedication

This chapter is dedicated to the memory of Marie Harris, who died in 2012. As a formidable character in her own right, and as Graham Harris's partner and wife of nearly 50 years, she sacrificed much on behalf of the workers who Graham was privileged to represent.

Note on Sources

The writing of this brief piece has been assisted by the recollections of a number of people. I am grateful to the following for agreeing to be interviewed: Des Heaney (8 August 2012, Canberra), Bill Kelty (13 September 2012,

Melbourne), Graham Harris (17 September 2012, Brisbane/ Pyap), and Laurie Carmichael (14 January 2013, Tewantin).

The chapter also draws on the following publications: T. Sheridan, *Mindful Militants: The Amalgamated Engineering Union in Australia 1920–1972*, Cambridge University Press, 1976; Ken Buckley, *The Amalgamated Engineers in Australia, 1852–1920*, Dept. of Economic History, Research School of the Social Sciences, Australian National University, 1979; C. Wright Mills, *White Collar: The American Middle Classes*, Oxford University Press, New York, 1951; and *Blueprint* (journal of AAESDA and ADSTE), 1951–1991.

In addition, the Melbourne University Archives provided invaluable resources relating to the various publications of AAESDA and ADSTE, especially its holdings of leaflets, working papers and publications on the amalgamation process.

Chapter 3

One Big Metal Union?

The Impact of Union Amalgamation in Western Australia

Bobbie Oliver

The story has been told elsewhere in this book of the amalgamation of the metal unions to form the Amalgamated Metal Workers Union, which took place in 1973. The proud bearer of the tradition of the 'metallies' is the Australian Manufacturing Workers Union. But what occurred in WA in this time? Given the popular perception on both sides of the Nullarbor that WA circumstances frequently differ from the eastern states (often referred to as 'West Australian exceptionalism'), this chapter examines the impact of successive amalgamations of the AMWU on WA members. Where did the impetus to amalgamate come from? Was it driven mainly by the federal organisation, or did some initiatives occur at local level? Who benefited and who did not? Did amalgamation impact upon union solidarity? Did members feel less loyalty to a new, amalgamated, industry-wide union than they had to a union of their specific craft or trade? Has amalgamation yielded the benefits that the organisers hoped for back in the 1960s when they orchestrated the 'first step' to achieving 'one big metal union'?

The unions involved in the amalgamation had been through the process before, with the AEU's predecessor, the Amalgamated Society of Engineers (ASE), joining with the Federated Ironworkers during the First World War – an alliance that occurred only in WA. The Boilermakers and the Blacksmiths united in one society in 1965. The 1973 amalgamation was initiated by the unions' federal bodies, and appears to have caused little dissention. Delegates at the Fourth Federal Conference of the Boilermakers and Blacksmiths Society in Sydney in April 1969 voted in favour by 579 to 55, as well as affirming the decision of the 1967 conference to explore amalgamation with the Shipwrights and other metalworkers' unions. The membership of both unions registered a majority of three to one in favour of amalgamation, while the journals of each hailed the achievement as a significant step towards 'fulfilling the aims and aspirations of Australian metalworkers over the past 50 years'– to form one big metal union.

The AEU was already WA's biggest metalworkers union. In 1970, the union had managed to negotiate site agreements with a range of employers in the Kwinana industrial strip, including Structural Steel, Forwood Down, Tomlinsons, Cockburn Cement, Alcoa, the BP Refinery, the Nickel Refinery, Vickers Hoskins, and all the fertiliser plants in WA. The construction agreement that the AEU brokered with employers in the Kwinana area of an allowance of $1.80 per hour for tradespeople from 1 May 1970 compared very favourably with the Award rate for other construction workers under the Metal Trades Agreement of $1.52 per hour and a shop rate of $1.44. Such agreements were formalised by an exchange of letters between the union secretary and the employer, with the letters then being registered with the WA Arbitration Court.

AEU Organiser Jack Marks toured the north-west in October – November 1970, travelling a distance of 8000 miles (12,874 kilometres), visiting Wyndham, Broome, Derby and Kununurra (where he was the first AEU organiser to visit in seven years). He reported to the union's January 1971 state conference that the membership had increased by over 2000 since September 1967. Consequently, there was a desperate need for more organisers, working an area that he picturesquely described as being 'bigger than NSW, Victoria, New Zealand and Tasmania put together'. Marks pointed out that the AEU employed fewer organisers than its rival union, the ASE (with only 4500 members and four full-time organisers). He forecast a dramatic expansion in the Eastern Goldfields and the Pilbara with the respective growth of the nickel and iron ore industries. Marks confidently predicted that 1971 would be an exciting year in which 'amalgamations [on] a scale never before witnessed in Australia's history will give rise to potentially the greatest single fighting force of the working class'.

But how did the rank and file feel about this arrangement? AEU historian Tom Sheridan devoted only a few lines to members' attitudes to this new union, when he wrote:

> While many members no doubt experienced a twinge of regret for the final passing of the old order, AEU activists now felt much better equipped to cope with the new era of industrial relations ushered in by contemporary radical changes in the arbitration and bargaining areas

and the appearance in Canberra of the first Labor government in 23 years.

Ideology was an important issue facing members contemplating the amalgamation of their union with others. 'Right'-wing and 'left'-wing unions did not make good bedfellows. In WA, as elsewhere, the AEU, BBS and SMWU were all aligned with the left. However, similar ideology did not make the process entirely trouble free. There had been way too many demarcation disputes between the three unions for members to be entirely gracious about joining forces. The rules of the AEU were used as the means of facilitating the amalgamation (being amended to incorporate the members and coverage of the two other unions). This may have been the source of possible dissension, but in the recollection of Gordon McIntosh, then president of the AEU, the rank and file of the three unions strongly supported the merger.

An immediate positive result was the foundation of an education committee in WA, which started a training program for shop stewards. This program predated Whitlam-era Labor Minister Clyde Cameron's initiative (which later became the Trade Union Training Authority) by at least two years. Shop stewards were trained in the structure and policies of their union, negotiation, how to hold meetings and public speaking. While many of these courses were conducted at the Labor Centre in Perth, others ran on mine sites in the north-west and elsewhere around the state.

In June 1972, officials of the new AMWU met with their counterparts in the WA Plumbers and Sheet Metal Workers Union (which was independent of the federal Sheet Metal Workers Union) to discuss amalgamation. AMWU Federal Joint Secretary Jack Heffernan observed that WA was unique because the sheet metalworkers and plumbers were not part of either federal body, but he saw 'few problems' in the sheet metal section of the union amalgamating at 'an early date', while safeguarding interests of the plumbers. The officials answered questions from assembled members of the union and resolved to expedite amalgamation as soon as possible. The Amalgamated Metal Workers Union of Western Australia [AMWU] was registered in the WA Arbitration Court on 2 February 1973, two months before the federal body was, finally, registered. In July, Assistant Secretary Frank Bastow reported to the AMWU State Council that amalgamation with the Vehicle Builders Union (again, a separate body from the Vehicle Builders Employees Federation, which operated in the eastern states) and the amending of the constitution to include the Sheet

Metal Workers was almost complete, but that some difficulties with awards had to be overcome. The Vehicle Builders Union was very small and after the closure of the Ford plant on Stirling Highway in the early 1970s, its members had been engaged mainly in constructing caravan bodies. The new arrangements required an award to cover all sheet metal trades workers employed by government departments across the state. Covering workers in private industry was more difficult, as their previous award applied only within a 25-mile radius of the Perth Post Office.

Initially, the impact of the amalgamations was extremely positive. Secretary Jim Mutton reported to the State Council in October 1973 that Organiser Colin Hollett had set up new branches at Karratha, Tom Price and Mt Newman – in the heart of the iron ore industry, where Marks had predicted phenomenal growth just two years earlier. In four months, 1122 members had been added to the union (engineering 760; boilermakers 179; sheet metalworkers 147; vehicle builders 36), and although 306 members had resigned, the net gain was 816 members. At the end of 1973, State President and Organiser Gordon Grenfell reported to State Council that the transitional period was over and the AMWU must be 'the most progressive and united organisation in the Commonwealth'. During the year, the union had made considerable gains for its members, including four weeks annual leave to all government workers, leave loading for both government and private sector workers, and an increase in over-award payments to all government workers. The union had also secured a new rate for apprentices based on a percentage of the relevant rate, with first year starting at 42 per cent. The Tonkin Labor state government had legislated full pay for workers compensation, including all over-award payments, and substantial increases in other benefits.

Despite these gains, however, the process of including the Shipwrights in an expanded AMWU was complex and protracted, providing another example of WA 'exceptionalism'. Although nationally, the shipwrights had their own union, the Federated Shipwrights' & Ship Constructors' Association of Australia, in the west they were part of the Maritime Workers Union of WA [MWU], a 1968 amalgamation of the Ship Painters and Dockers', the Seamen's, and the Shipwrights' and Watchmen's unions, with just over 300 members (70 of whom were shipwrights), and only two paid staff, a full-time secretary and an office typist. Although a national membership ballot of the shipwrights on 31 August 1976 recorded 588 in favour of amalgamation with the AMWU, there was a sizable 'No' minority of 340 members – almost 37 per cent. The appeal period against the decision to amalgamate was only one month, which was half over by the time the minute advising proceedings arrived in the west; the federal body seemed anxious to complete the process as soon as possible.

The amalgamation had negative consequences for the MWU. With such a small membership, administration costs of approximately $2000 per month and dues of $20 per quarter, there was very little surplus. The loss of 70 members was potentially devastating. There were further difficulties because half of the shipwrights were employed at Fremantle on a 35-hour week, while others worked a 40-hour week. Shipwrights in the port area who worked for the state government were covered by the State Ship Painters & Dockers' award, which granted a 35-hour working week, a 25 per cent leave loading, and other benefits such as payment of meal monies. The MWU normally negotiated on behalf of dockers and shipwrights as one body of workers, rather than separating two. When an agreement was reached, the Ship Painters & Dockers' award was amended and the shipwrights also got those conditions.

Seagoing shipwrights were employed when required by shipowners and worked under different conditions; therefore, to ensure that amalgamation was in everyone's interests, they were granted a separate ballot, giving them a choice of amalgamation either with the AMWU or with a seagoing union. MWU Secretary Chris Wells argued that it seemed best for shipwrights on a 35-hour week to remain in the MWU to enable the union to function as a unit and at the same time protect their conditions. JD Garland, joint national secretary of the AMWU, suggested a solution in which the AMWU in WA recognised the MWU's problem of remaining viable after its shipwright members departed. In turn, the MWU must acknowledge that nationally shipwrights had voted by a large majority for amalgamation with the AMWU, and that only the special circumstances existing in WA warranted those members remaining in the MWU unless the union could maintain its operations without them. In that case, the shipwrights would transfer to the AMWU. Internal union correspondence for the period indicated a fear that the Waterside Workers Federation (WWF) was moving in on the MWU, and was likely to snap up the shipwrights' membership. This merger did not occur until 1993. It involved the WWF, the Seamen's Union and several smaller maritime unions, and resulted in the Maritime Union of Australia [MUA]. The official merger of the AMWU with the shipwrights' section of the MWU occurred on 9 September 1977; the union changed its title to the Amalgamated Metal Workers and Shipwrights Union (AMWSU).

The next amalgamation discussions involved the ASEM&FWU, a metalworkers union that had formed from an amalgamation of the Australasian Society of Engineers (ASE) and the Moulders & Foundry Workers Union in 1979. The ASE not only historically competed for membership, but was also ideologically poles apart from the AMWU. A long, rancorous history between the unions in WA contained such flashpoints as the 1952 metal trades strike, in which the AEU, the Boilermakers and the Blacksmiths took a leading role, but the ASE and the moulders both refused to take part. The parties met in April 1980 at the State School Teachers Union premises in Adelaide Terrace, Perth. With AMWU State President Harold Peden in the chair, the unions' representatives discussed proposals put forward by ASEM&FWU: no redundancies among existing staff and officials (although some retiring workers might not be replaced); the adoption of a new superannuation scheme; and the computerising of joint membership records. The ASEM&FWU were keen to retain a separate identity within the AMWSU, which would include altering the name to accommodate them as had been done for the shipwrights. The AMWSU, however, responded that the name would be too long and unwieldy and could delay amalgamation with the federation; none of the other original AMWSU amalgamating unions were recognised in the title.

The meeting also discussed contributions and salaries. AMWSU contributions were marginally more, but the salaries of their paid officials were lower than those of the ASEM&FWU. A six-member committee, consisting of three representatives from each of the unions, would be set up for further discussions. Negotiations continued until November 1983, when the membership of each union was scheduled to vote on amalgamation.

From June 1983, the unions circulated pamphlets to their memberships, putting the case for amalgamation. The first of these pamphlets, headed 'One Metal Union for all WA Metal Workers', gave as reasons, 'solidarity' and 'service' – or frugality:

> (a) Solidarity. Over recent years, the trade union movement has borne the brunt of unprecedented attacks by both [sic] government, employers and the media. It has become obvious that while we are divided our backs will always be to the wall. However, a UNITED METAL TRADES UNION will be in a much better position to protect the interests of ALL West Australian metal workers.
>
> (b) Service. Two unions duplicating services to a membership that has virtually the same interests at heart and often employed in the

same workplace is a shameful waste of members' funds. Funds that could be much better employed in providing an efficient more professional service and in better promoting the interests of ALL West Australian metal trade workers.

Another flyer, titled 'Changing Role of the Metal Trades Unions', asserted that the role of unions had changed from the 'luxury' of servicing members with benefits, wage rises and improved working conditions to the 'retention of jobs and conditions' and trying to assist unemployed members. It quoted a figure of 75,000 jobs lost in the metal trades alone in Australia in 1982, and also raised the issues of 'major youth unemployment', and 'third world countries dumping metal products in Australia supported by massive subsidisation by their respective governments and multi-national companies'. The flyer argued that there was a need for a strong, united approach that would be achieved only by the two largest metalworkers' unions amalgamating. Another leaflet asked: 'Why Amalgamation?' and answered, in strong rhetorical language 'Historically!!!' Ever since unions formed, there had been mergers, the leaflet argued. The old cliché 'Unity is Strength' was 'as evident to the movement's pioneers as to today's members'. The AMWSU, the ASEM&FWU and the Federated Engine Drivers and Firemen's Association had worked together in a Joint Research Centre since 1982. The 'next logical step' was to amalgamate the two major unions in the metal industry in WA.

This was a WA initiative, and it encountered a major problem because, while the AMWU was a state branch of a national union, the ASE structure was more autonomous, with states being members of a federated body. The amalgamation between the ASE and the M&FWU that had taken place in WA in 1979 had not happened in the eastern states, where the two unions had remained separate, and where the moulders were now covered by the AMWSU. The *Engineering Trades Newsletter* of August 1983 pointed out that talks between the ASEM&FWU and the AMWU (Australia's 'largest metal trades union') had been going on for two years and it was time that members voted in favour of amalgamation.

How did the membership of the two unions involved respond to this campaign? Organisers reported 'isolated pockets' of opposition at companies such as Forwood Down, Westrail and the Paraburdoo mine site, and emphasised the 'need to make a proper job of the ballot'. But elements in the ASE launched a campaign opposing amalgamation. The 'Committee to preserve the ASE in WA' addressed the membership, in a leaflet titled

'Don't vote ourselves out of existence'. It asked, 'Why should members of the ASE be swallowed up by a giant union which is communist controlled and always acts in the most militant way possible?' The leaflet predicted that the only result would be involvement in militant strike action and loss of wages and conditions. It stated: 'Amalgamate with the AMWSU and you join a punch drunk strike machine', and 'the ASE doesn't even get a mention in the new name'. But the ASEM & FWU's paid officials urged members to vote 'yes'.

Some AMWSU officials, too, were unenthusiastic about the prospect of a merger with the old enemy. Ten days before the 28 November ballot, Peter Procter, the union's state organiser, complained that 'Yes' vote campaign pamphlets had been left unpacked and undistributed at the union office, and he urged all officials to give publication of the ballot top priority. But the anti-amalgamation propaganda won the day, with a majority of ASE members voting 'No'. The Moulders and Foundry Workers, however, voted to amalgamate with the AMWSU, and coincidentally in April 1984, the union title had been altered to accommodate them as well as the Federated Moulders Union. It was now the Amalgamated Metals, Foundry and Shipwrights Union (AMFSU).

The AMFSU still did not give up hope of amalgamating with the ASE. In May 1986, President Keith Peckham wrote to ASE Secretary Norm Xavier, that the relationship between the unions had 'improved' in the past three years, owing to the formation of the Metal Trades Joint Research Centre and its modern approach to research and computerisation. Elected officials represented each other's unions in negotiations, commission and court appearances, and there was a belief that the future needs of the membership would be best served by amalgamation 'at an appropriate time'. It never occurred. Eventually, the ASE in WA merged with the Electrical Trades Union – not with the AWU as in the eastern states. Ironically, during the 1980s, the AMWU had considered amalgamating with the ETU. The two union presidents Keith Peckham and Rivo Gandini were keen, but the federal ETU objected.

By the mid 1980s, trade unions were fighting for survival against attacks on working conditions and workers' rights to organise. One of the most concerted attacks commenced in December 1986, when Robe River Iron Associates, a subsidiary of the US company Peko Wallsend, sought to reduce already poor pay and working conditions at Cape Lambert and Pannawonica. The dispute, involving the AMWU and other mining unions, dragged on for years without resolution.

In 1989, the Building Workers Industrial Union published a report, titled *Can Unions Survive?*, showing a decline in union membership from 51 per cent of the Australian workforce in 1976 to 42 per cent in 1988. A number of factors combined to produce this statistic: technology had replaced much unionised manual labour with computerised systems – a trend that was especially marked in such occupations as wharf labouring and seafaring, but also in the transport industry. Over three or four decades, railways, where many AMWU members were employed, had passed from very labour intensive steam, through dieselisation to electric, and railway workshops around Australia had seen the near-disappearance of old trades such as blacksmiths and carriage makers when fibre glass and aluminium replaced wooden carriages and wagons. This was accompanied by government moves to outsource contracts to private manufacturers, resulting in the closure of many government railway workshops, including Midland (WA), in the last two decades of the twentieth century.

The change in the workforce, caused by a greater proportion of non-manual occupations, a decrease in public sector employment in traditional blue-collar jobs, and a youth culture that doesn't seem to think about joining a union were other factors. In his 2005 study on the state of the Australian union movement, Michael Crosby showed that, while union density stood at 22.7 per cent of the workforce in 2004, it varied from 46.4 per cent in the public sector to just 17.4 per cent in the private sector.

The AMWU's major amalgamations were completed by 1995, although the union underwent further changes in both composition and name in the process of becoming the Australian Manufacturing Workers Union. How had the union fared? A report on Australian manufacturing and trade unionism in the 1990s, delivered to the union's Biennial Conference in July 1994, did not paint an optimistic picture. The downsizing and closures of factories had the most profound impact on manufacturing union membership and union finances. In WA in 1990, 58.9 per cent of the blue-collar workforce in large enterprises was unionised. In 1993, this number had dropped by more than a third. Despite forecasts that the remainder of the 1990s would see the continued expansion of WA manufacturing employment, between 1986 and 1993 the AMWU lost almost 4000 union members in manufacturing (a drop of 14.3 per cent), while the number of non-unionists employed in manufacturing rose by more than 7500 (19.4 per cent). From 1976 to 1993 the proportion of WA manufacturing employees who were unionised dropped from 54 to 33.6 per cent. This was the lowest percentage in Australia, followed by Queensland – a splendid irony considering that these were the two states

Figure 3.1 (top) 'The war on the wharves', as the 1998 dispute between the MUA and Patricks became known, demonstrated union solidarity.

Here, MUA Assistant Secretary Paddy Crumlin (back to camera) talks with AMWU officials (L to R) John Sharp-Collett; (unidentified); Keith Peckham; Doug Cameron; Dave Hicks (behind); Jock Ferguson; Ron Knox. The AMWU had marched from their State Conference to the picket line at North Wharf, Fremantle, to show solidarity with the strikers.

Figure 3.2. The famous caravan that was the early focus of the Workers' Embassy in the 1997 'Third Wave' dispute featured the other protests, such as the Amcor Box dispute in September 1998.

where manufacturing continued to expand. Australia-wide, the number of blue-collar manufacturing workers fell by more than 100,000 (21 per cent) and the number with union coverage fell from 64.6 per cent to 56.5 per cent. So, although Jack Marks's optimistic predictions had in fact been realised with regard to 'phenomenal growth' in the state, the 'greatest single fighting force of the working class' was in drastic decline.

There were, of course, many reasons for the union movement's continuing decline that impacted upon the whole of the continent, not merely its western third. Economic rationalism, especially as embraced by conservative political parties in Australia, has often been blamed. From the 1980s, the federal Liberal Party, under John Howard's influence and (sometime) leadership, argued that the arbitration system and strong unions posed 'the greatest threat to Australia's economic performance'. Crosby commented that the success of this 'extremist' message was surprising, coming as it did when 'the Accord was in force and Higgins' legacy bore fruit – controlling wages and promoting a modernisation of the Award system'. During the 1990s, as successive states voted in Liberal and Coalition governments, premiers embarked on destroying the arbitration system in their states, none with greater vehemence than Richard Court in WA.

The last amalgamation to take place occurred in 1995. The Printing and Kindred Industries Union (PKIU) – its ancestor, the WA Typographical Society, was founded in 1888 – was a product of a 1966 amalgamation between two earlier printing unions, which had been instigated by technological innovations creating an overlap of the unions' traditional work demarcation. Most WA members of the PKIU clearly felt that amalgamation was the best step to take. One said that he believed it would make the union 'more relevant' in smaller workplaces if it were a section of a much larger, more powerful union. Nation-wide the membership had already declined by 8000 between 1982 and 1992. The WA members voted strongly in favour of amalgamation (92 per cent), and the 62 per cent of returned ballot papers was the highest response in Australia.

There were significant reasons for the membership decline in printing. Australia-wide, the number of printing and kindred industries members (now the Printing Division of the AMWU) dropped from 43,370 in 1992 to 25,000 in 2007. In WA, there is evidence that the decline of union membership in private commercial firms, the Court government's assault on industrial legislation, and the introduction of individual workplace agreements during the Howard era, as well as advances in technology, influenced these figures. For example, when the private company Perth

Print bought out the *Sunday Times* printing operation in 1995, it refused to apply the commercial printing award rates and conditions to its employees and informed them that a union presence would not be tolerated. However, officials also mentioned the difficulty of organising membership in the small printing businesses (employing 12 or fewer workers) that comprised the majority of the industry in WA, as well as redundancies brought about by technological innovation and economic restructuring.

Conclusion

It is evident that the impetus to amalgamate came from various sources. It was sometimes a federal initiative as in the 1971 amalgamation of the AEU, the SMWU and the BBS; sometimes prompted by local interests, as in the negotiations with the plumbers, the sheet metalworkers and the shipwrights over several years.

Whether amalgamation has yielded the benefits that the organisers hoped for back in the 1960s when they orchestrated the 'first step' to achieving 'one big metal union' is more difficult to assess, because it is impossible to judge what the results of the alternative scenario – the continuing multiplicity of unions in related industries – would have been. But it is hard to imagine that smaller unions would have survived in the hostile climate of the twenty-first century, when larger unions have failed to prevent the erosion of wages and conditions. The aim of 'one big metal union' was achieved, and it remains one of the largest and most powerful unions in Western Australia.

References

Australian Manufacturing Workers Union (AMWU) Papers, J.S. Battye Library of Western Australian History Collection, Accession numbers 7673A, 7746A.

Conversations with former AEU/AMWU officials Neil Byrne, Keith Peckham and Gordon McIntosh.

Bertola, P & Oliver, B (eds), (2006), *The Workshops: A history of the Western Australian Government Railway Workshops*, UWA Press, Perth.

Crosby, M (2005), *Power at Work. Rebuilding the Australian Union Movement*, The Federation Press, Annandale, NSW.

Davis, M (2020), 'Unions Face Fight on a New Front', *Sydney Morning Herald*, 23 September 2010, available at http://www.smh.com.au/opinion/politics/unions-face-fight-on-a-new-front-20100922-15mex.html

Macintyre, S (1984), *Militant: The Life and Times of Paddy Troy*, Allen & Unwin, Sydney.

Moy, T (2008), 'Union Amalgamation and its Impact upon the Printing Industry's Trade Union Spirit and Identity: A Case Study of the Western Australian Branch Experience', *Papers in Labour History*, no. 31, March, pp. 19–31.

Oliver, B (2003), *Unity is Strength. A History of Australian Labor Party and the Trades and Labor Council in Western Australia, 1899–1999*, API Network, Perth.

Sheridan, T (1975), *Mindful Militants. The Amalgamated Engineering Union in Australia, 1920–1972*, Cambridge University Press, New York.

Tomkins, M (1999), 'Trade Union Amalgamations: Explaining the Recent Spate of Mergers in Australia', *Labour and Industry*, vol. 9, no. 3, April, pp. 61–77.

Chapter 4

Off to the Mystery Picnic

Mobilising Young Engineers in Victoria, 1941–1961

Keir Reeves

Almost 20 years ago I was lucky enough to interview a number of former Amalgamated Engineering Union (AEU) members who were involved in the AEU Youth Committee. At the time I was an earnest university student trying to make sense of the politics and culture of one of the most fabled unions in Australian history. One organisation was the union's youth committee, particularly its Melbourne district branch. The youth committee served the dual purpose of winning apprentices over to the AEU philosophy and also identifying future leaders in Victoria. Any understanding of the internal operations of union activities is not possible without the consent and cooperation of officials and ordinary members. This chapter is an invaluable record of the thoughts and recollections of a number of active members on the youth committee, many of whom have subsequently died since the original interviews.

The passing of almost two decades has led me to reflect upon my talks with former youth committee president Bruce McKissack in Chiltern near the Murray River in the early 1990s. At the time Bruce was terminally ill, but still had fire in his belly and an outspokenness and practical pragmatism that was apparent to me even as a young man. Despite his illness he was still ably equipped to vigorously engage in union politics and industrial struggles.

Other memorable discussions included those held with Bruce Armstrong, whose apprenticeship was with Otis elevators. Bruce served as both an elected official and as the editor of the *Young Engineer*, the official publication of the AEU Youth Committee. One day he told me that one of his earliest jobs as a young apprentice working for Otis had been winching an elevator car up a building with another teenage worker for almost eight hours and then later going to night school to get further technical training.

Issued FREE

Issued by AEU Melbourne District Youth Committee

OCTOBER, 1953

A.E.U. Youth Committee Formed

MOVE TO INCREASE WAGES

"The District Committee congratulates those apprentices and other members of the Union who have set about to build the AEU Youth Committee. We appeal to all members—young and old—to take an active interest in building this committee." These were the words of Bro Tennant, District secretary, when he opened the first meeting of the Youth Committee about six weeks ago.

Already this appeal by Bro Tennant has been taken up in a number of shops, branches, and amongst young members on the job.

Although under way for only a few weeks the Youth Committee has entered into a program of action for increased wages, etc. We know from our own experience how hard it is to make ends meet on the low wages of apprentices and young workers. We pay the same fares, same prices for food, clothes, entertainment, etc, as older people, but only receive a portion of their wage. In many cases we do the same work as adults, yet only receive a small portion of the adult rate.

DEMANDS

The Youth Committee puts forward these demands for all apprentices and young workers:—

● £1 a week increase for all young workers.

● Apprentice rates based on tradesmen's rates not basic wage.

● Free protective clothing (overalls, etc).

● Free tool kits.

● Military training to be voluntary.

These five points head a fine list. Now we must set about making these demands a reality, and only our strong united voice will make the bosses listen.

Now is the time for action.

(1) Make sure you are a Union member.

(2) Read The Young Engineer and pass it around.

(3) See your shop steward and elect a delegate to the Youth Committee.

(4) Discuss the Youth Committee program on your job.

(5) Support the Youth Committee functions.

SPORTS AND SOCIALS

Along with the activities around our demands, the Youth Committee is setting out to organise sporting and social activities where our member can get together.

Sports days, hikes, picnics are on the way, and cricket and football competitions are being planned.

A gay social life is in store, with dances, films, socials, etc. A dance and Xmas party will be coming off shortly.

This paper will be a regular publication, putting forward the activities of the committee and your views.

A good start has been made; let us continue to build the committee and make it a real fighter in our own interest.

YOUTH UNITE.

Mystery Picnic

SUNDAY, NOVEMBER 8, to ? ? ? ?
Sports, Games, Fun, etc.—Bring lunch and friends.

BUSES leave State Theatre, City, at 10 am.

The Young Engineer

By BARRY EVANS

What is The Young Engineer? Who runs this paper?

THE answer to the first question —very briefly—is that The Young Engineer is the paper of the Melbourne District Youth Committee — a committee of young AEU members working to bring all young AEU members together in sporting and social activities around the program of demands for improved wages and working conditions.

THE answer to Question 2. — The paper is run by the Youth Committee and YOU; so let us have your ideas on the paper.

Write articles on your job, your hobby, interest or anything you like. Any suggestons you have on improving the paper and building the Youth Committee.

This is OUR paper, determined to fight for OUR welfare, for better wages and a better life for young engineers.

Next Issue

The next issue of The Young Engineer will be in one month, and will be four pages instead of two like this one. It will include—

● Latest information on the actions of the Youth Committee for the £1 increase.

● An article by Frank Johnson on Jazz.

● Film and sports reviews.

If you have any ideas, stories, jokes, etc, send them to the Editor, C/o AEU, Collins street, Melbourne.

THIS IS YOUR PAPER.

NEXT YOUTH COMMITTEE MEETING
Friday, November 20, at 8 p.m., in A.E.U. Rooms
Make Sure Your Shop Has a Representative

Figure 4.1 *Young Engineer.*

Exhausted, Bruce sometimes missed the tram home and ended up walking from the city to South Melbourne. Such days could be upwards of 14 hours. (During the wartime era it was not uncommon for apprentices to work up to 56 hours per week plus attend their evening classes.) It was during this conversation I realised that for people such as Bruce and others (including Laurie Carmichael, John Halfpenny and later Max Ogden), their experience of the union was Labourite and Marxist politics. However, there was also a practical side to their thoughts and this was the desire for changes in wages and conditions such as daytime training for young people to avoid the workplace deprivations they experienced.

These were lofty objectives and the AEU, and its youth committee, pursued progressive political agendas during and following the Second World War and on into the early 1960s. Many of these agendas were driven by the AEU Youth Committee; it also demanded votes for all 18-year-olds, wage parity for men and women, and Sunday sport. Yet practical successes were limited to industrial initiatives, the most notable being the provision of daytime training.

One key legacy was the way in which the youth committee, in a manner not unlike the Victorian Labour College (described below), provided the education, particularly political, and experience that served as a proxy for university. Tertiary training has become the more conventional route of progression for some union organisers and activists during the past 30 years. However, under the auspices of the youth committee a number of members went on to play prominent roles within the union and the labour movement. Possibly the best known of these was John Halfpenny, who rose to become Victorian State Secretary of the AMWU and then of the Victorian Trades Hall Council during a particularly active, albeit divisive, era. Ultimately, the tension was between pragmatic trade unionism and idealistic propagandising intellectualism. Clearly, the youth committee required elements of both – a position not always readily accepted by competing political interests.

The AEU Melbourne District Youth Committee

Political youth organisations exist to attract young people to the ideals of their respective parties. They are also a means of recruiting new members and source of dynamic political activity. While this is usually understood in terms of the political parties it is equally applicable to counterparts in the industrial arena. In a long-established and traditional craft union such as the AEU the youth committee was regarded as a source, sometimes unwanted, of new ideas to the union. Key union officials in Victoria envisaged the youth committee as a source of political expression for the young engineers that would also serve as a way of organising them.[88] This twin objective has echoes in other organisations such as Young Labor, the Eureka Youth League (the youth branch of the Communist Party of Australia (CPA)) and the Young Liberals.[89]

The Second World War mobilised the union, in particular the political committee, which 'undertook a little experimentation in new ways of political expression'.[90] This entailed more direct methods of influencing the ALP to carry out policies for a widening of the welfare state. Another aspect of the union's political committee was the formation of the Melbourne District Youth Committee aimed at bringing younger members into the life of the union. Concurrent with the advent of the youth committee was the inception by the Sydney District Political Committee of an educational and cultural service, in conjunction with the Henry Lawson Labour College (opened by Frank Forde on behalf of John Curtin with the express purpose of training future labour leaders).[91] The Commonwealth Council, the AEU's peak decision-making body, solemnly endorsed the groups with the rationale that the study of labour affairs would strengthen the union.

More specifically, it is clear that during the 1940s the union made a conscientious effort to politicise its younger members. This was due to the combination of the radicalisation that occurred during the war, the role of the CPA in the politics of the union, and the rising militancy of the AEU during this era.

The views and political stance of the youth committee, like the union, was formed in this volatile political climate. 'Cup' Southwell, a former AEU Melbourne District organiser, observed that the views of many during this era, particularly those of young apprentices, were best understood in the social context of the late 1930s and early 1940s.[92] For apprentices, the legacy

---

[88] Hemingway, J 1978, *Conflict and Democracy*, Oxford University Press, Oxford, p. 1.

[89] National Foundation for Australian Women (NFAW), 'Eureka Youth League', *The Australian Women's Register*, available at http://www.womenaustralia.info/biogs/AWE0 227b.htm, accessed 4 January 2013.

[90] Sheridan, T 1989, *Division of Labour: Industrial Relations in the Chifley Years 1945–1949*, Oxford University Press, South Melbourne, p. 6.

[91] Blake, A nd, *Notes on the Development of the Eureka Youth League and Its Predecessors*, unpublished manuscript, in The University of Melbourne Archives, Eureka League Collection, Brunswick; 'College to Train Labour Leaders Opened in Sydney', *The Argus*, 5 February 1945, p. 4.

[92] Southwell, C 1994, Response to questionnaire, 30 September.

The A.E.U. Melbourne District Youth Committee 1944.

Back row left to right:
(1) Max Hannon. (2) ? (3) R. Owen. (4) ? (5) ?
(6) Angus Tennant. (7) L. Campbell. (8) ?

Front row left to right:
(1) John Rowe (Secretary). (2) Bruce Armstrong, editor of
Young Engineer.
(3) Pauline De Campo. (4) K. Courtney. (5) Ed. Finigan.

Absent: President, Bruce McKissack.
The founding secretary, Fred Thompson, had volunteered
for the Armed Services at the time this photograph was
taken.

Figure 4.2 Second World War AEU Youth Committee 1944.

of the First World War was immediate, with many growing up around war casualties. The hardship was further compounded by the experience of the Great Depression. It was these events that gave many apprentices a natural inclination towards socialism. This often resulted in an attraction to the CPA, particularly through membership of the Eureka Youth League. This was particularly the case following the German invasion of the Soviet Union that led the CPA to unambiguously support the war effort.[93]

---

[93] Symons, B 1991, 'All Out for the People's War: "Red Diggers" in the Armed Forces and the Communist Party of Australia's Policies in the Second World War', BA Honours

In Victoria, the AEU maintained a progressive outlook that in part explains why the youth committee persisted long after its Sydney counterpart ceased to exist. Until the split in the Australian Labor Party in the 1950s, AEU members in Melbourne 'revealed a sophistication rare in the union world by simultaneously electing from the same constituency both communist and anti-communist full-time officials'.[94] While the youth committee was more polarised and radical in its politics (it had more communist sympathisers) than the main body of the union, it continued to receive support from the Melbourne district branch.

This support was not always unanimous, as there was always a craft mindset in the union despite its progressive stance on a number of industrial and political issues. Essentially, some in the AEU regarded the youth committee as an undesirable break from the tradition. An understandable stance, given the AEU in Australia traced it roots directly back to the New Model unions of the 1850s.

Copies of the wartime era *Young Engineer*, the official publication of the Melbourne District Youth Committee, highlight both the strengths and weaknesses of the committee.[95] Clearly, they were erudite young working men and women who were organised in a manner that could ensure industrial success. Founding Secretary Fred Thompson (referred to elsewhere in this book) was already challenging more senior AEU union officials. His career was only interrupted by his enlistment in the Australian Army.

Throughout the pages of the *Young Engineer* there is a sober zealousness that clearly took the motto of the union 'Organise, Educate, Control' to heart. For committee intellectuals such as John Rowe and Bruce Armstrong and other political aspirants including Laurie Carmichael and, later, John Halfpenny, the politics and promotion of CPA agendas and the linking of the Eureka Youth League and AEU Youth Committee were paramount. Yet this missionary zeal was not always successful in a trade union setting. Committee member Pauline Potter (nee De Campo) recalls communists manipulating the committee. While she did not object, others expressed their concern.[96] Ultimately, communists were tolerated as long as they pursued union objectives. This was easy enough during the Second World War where there were common political and industrial objectives, but it became more divisive

---

Thesis, University of Wollongong, p. 34.

[94] Sheridan, T 1989, *Division of Labour*, p. 127.

[95] *Young Engineer*, April 1943, pp. 1–4.

[96] De Campo, P 1994, Letter and response to questionnaire, 13 July.

ABOVE:
Eureka Youth League weekend study group, Greensborough, 1948.
The tutor was Bernie Taft, then Director of Marx School, Communist
Party education centre, front row third from the right. Three
other participants of interest: Front row, extreme left, John
Rowe (a former Youth Committee secretary); Laurie Carmichael
(holding a book), (former Youth Committee president); Max Lorkin,
second from the right (former Eureka Youth League secretary,
later A.E.U. organiser).
BELOW: Second left, Laurie Carmichael, Third left, John Rowe.

Figure 4.3 The Eureka Youth League Study Group.

following the war. In part, this trend explains why the youth committee temporarily disbanded in the early 1950s once it key objectives were realised. It was soon reconstituted in 1953 with a new cohort of young engineers.

Bruce McKissack recalled that the committee had extensive sporting and social organisations, including a football league that was the lifeblood of the committee, but was only 'grudgingly tolerated by the politically very correct comrades of the youth movement'.[97] It was these organisations that helped maintain the interest of the politically uninvolved apprentices. McKissack recalled a group of AEU apprentices at the Johns and Waygood workshops in South Melbourne being addressed in a proselytising fashion by a group of Eureka Youth League members. So unsuccessful was their approach that McKissack told them 'that's not the way you win people ... you've got to talk young people's language'.[98] Later in the 1950s the *Young Engineer* seemed to strike a balance between the two positions when it prompted a new campaign to increase apprentice wages while also advertising the mystery picnic 'to????'.[99] In this respect the social activities could be seen as facilitating the youth committee agenda, something that was underplayed by the more politically oriented committee members.

A Progressive and Independent Tradition

To understand the significance and radical nature of the creation of the youth committee it is necessary to refer to the history and structure of the union, which is described in Chapter 1 by Balnaves and Patmore. A feature of the both the British and the Australian branches of the AEU was the emphasis placed on the 'democratic checks and balances against executive autocracy'.[100] This was attributable to the domination of tradespeople who wanted to emphasise the democratic and independent structure of the union. The autonomous structure and hierarchy of the AEU was enshrined in its constitution, and emphasis was placed upon the importance of the district committee. These were reinforced through the conventions that developed regarding the autonomy of shop stewards.

This meant in turn that low-level organisation in the union such as the youth committee had a clear role and a degree of independence, particularly in regard to the welfare of young apprentices. Moreover, the nature of the

[97] Armstrong, B 1994, Interview, Chadstone, 26 September.

[98] McKissack, B 1994, Interview, Dallas Brooks Hall, Melbourne, 14 March.

[99] *Young Engineer*, October 1953, p. 1.

[100] Sheridan, T 1989, *Division of Labour*, p. 127.

union, renowned for its independence and strategic importance industrially, approved of rank-and-file action. This included the activities undertaken by the young engineers.

Because of its immense bargaining power it was observed that the AEU was a pacesetter with demands. This sometimes led to a situation where 'kindred unions were left floundering in its wake'.[101] Nonetheless, the single-mindedness and industrial power of the AEU meant that a climate existed where experiments such as the youth committee were realised and supported. It is unlikely that the youth committee and its manifesto of political and industrial demands would have emerged in other parts of the Australian labour movement during the 1940s. The approving culture and organisational mechanics of the union, the political temper of the times and the increased political consciousness of working class apprentices due to the rise of fascism and the onset of the Second World War all contributed to the rise of the youth committee and its sustained success for the next 20 years.

Former member Jack Hutson was the conduit between the youth committee and the district committee. Hutson felt that the youth committee received support from the AEU leadership as its members had an appreciation of how the union functioned. He also credited the success of the AEU to a principled set of values that were premised upon independence. Accordingly, the youth committee was another progressive experiment that only came about because of the independent stance of the union. The AEU policy of shared leadership also emphasised consensus. Unlike the Ironworkers Union, whose communist leadership purged the executive of non-communists during this period, the AEU realised the diversity of views among its membership meant that its leadership needed to represent a wide range of interests.

Young Apprentices during the 1950s

During the 1950s attitudes towards apprenticeship were framed within the context of demands for improved wages and conditions. With the long boom in full swing and Australia enjoying a period of full employment, many apprentices were not interested in undertaking four- and five-year apprenticeships on low wages when other occupations offered higher wages with little or no formal training. The situation is analogous to those who are now attracted to working in the mining industry in the early twenty-first century. Employers were keen to employ the cheap labour of apprentices, but

---

[101] Sheridan, T 1972, *Mindful Militants: The Amalgamated Engineering Union in Australia, 1920–1972*, Cambridge University Press, Cambridge, p. 56.

found many rejected the notion of entering a trade.[102] This was a situation realised by both state and federal governments and, in order to counter this negative trend, the terms of apprenticeship were reconsidered and more favourable terms were won for apprentices.

The youth committee also provided a forum that gave future leaders of the union movement a political grounding. This was particularly the case during the 1950s. One of the more notable identities was John Halfpenny who edited the *Young Engineer* and served in a number of official positions as a committee official. Founding member Angus Tennant observed that the committee was intended to bring young engineers into the life of the union. During the 1950s the AEU began to contemplate the series of amalgamations that led to it becoming an industrial union as opposed to a predominantly craft-oriented one. These changes meant that the leadership of the union was concentrated upon a broader political agenda. This in turn facilitated the youth committee's aims of asserting itself within the union hierarchy and also pursuing issues of a political nature.[103]

Despite this, the late 1950s witnessed a decline in youth committee activity. Throughout the decade it had continued its campaign to have apprentice wages calculated as a percentage of the tradesperson's rate under the award. This had been informally in place since 1955, but was later ratified and in a sense the young engineers were left without an agenda. The success of the young engineers led to the Plumbers Union creating a similar body.

However, sectarianism between communist and ALP members and sympathisers by this stage was rife in the youth committee as it had been for a large part of the 1950s. The lack of tolerance towards the Young Christian Workers in the youth committee resulted in a bitter internal conflict that effectively divided it and rendered it largely dysfunctional. This was compounded from 1959 onwards when the AEU neglected the committee, in the process hastening its demise. By the early 1960s the youth committee was an inoperative body. It is unclear when it actually ceased to exist; however, it had not functioned effectively since the late 1950s.

Despite its gradual disappearance, the youth committee served a useful purpose in that it gave its members formative political experiences and a grounding in union culture. It also helped to shape its members' political beliefs. The committee provided a forum for young engineers to engage

---

102 Armstrong, B 1994, Interview.

103 Massey, RN 1994, 'A Century of Laborism, 1891–1993: An Historical Interpretation' in *Labour History*, 66, pp. 45–71.

socially and politically. Of course, this is not a unique situation as most organisations aim to attract members to their ideals. What was significant about the youth committee was the extent to which the ideals of union manifested themselves in the activities of the youth committee.

It would be a mistake to emphasise the achievements of only a few noted individuals, when in fact the youth committee was an organisation that broadened political awareness among the majority of its members. Max Lorkin, an AEU organiser during those years, when asked whether the youth committee was a political training ground stated, 'virtually that was what it was', while Bruce McKissack recalled that 'the number of union officials and activists that came through out of the Youth Committee was unbelievable'.[104]

Max Ogden, a former youth committee president, argues that it was an organisation that provided him and many others with political training. In 1959 he was the youth committee representative to a youth festival in Vienna, and upon his return he reported to the union. Max's selection for and attendance at this conference exemplifies the practical experience that was otherwise unavailable to young people of the era. Moreover, Ogden's early career highlights how engineering apprentices gained a political and general education that otherwise would not have occurred. Ogden also recalls how others such as John Halfpenny used the youth committee as a springboard to other opportunities. For many metal trades apprentices the youth committee and the Eureka Youth League (the crossover was great as many of the politicised young engineers shared communist sympathies) 'was almost like a replacement for a liberal university education.[105]

Alistair Davison argues that the history of communism in the Australian trade union movement is separate from CPA political history. In the industrial sphere the CPA achieved success because its political activities 'were tactical rather than principled in basis'.[106] Thus the gains that were made were of limited use in terms of political currency for the CPA because they were approved by the union membership in terms of industrial policy, not as great victories of the party. This ultimately meant that the 'translation of union activity from industrial to political activity could not be made'.[107]

---

[104] McKissack, B 1994, Interview.

[105] Ogden, M 1994, Interview, Melbourne, 25 October.

[106] Davidson, A 1969, *The Communist Party of Australia: A Short History*, Hoover Institution Press, Stanford, pp. 98–99.

[107] Davidson, A 1969, *Communist Party of Australia*.

The experience of the youth committee bears this out in that the industrial campaigns were successful where the social and political ones were not. However, the youth committee was successful in energising and politicising a generation of young apprentices and the political significance of this was an enduring one even if it is difficult to gauge.

The youth committee was an integral part of the union for 20 years between 1941 and 1961. While communist members of the committee agitated for a broader political agenda it is worth reiterating that the committee was always primarily a union body and consequently there was a tension between Labourite and communist principles. This tension in part explains its ultimate demise. Its industrial campaigns were extremely successful and its political campaigns, while innovative, were not. Yet, as mentioned earlier, the AEU and its youth committee was ahead of its time in many of the social policies it advocated such as gender equality, votes to all at the age of 18, wage parity and challenging the wowser observance of the Sabbath and bans on Sunday sport. Besides the politicisation and training of a cohort of key left-wing Victorian activists, the achievement of daytime training was a major union victory. The youth committee was a key part of the Carlton Apprentices Committee headed by Jack Williamson who led deputations to parliamentarians and unions to seek the abolition of evening training.[108]

The other major victory was the award of the proportion of the tradesperson's rate for apprentices that significantly improved their incomes. The last of these received a commendation from UNESCO in a report entitled *Education in a Technological Society* where the apprenticeship model, regulated by government, was cited as 'changing the conditions by means of part-time general technical training courses at the technical colleges'.[109] By way of comparison these improvements to the apprenticeship system meant that the Australian system was renowned as the best in the world until the 1960s when West Germany and Scandinavia developed superior schemes.[110] Yet, like so many political groups that advocated change before their time, it was destined not to fully realise its objectives.

---

[108] Williamson, J 1994, Interview, Pascoe Vale, 10 May; *Young Engineer*, July 1943, p. 1.

[109] UNESCO 1952, *Education in a Technological Society*. Apprenticeship Commission of Victoria, *Twenty-Fifth Annual Report for Year Ended 30th June*, Victorian Government, Melbourne, 1953, p. 22.

[110] Armstrong, B 1994, Interview.

Conclusion

At an AEU Retirees Association Annual Labour Day Dinner at Dallas Brookes Hall in the early 1990s, more than 50 years after the creation of the Melbourne District Youth Committee, I observed a few of the former members talking about old times. Immediately I was struck by the sense of pride they had in the youth committee and the union, of their camaraderie that had been sustained over five decades. They still referred to each other only half-jokingly, and certainly not casually, as 'Brother', and 'Sister', just as they were solemnly referred in the *Young Engineer*. These were men and women who had spoken out against fascism, who had worked for and in many cases fought in the Second World War, and as a group advocated for a raft of progressive politics that in some cases were 30 years ahead of their time and others are yet to come to pass. They endured deprivation as children of the depression and they experienced the Second World War. There was a certainty about their political convictions that were borne of experience and perhaps the legacy of dealing with setbacks as part of the Australian left over a long period of time. They were also proud and assured of the achievement of the union, albeit this was tempered by a wistful cynicism about the long-term significance of the youth committee that ran along the rhetorical lines of 'was it all worth it'?

Clearly it was.

Acknowledgements

Warm thanks to the surviving former members of the AEU Youth Committee, particularly Bruce Armstrong.

Chapter 5

The Female Confectioners Union, 1916–1945

Cathy Brigden

On Tuesday 26 September 1916, a meeting of female confectioners at Temperance Hall in Russell Street, Melbourne, drew 47 people. The focus of the meeting was the state of the wages and conditions for women in the trade. Among the speakers was Sara Lewis, who was the secretary of one of the women's unions in Victoria, the Female Hotel and Caterers Union. Also addressing the meeting was Isaac Johnston, a former secretary of the Federated Gas Employees Union, who described the 'serious' effect of the 1914 Confectioners Wages Determination on their wages and conditions. He encouraged those present to form a union that would affiliate with the Melbourne Trades Hall Council (THC) and register under the Commonwealth *Conciliation and Arbitration Act 1904* to enable legal action to secure 'some measure of justice'.

The record of this meeting appears as the first entry in the minute book of the Female Confectioners Union. Showing some prior organising and planning, Isabella Parker, who was chairing the meeting, submitted a list of 116 workers willing to be members. A committee was elected with Isabella Parker and Isaac Johnston elected president and secretary respectively. A set of rules was also considered. While the union was clearly formed to represent female confectionery workers, the rules were drawn broadly to include anyone 'employed in the production, sale and distribution of chocolate, cocoa and confectionery'.

From the outset, notwithstanding the male leadership it drew on, the union was a women's union: a union for women and led by women as paid and honorary leaders, on its various committees, in the branch office and in the workplaces. It would remain one for its 30-year life. This formation of a women's union was not unusual, as a number of women's unions had been formed in the early 1910s as part of a push to organise women workers both by trade unionists and female activists, following the achievement of

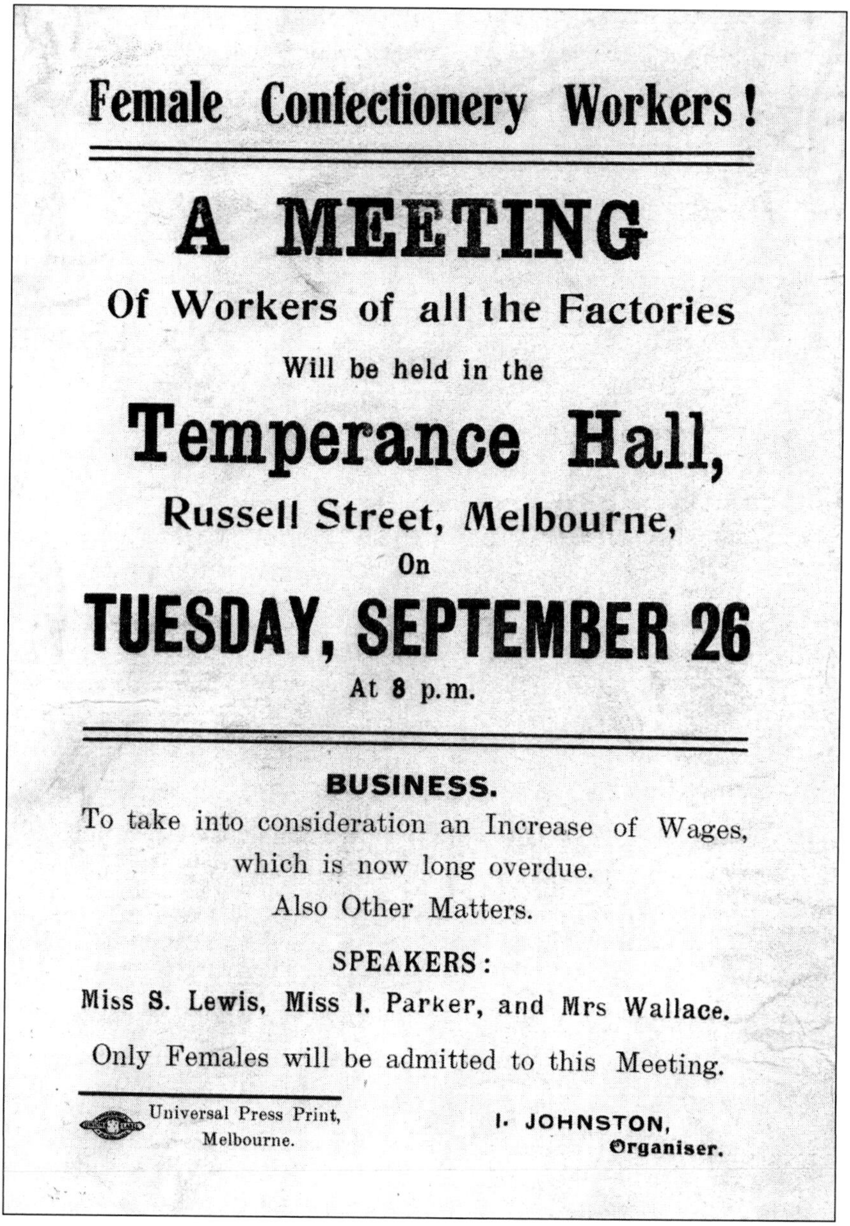

Female Confectionery Workers!

A MEETING

Of Workers of all the Factories

Will be held in the

Temperance Hall,

Russell Street, Melbourne,

On

TUESDAY, SEPTEMBER 26

At 8 p.m.

BUSINESS.

To take into consideration an Increase of Wages,
which is now long overdue.

Also Other Matters.

SPEAKERS:

Miss S. Lewis, Miss I. Parker, and Mrs Wallace.

Only Females will be admitted to this Meeting.

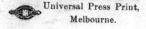 Universal Press Print,
Melbourne.

I. JOHNSTON,
Organiser.

Figure 5.1 Handbill advertising the meeting at which women employed by MacRobertsons, Hoadleys, Allans and other city confectioners formed their own union.

Reproduced with the permission of the University of Melbourne Archives female suffrage in Victoria in 1908. Organising along gender lines, often described as 'separate organising', is argued to be an important strategy for advancing the interests and voices of women, something not always possible or supported in mixed sex trade unions. A theme running through the union's existence was the commitment to 'separate representation', expressed by both the leaders and the members time and again.

The female confectioners' commitment to have their own trade union and to be active unionists was demonstrated by the membership growth seen in the union's first few years and the willingness of members to take on workplace and management committee leadership roles. From those first 116 workers on Parker's list, three months later the union had more than 400 members and by the end of 1917, membership had grown to 900. At the union's first meeting, workplace leadership roles were taken on by nine women volunteering to be shop stewards at four firms: MacRobertson's (Miss I Hunter and Miss Agnes McVeigh), Hoadley's (Miss Keystone and Mrs Hales), Allans (Miss Finlayson and Miss Elsie Mulcahy), and Long and Smith's (Miss Eva Forrest, Miss Tucker and Miss P White). Five of these women – Hunter, McVeigh, Mulcahy, Forrest and White – were also on the initial management committee. There were 34 women who went on to serve on the management committee between 1916 and 1922 (General meeting minutes, various).

One of the key motivations for the union's formation was in response to female confectionery workers' 'sweated' conditions (a term used to denote exploited labour) and the desire for better representation of their industrial concerns. These concerns were reflected in the calling for a royal commission into the sweating of women in the confectionery trade at a Trades Hall Council meeting in 1917. Complaints were also made to the state Minister for Labour about the women's very low wages and poor conditions.[111]

Although there was a union presence since the early 1880s, when the Victorian United Confectioners' Society organised in 1883 (after an earlier short-lived attempt in 1880), by the First World War mechanisation of the trade had completely transformed it from male-dominated to female-dominated, where women and girls outnumbered men and boys by two to one.[112] The trade was also highly sex-segregated with women and girls concentrated in 'women's' jobs, in particular as dippers, wrappers and packers. It was also tedious work:

---

[111] THC Council minutes, 28 June 1917; *The Argus*, 4 October 1917, p. 4.

[112] *The Argus*, 8 May 1933, p. 8.

Probably no employment could be found that is of a more monotonous character than chocolate dipping (where girls are compelled to sit for very long periods doing the same kind of work for hour after hour with almost clock-like regularity). Wrapping is also a most monotonous and tiring occupation. In many cases girls are compelled to support a large box on their knees. Pressure has to be exerted by the body upon one side of the box; the other side being jammed against the table in order to keep it in position. The use of these boxes have a very injurious effect upon their health.[113]

There is some evidence of various attempts at union organisation. In 1900, as part of the THC organising committee's activities to form women's unions, it was reported that female confectionery workers had formed a union with at least 150 members.[114] One reference can be found to a 'Women's Branch of the Confectionery Trade' in the 1911 minutes of the Eight-Hour Anniversary Committee.[115] But apart from these isolated references, there are no details about these earlier bodies.

By 1916, the Confectioners Union's secretary, Mr Geddes, having held office since 1889, had seen industry transformation but not an accompanying one for any women members in terms of their working conditions. Indeed, it was the female wages in the 1914 Wages Determination made by the Confectioners Wages Board that became the particular catalyst for action, where male Confectioners Union leaders were the employee representatives. Some of the wage rates were described as below the living wage, which 'no female who desired to get respectable board and lodging could live on'.[116] Even the prime minister was moved to observe that if such a wage was being paid, it was 'obviously insufficient for subsistence'.[117]

The union mounted a successful appeal, with 'considerable increases in rates of pay' from 2 January 1918 resulting from the amended wage determination.[118] However, the next attempt to increase the female rate at the Wages Board was hindered by the men's union delegates voting with the employers – a clear sign of the lack of union solidarity that only reinforced the female confectioners' reliance on separate organising.[119]

---

113 *The Woman's Clarion*, 20 September 1923.

114 *The Argus*, 27 November 1900, p. 9.

115 Eight Hours Anniversary Committee minutes 1911.

116 *The Argus*, 4 October 1917, p. 4.

117 *The Argus*, 19 September 1917, p. 9.

118 *The Argus*, 15 December 1917.

119 Wages Board minutes 19 June 1919.

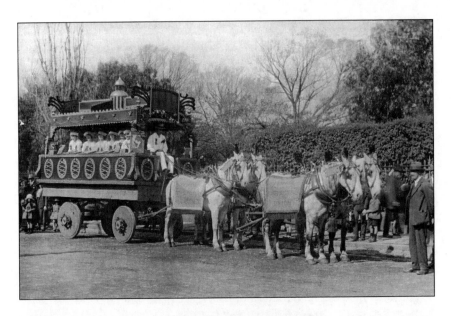

Figures 5.2 and 5.3 It is unlikely that members of the Female Confectioner's Union ever had their own banner but this highly ornate trade display became a feature of the Melbourne Eight Hour processions during the 1920s.

Reproduced with the permission of the University of Melbourne Archives

The union had a difficult start. Although the appeal was successful, the choice of Johnston as secretary proved unwise and there was extensive unemployment in 1917 as a result of a seamen's strike. A test of the commitment to separate representation and women's unionism came when internal conflict beset the union late in 1917. A disagreement with a sacked shop steward led to a challenge to Secretary Isaac Johnston's leadership. Despite being comprehensively returned as secretary in the union elections in December 1917, growing membership concerns over his actions and allegations of impropriety, obstructive behaviour and a damaging leadership style ('his personal conduct was conducive of disorder among members rather than for harmony') led to an inquiry by the THC in early 1918.[120] As a consequence, the members voted to wind up the original union and to reorganise it, once more as a women's union.[121] The THC actively supported the new union by offering the service of EHA (Harry) Smith, who was an experienced union organiser. The members accepted Smith and he was elected secretary. Harry Smith would lead the union for the next decade until his untimely death in 1927.

Smith immediately set about negotiating with MacRobertson's, one of the leading confectionery firms, and the industry's employer association, the Victorian Manufacturing Confectioners Association (VMCA). These direct negotiations with MacRobertson's led first to agreed union right of entry and appointment of a shop president, and then a closed shop agreement, while union recognition, agreed dispute resolution processes and a means for managing piecework changes were outcomes of negotiations with the VMCA.[122]

With only an estimated 200 members when Johnston departed, rebuilding the union was successful with membership climbing to over 1000 by March 1919.[123] While demonstrating support from female confectioners for the revival of the union, this growth also entitled the union to an additional THC delegate. Five years later, the union had 1828 members (annual conference 1924). Identification with the new union was boosted with a union badge (a three-colour badge for 3 shillings). In 1921, a union journal,

---

[120] THC special committee report 1918.

[121] While proceedings in the Commonwealth Court of Conciliation and Arbitration finally led the union not to deregister, to all intents and purposes, the union under Smith's stewardship was the 'new' union.

[122] Executive Committee special meeting, 1 July 1918 general meeting, 20 January 1919.

[123] Management Committee 17 March 1919.

The Woman's Clarion, was launched 'with unpardonable pride'.[124] It was used to encourage activism as 'organisation and unity of action are the only means by which you can secure results'.[125]

In a show that the union's support had been extended to its members, Margaret Wearne was appointed to the new role of assistant secretary from 1919, as 'someone should be in constant touch with the members and to generally act as an Inspector of the Factories'.[126] Margaret Wearne, already the general secretary of the federally registered union, would go on to play a central leadership role in the union. Together with Harry Smith, and then after his death, as secretary with a solid group of women honorary officials, she would lead the union until the 1945 amalgamation.

A test for the leaders came with the second agreement with the VCMA when it came before the Wages Board for endorsement. Accused by the men's union of accepting wage rates set by one of the employers and Smith going 'behind the members' backs', the executive called a membership ballot. The result was overwhelming support for the executive's action: not only did 96 per cent support the action, but 751 members voted.[127] It was compliance with the 1920 VMCA agreement that led to one of the few times where the Female Confectioners Union threatened industrial action. Reports in *The Argus* told of the threats to withdraw labour with firms given a deadline by which to comply with the agreement.[128] The tactic proved effective with the action averted as firms agreed to adhere to the agreement.

The union expanded into Tasmania in 1923, prompted by the arrival of the British firm, Cadbury. A similar model whereby the secretary was an experienced male unionist supported by an all-female committee was followed. Charles Culley, who combined his industrial role as secretary of the Hobart Trades Hall and Labour Council with his parliamentary duties as the state member for Denison, would lead the Tasmanian branch until just before the amalgamation. An agreement was soon secured that 'meant a good deal to the girls. The rates of pay and conditions were very much improved'.[129] Despite Culley and the committee's efforts, the branch did not flourish, through a combination of fluctuating employment, activist

---

124   *The Woman's Clarion,* 7 November 1921.

125   *The Woman's Clarion,* 20 May 1922.

126   Management Committee 13 January 1919.

127   General meeting minutes 31 March 1919.

128   23 February 1923, p. 8, 6 March 1923, p. 10.

129   *The Woman's Clarion,* 20 October 1923.

turnover (commonly due to marriage), active poaching of members by a hostile men's union and worker apathy.[130]

Antagonism between the two unions continued with intermittent breaks in hostilities to consider amalgamation. While this may seem paradoxical, overtures were made by both unions at different times. Common to the Female Confectioners Union's demands was protection of their sectional interests, which included not only separate structures and officers, but also the capacity to directly negotiate with employers. There was an ongoing fight over representation on the Wages Board in the 1920s, where the men's union continually agitated for more delegates than the Female Confectioners Union, despite the membership disparity (said to be 1105 females and 609 males in 1917). Poaching by the men's union, particularly at Hoadley's, just added to uneasy relations. Also working against the union was the impact of the broader economic conditions in the early and late 1920s, and particularly in the 1930s as the Great Depression took hold. With periods of slack trade and unemployment, there was little bargaining power that could be harnessed.

Women as Leaders, Activists and Members

The Female Confectioners Union, as a women's union, the role of women in sustaining it was obviously critical. As said above, in its early days members were instrumental in creating a workplace profile for the union and running the organisation. Protective of the organisation, the members stood behind its reorganisation and worked to rebuild it. While two men were the initial secretaries, this brought organising experience to the union. By the time of Harry Smith's death, the women were capable leaders and did not need to accept the offer by Percival J Lucas to be a candidate for secretary (the same PJ Lucas who was later the federal secretary of the Confectioner's Union).[131] As Jean Daley's obituary for Harry Smith observed, he had 'made a fine and self-reliant group of women who can take up the battle where he laid it down, intelligently and militantly'.[132]

Initially, the president was also the organiser. Isabel Parker, aged 41 in 1916, experienced resistance not only from management but male workers, who at MacRobertson's were 'telling the girls not to join'.[133] Following a visit

---

[130] See Barton, R 2001, 'Gender, Skill and Trade-Unionism: Women Workers at Cadbury in Tasmania, 1920–51', *Historical Studies in Industrial Relations*, 11, pp. 37–62.

[131] Management Committee, 7 June 1927.

[132] *The Woman's Clarion*, June 1927.

[133] Members meeting, 22 January 1917.

Figure 5.4 The Female Confectioners Union National Executive, c.1925, taken from the union's journal *The Women's Clarion*.

Reproduced with the permission of the University of Melbourne Archives

to Sydney by Secretary Johnston, which found female wages and conditions in a 'very bad way', Parker was dispatched on an organising tour 'for at least three weeks'. Nothing came of this, but more importantly, Parker then suffered a nervous breakdown and was absent for a number of months.[134] Although her position was kept, she returned when the initial trouble with Johnston had begun. Despite running for election as secretary, she was not able to regain membership support and lost to both Johnston and then Smith. After the reorganisation, she disappeared from the union, and from the union's public record. Elizabeth Burns, a confectioner also in her forties, was the first post-reorganisation president and organiser (part-time because of financial constraints). Attempts to organise Hoadley's where Burns worked proved slow as 'Mr Hoadley was a very difficult man to deal with' in Smith's view. She also worked 'undercover'. When it was suspected that an employer was paying less than the Wages Board wage rate, she worked at the Chocolate Bowl 'for a few days to prove that it was so' with the employer subsequently fined.[135]

---

[134] Meeting 6 August 1917, 20 August 1917.

[135] Management Committee 6 October, 3 November 1919.

Workplace leaders were publicly acknowledged. Daisy Diwell, the union treasurer and MacRobertson's shop president, was praised by Secretary Smith: 'the members all agreed that most of the success of the union in that factory had been due to the great energy and tact she has displayed on all occasions, she had given her services ungrudgingly'.[136] However, this took a toll on Daisy and, prompted by ill health, she stepped away from active union work. Her health, it was felt, was affected by her missing lunch in order to interview workers: 'it is little wonder that her health suffered in consequence'.[137] Miss Nellie Black (aged 23) and Miss Mary Moss were 'congratulated … on the courage they had displayed' as they had 'put up a splendid case' during a dispute at MacRobertson's in 1920.[138] Margaret Wearne, while a shop steward at MacRobertson's, was said to have enrolled 95 per cent of her department. In 1921, Secretary Smith paid tribute to the many women who 'have rendered yeoman service, notably Flora Wearne, Elsie Hood, Maud Hood, Jane Elliott, Nellie Black, May Webber, Ruby Gay, Lalla Steele, Sis. Anderson, Gladys Robinson, Vera Watts, Olive Phillips, Grace Hanson'.[139] No mention was made of Isabel Parker with Margaret Wearne and Daisy Diwell described as 'pioneers' of the union.

While Parker and Burns were in their forties, many young women took up leadership roles. This was important given the age profile of members. The trade was dominated by young women and girls, with nearly 80 per cent of female confectionery makers less than 25 years of age, and more than two-thirds of those aged 10 to 19 years of age, according to the 1921 census.[140] When she assumed the role of assistant secretary, Margaret Wearne was 26 years old, as were Daisy Diwell when elected treasurer and Maud Hood when she joined the committee. Maud followed her younger sister Elsie who was only 20 when she was elected a trustee in 1918, and 22 when elected vice-president. The Hoods were both elected on to the Wages Board in 1920. While ill health prematurely brought Daisy's involvement to an end, it was marriage for the Hood sisters that saw them retire from office. There were also personal ties between these three, with Daisy for a time living with Maud, Elsie and their family.

---

[136] General Meeting 20 January 1919.

[137] *The Woman's Clarion*, 7 November 1921, p. 3.

[138] Special General Meeting, 10 May 1920.

[139] *The Woman's Clarion*, 7 November 1921, p. 3.

[140] Australian Bureau of Statistics (ABS) 1921, *Census of the Commonwealth of Australia*, Cat. 2110.0, ABS Canberra.

After the high participation, but also high turnover of activists on the branch committee that marked the union's early years, a period of stability emerged in the early to mid 1920s. Joining Margaret Wearne was Flora, her older sister by two years, who succeeded Daisy Diwell as treasurer. Flora, together with Miranda Hill, Ruby Warway, Ivy Heath nee Chapman and Maud Howard would form the core of the union's honorary leadership group until the 1945 merger. Between 1926 and 1944, Ruby Warway and Maud Howard would serve as president for 13 of those 18 years (the presidency being an annual term). Miranda Hill started as a committee member in 1922, was then vice-president and president before being elected assistant secretary after Smith's death in 1927. She held this position until 1942, stepping down only to help the union financially when she was asked to work for the Department of Labour and National Service. Jean Elliott (1918–1932) and May Webber (1920–1937) also played important roles in this period. Taking on a slightly different role was Jean Daley. From 1926, she was one of the union's THC and ALP delegates, but was not engaged in the day-to-day leadership of the union. Other than Ivy and Jean, who worked in retail confectionery, all were employed in confectionery manufacturing.[141]

Apart from Maud Howard, a 40-year-old British migrant, and Ivy Chapman, who was about 31, these women were in their twenties when they took initial office. They drew on experience as shop stewards and presidents, and continued in those roles. Most were unmarried and had no children. Only Ivy Chapman and May Webber married and, despite their concerns that marriage might affect their involvement, they continued in their honorary roles. Both continued to use their maiden names. It was about eight years before the union records showed Ivy using her married name of Heath.

Like Daisy and the Hoods, these women had both organisational and personal relationships. The Wearne sisters lived together, with their mother and various siblings, until they were in their fifties. Ruby Warway and Miranda Hill shared a house for many years. Ruby had moved in with the Hill family in the early 1920s, the two women possibly meeting at work at A.W. Allen's. They would continue to share residences with Miranda's mother and/or siblings, and then on their own until Miranda's death in 1973.

---

141 For more details see, Brigden, C 2012, 'Tracing and Placing Women Trade Union Leaders: A Study of the Female Confectioners Union', *Journal of Industrial Relations*, 54, pp. 238–255.

This group formed the backbone of the union. Without such committed honorary officials, the union would not have survived or been able to withstand the pressure placed on it by the often hostile or at least unhelpful behaviour of the men's union. While it was certainly no pacesetter, the union grappled with a number of issues well recognised as impediments to workplace organising. Although there were large employers such as MacRobertson's, the industry was also one in which small firms were common. The comparatively benign managerial attitude at MacRobertson's was in sharp contrast to Hoadley's, where the union continually encountered barriers. The membership profile also posed challenges with the large number of girls and young women who, it was said, did not always appreciate the work of the union or the need to support the union. Harry Smith commented that 'It must be always understood that a women's union consisted of a large proportion of very young girls who by the very nature of things had a very light sense of responsibility which made the difficulties about twenty times greater than that of a men's union'.[142]

Fluctuations in employment meant that, while in 1924 there were 1828 financial members, it was estimated that if all members on the books paid their arrears, membership would be over 5000, even though there were only 1800 female employees in the trade:

> This showed an astounding indication of the ebb and flow that takes place amongst women in the Confectionery Industry and a surprising indication of the huge difficulty that continually confront the Union in its efforts to combat these [sic] and create a successful organisation amongst women and girls ... The organisation of women, more particularly in unskilled and semi-skilled occupations, will always be a matter of extreme difficulty.

Smith would add, 'I most confidently assert that our Union has achieved greater success in the organisation of women and girls than has ever been accomplished by any other Union, in any industry'.[143]

While other women joined the committee in the 1930s and 1940s, and were elected to senior roles as vice-president and president, they did not displace the core group. Notable among those who came on to the committee in the 1930s were Aileen Callick and M Hishon. After two

---

[142] Annual meeting, 12 February 1923.

[143] Victorian–Tasmanian branch annual conference 9 March 1924.

months on the committee in 1933, M Hishon[144] was elected vice-president. She was president in 1935 and again in 1938, and continued as a committee member until the amalgamation. At the age of 27, Aileen Callick brought youth to the committee when she joined in 1937. She was married but, like Ivy and May, used her maiden name as a union activist (she only signed the minutes as Mrs Connelly once). A shop steward at Bush's confectionery, Aileen too was welcomed by the core group, elected first as vice-president in 1938 before becoming president, roles she would hold again in 1941 and 1942. Her resignation in 1943 because she was 'leaving the industry' was subsequently explained by the birth of her son. Helen Bull and Ethel Skipper were married women in their forties when they came on the committee in 1943. Ethel had a teenage son and an older daughter, while Helen did not have children. Though similar in age to the core leadership group, Helen and Ethel reflected the increasing number of married women working in the trade due to the war.

All of these activists were absorbed into the leadership structure and were elected unopposed. Not since 1920 had there been a contested election. This changed in 1944 when, just as amalgamation discussions were reaching finalisation, there was a challenge to the leadership from two members from MacRobertson's. Gladys Thomas nominated for president and federal council, and Grace Keamy for the THC delegation and picnic committee.[145] They were successful in each contest, the most dramatic being Thomas's defeat of Miranda Hill who had most recently taken leave from her Department of Labour job to return to the union office so Margaret Wearne could enjoy some annual leave.[146] Gladys was elected as a federal councillor, again defeating Miranda as well as Maud Howard and Helen Bull. That the amalgamation was the impetus was evident at the special meeting in January 1945 to consider the amalgamation scheme. The members rejected the scheme that the leadership saw as 'safeguarding' a women's section by a vote of 63 to 11. Unwilling to walk away from the amalgamation, the executive pushed on and recommitted the resolution to the next general meeting. At this meeting, using her authority as president, Gladys Thomas challenged Margaret Wearne, and again won the support

---

[144] There is no mention of her name in the union records, her marital status is unclear and a search of genealogical records has to date been unsuccessful in tracing her.

[145] General meeting, 11 December 1944.

[146] General meeting, 13 November 1944.

of the members.[147] While there are no union minutes indicating how this was resolved, the amalgamation took place in April 1945. The core group retained its dominance with Gladys Thomas absent from the post-amalgamation committee in July 1945. Margaret Wearne was assistant secretary, Miranda Hill junior vice-president, Flora Wearne a trustee and Ruby Warway, Maud Howard, Helen Bull and Ethel Skipper were committee members.

An Integrated Union – The Female Confectioners' Labour Movement Ties

From the outset, the union saw itself as part of the union movement and was embraced by other unions. While the union's first campaign was its industrial campaign, the second issue was a political one: the anti-conscription referendum with members being encouraged, and to encourage others, to 'vote no' in line with the THC.[148] It affiliated with the THC and elected its first delegates, Matilda (Tilly) Higgs and Isobel Parker, in late November 1916. Members' meetings were held in the Trades Hall almost immediately with the union. Seeking Trades Hall tenancy in 1918, by 1921 they were residents in room 12, which was a 'very large and commodious' room, large enough to hold general meetings, located upstairs in the new building in the north wing.[149] After Harry Smith died, the THC delegation comprised Margaret (a delegate since 1918), Jean Daley and Miranda Hill (who was replaced by Maud Howard in 1942). For many years, Margaret (1929–1938) and Jean (1925–1939) were elected to the THC's Labour Day Committee, often receiving the most votes.[150]

In the 1919 Eight Hours procession, a 'fair show was made by the members of the Female Confectioners' Society, who looked smart in white hats and blouses, with red bands and belts'.[151] Financial support for the wage determination appeal came from a broad range of unions, with 18 donations: including £10 from the Fellmongers, £2 each from the Stone Masons and Sheet Metal Workers. The largest donation came from the Wharf Labourers, which donated £62-10-0 'to assist the girls in their fight

---

[147] General meeting, 19 February 1945.

[148] Meeting, 3 October 1916.

[149] *The Woman's Clarion*, August 1922.

[150] THC minutes, various.

[151] *The Argus* 8 April 1919, p. 3.

for better conditions'.[152] For its part, for example, the union donated £5 to the 1920 Women Bookbinders strike for a 44-hour week,[153] while a euchre party and dance was held to raise money for the timber workers in their 1927 dispute. A dinner was organised for expatriate journalist and union activist Alice Henry when she visited in 1925, with all the women THC delegates invited by Margaret and Jean.[154]

In 1925, the union affiliated with the ALP, Victorian branch and became active in the its Women's Committee, the Women's Central Organising Committee (WCOC). For a decade, the union's delegation included Miranda, Maud, Ruby, Flora, Margaret Wearne and Jean Daley. Miranda and Margaret served as WCOC committee members, with Miranda president in 1940 and Jean Daley its secretary from 1932 to 1947. At the 1938 annual WCOC conference, 'Miss Hill held the conference by her forcible exposition of the labour women's angle on social service'.[155]

Conclusion

The union thus often faced a challenging external environment, while having to grapple with a competing union added innumerable tensions. Despite this, the Female Confectioners Union was a union that persisted in trying to advance the interests of women workers and that saw dedicated service by a group of committed honorary officials: among them, 'loyal' and 'earnest' Ruby, 'reliable' Flora, 'staunch' and 'energetic' Aileen, plus Miranda who had 'no regard whatever for a non-unionist and they have to quickly join the Union if they desire peace', and the 'calm' and dignified Margaret Wearne.[156]

---

152 Victorian sub-branch committee meeting, 11 June, 6 August 1917.

153 Management Committee 8 March 1920.

154 *The Woman's Clarion*, June 1925, p. 4.

155 *The Argus* 7 March 1938, p. 40.

156 *The Woman's Clarion*, March 1924, p. 10; general meeting, 12 July 1943; annual conference, 9 March 1924.

Chapter 6

The Melbourne Typographical Society and the Melbourne Trades and Labour Council, 1874–76

Andrew Reeves

From their earliest years, Australian trade unions reflected their British origins. The influence of migrant workers has been evident within the Australian labour movement for a century and a half, and the methods of organisation and industrial practices adopted by Australian unions have also reflected the links between Australian unions and their British counterparts.

Unlike the history of union development in Continental Europe and North America, where union peak bodies, divided by ideology, religion and regional affiliation, competed for the allegiance of organised workers, Australian experience reflected the authoritative role of the Trade Union Congress within British unionism. The Australian Council of Trade Unions (ACTU) has faced no serious challenges to its national leadership of the union movement throughout its 85-year history, while trades and labour councils in each capital city can claim up to 150 years leadership of state and regional union movements.

Yet for a brief period, in the mid 1870s, Melbourne had two rival, if not antagonistic, union organisations that represented different unions and alternative industrial programs competing for power. Although short-lived, such competition reflected a significant debate among Victorian unions on the political direction of an increasingly powerful movement, and raised questions of industrial strategy and political representation that would not finally be resolved for a further decade.

Melbourne's Trades Hall Committee, forerunner of the Victoria Trades Hall Council (THC), had developed out of the industrial ferment that accompanied the building tradesmen's successful campaign to win an eight-hour working day during 1856. The eight-hour day represented the talisman of the Trades Hall Committee. For many unions, possession of the eight-hour day represented permanence and legitimacy, as well as a necessary credential for membership of the Trades Hall Committee. In the 1870s the Trades Hall Committee did not purport to represent the majority of Victorian trades unions. Instead, the committee relied upon an unofficial, but effective, policy of restricted membership. Nor did the committee involve itself in industrial conflict, believing instead that industrial action remained a matter for individual unions.

This preference was reinforced by the impact of the protracted depression that began in 1859. Survival itself had proved a major achievement, while possession of an eight-hour working day was understood as a mark of social acceptance at a time when the Trades Hall Committee's own interests extended little further than the prospect of building a permanent hall on the trade societies' site at the corner of Lygon and Victoria Streets in Carlton. In fact, the notion of permanence lay at the heart of the Trades Hall Committee's erratic development and its ambivalent attitude towards some unions. For the committee, the construction of a permanent hall provided an appropriate focus for union activity while also demonstrating unionism's stability and achievements. On the other hand, the committee's outwardly reasonable demand that affiliated societies meet at the Hall, coupled with its refusal to involve itself in strike action, presumed a permanence or stability that relatively few unions possessed.

While late in the nineteenth century Eight-Hour Day celebrations had become large and popular public festivals, during the 1870s the Melbourne celebration had began to outgrow the exclusiveness that marked its origins. Although the eight-hour day represented the most important industrial achievement of nineteenth-century Australian unionism, the need to extend the eight-hour system did not provide sufficient cause for cooperative effort between colonial unions until well into the 1880s. Instead, unions appeared to rely upon some internal process within individual trades to produce the necessary pressure for acceptance of an eight-hour day by their employers. But such acceptance was conditional. Only where employees could maintain some control of the labour and pace of work was such pressure even conceivable. As a consequence, unions of unskilled and factory workers generally remained beyond the pale of the eight-hour system.

It is conceivable that the Trades Hall Committee could have evolved into little more than a building management committee, lacking any more fundamental relationship with its affiliates. However, a number of pressures upon the committee to assume a prominent role in local industrial and political activities after 1870 made this unlikely. Among these was a short-lived organisation known as the Melbourne Trades and Labour Council (MTLC), sponsored principally by the Melbourne Typographical Society (MTS). Other than the historians of the printing trades unions, little attention has been paid to this organisation. At best it has rated a passing mention in labour studies of this period: at worst, it has been confused with the Trades Hall Committee and its own particular character ignored. The historian of the national printing unions, Jim Hagan, treats the MTLC in a rather perfunctory, dismissive manner. Referring to the regret of the Ballarat Typographical Society at the 'decay of the Trades and Labour Council' he comments, 'disaster had followed its only major action, failure had attended all its small affairs'.[157] Ron Fitzgerald's *The Printers of Melbourne*, concentrating on the Melbourne Typographical Society and published a year after Hagan's volume, captures the spirit of the times and the motivation of the MTS rather better. His brisk summary of its early progress provides a snapshot of its ambitions and influence:

> By 1890 their new union had proved itself to be one of the colony's best organized and most influential bodies. A leading force in coordinating working class activity, the Society had set up a Trades and Labour Council in the seventies, had attempted to do so again in 1880 and in that year had also founded one of the first of Australia's federated organizations, the Australasian Typographical Union. The printers during the eighties also helped to initiate the public campaign which led to the passing of Victoria's first effective industrial legislation. They also worked to extend the power and influence of the Melbourne Trades Hall Council.[158]

Fitzgerald acknowledges the relative lack of success that attended the MTLC, but sees greater importance in locating it within a context of a series of attempts by unions at wider organisation. He refers to the short-lived predecessor to the MTLC, the United Trades Association, which in 1873 briefly joined tinsmiths, cabinetmakers, tailors, boot-makers and, latterly, printers in an attempt to create a central union organisation allowing unions to negotiate with employers on something approaching equal terms. He also places greater significance on its democratic structures, but ultimately concludes that the organisation was ahead of its time, seeking from individual

---

[157] Quoted in Hagan, J. 1966, *Printers and Politics*, ANU Press, Canberra, p. 48.

[158] Fitzgerald, RT 1967, *The Printers of Melbourne*, Pitman, Melbourne, p. 23.

unions a measure of discipline that they could not provide, to the detriment of the MTLC's own effectiveness.

The Trades and Labour Council's anonymity can be explained partly by the paucity of records detailing its activities. This chapter is based on the Trades and Labour Council's minute book, which fortuitously survived in the archives of its major sponsor, the Melbourne Typographical Society, later the Printing and Kindred Industries Union and now the Printing Division of the Australian Manufacturing Workers Union (AMWU). As with many other early documents of this sort, it survived as a consequence of the parsimony of union secretaries. A decade later this minute book would be reused as an attendance register for Typographical Society Committee meetings and as a consequence would be preserved in the society's archives. Alternative sources of information are equally fugitive. The Typographical Society's *Journal* is possibly the only other source deserving close study, while scattered references in Melbourne's daily press complete this short list.

If the Trades Hall Committee found legitimacy in that distinctly Australia achievement – the eight-hour system – then the Trades and Labour Council represented a local expression of contemporary British concerns, in particular the legal recognition of trade unions and the legal right to picket during industrial disputes between employers and employees. These were issues that had been adopted by British unions during the years of good trade and increasing union membership. The success of the 1874 Sheffield Trade Union Congress, which represented the high-water mark of cooperative union action over these issues, attracted the keen attention of the Melbourne Typographical Society. In its June 1874 manifesto, urging the formation of an amalgamated trades union, the society referred to its pleasure at the success of the Sheffield Congress, arguing that their intention was 'to follow in the wake of a similar union so successfully operating in England'. In reality, the society's objective was cooperation between unions rather than amalgamation.

> One principle (of cooperation) must be … either a combination of trade interests on a financial basis – that is by stated contributions so as to assist trades in dispute – or simply on a system of mutual interest by moral influence and support, and voluntary contributions in time of need … Another principle is clearly shown – the settlement of disputes by arbitration.[159]

---

[159] MTLC minutes, 13 June 1874.

While British experience certainly acted as a catalyst, local factors were also important. Local economic improvement after 1870 underpinned increased union membership and renewed union optimism, but even during such years of opportunity, different union objectives often resulted in contradictory strategies.

Eighteen unions were represented at the Trades Hall meeting that discussed the Typographical Society's proposals. Twelve were also affiliated to the Trades Hall Committee, or soon would be, while others, such as the Typographical Society and unions of millwrights, shipwrights, cabmen and grocers could claim neither affiliation to the Trades Hall Committee nor, with a single exception, an eight-hour working day. Many of these unions that represented trades or industries are now covered by the AMWU. That they involved themselves with these discussions is indicative of the early origins of so many AMWU unions and their participation in the debates and strategies that shaped the labour movement in the nineteenth century. In addition to the Typographical Society, these included the coachmakers, the shipwrights, ironmoulders and tinsmiths societies.

In the estimation of the Typographical Society, cooperation in the form of a Trades and Labour Council represented the best opportunity of establishing an effective means of regulating industrial relations while simultaneously reducing union reliance upon strike action. This position attracted the support of a number of recent Trades Hall Committee affiliates that, while having enjoyed industrial success, nevertheless lacked the financial and industrial resources more characteristic of Melbourne's strong building trade unions. Unsurprisingly, many of these building unions, led by the Stonemasons Society, objected to the Typographical Society's promotion of arbitration. Such objections were raised at the council's inaugural meeting on 13 June. A Stonemason's delegate complained that:

> The promoters had not taken into consideration a subject which he considered of much greater importance than arbitration. (In) case of disputes he thought it would be more profitable to endeavor to secure for those trades who have not already got it, the eight-hour system.[160]

With other unions unwilling to concede this point, the stonemasons and bricklayers societies withdrew from the council at its next meeting. The ironmoulders and basketmakers declined to join.

---

[160] MTLC minutes, 12 June 1874.

Throughout the nineteenth century the possession of an eight-hour working day, however nominal, separated the haves from the have-nots among Melbourne's trade organisations. Winning the eight-hour day represented a source of considerable strength and was a sign of superiority over the achievements of other unions. It became something of a universal panacea. For many unionists an eight-hour day represented the key to social integration and respectability. Even if protagonists of the Trades and Labour Council looked to British experiences for models of industrial regulation, the majority of eight-hour trades remained ambivalent. While accepting the right of artisans and tradesmen to contribute to and benefit from the social progress inherent in Britain's imperial power, in their eyes possession of the eight-hour day also marked their colonial society off from the many evils of British working-class life.

The proposals advanced by the Trades and Labour Council highlighted the differences many in the union movement saw at that time between two alternative paths to security: the eight-hour system, with its overtones of trade independence; and arbitration, with its inherent acceptance of the organisational and industrial limitations to trade union strength. After the strike defeats of 1891–94 any sense that these two union strategies were, in fact, alternatives became irrelevant, but in 1874 the absence of any central authority ensured that individual unions needed to establish their own guarantees of permanence.

Trades societies representing more than 3600 unionists had initially responded to the Typographical Society's invitation to establish a Trades and Labour Council, but by the July delegates' meeting defections and rejections had reduced the council to 13 societies with an approximate membership of 1800. Prominent among its affiliates were the Tailors' Trade Protection Society (350 members), the Carpenters' and Joiners' Society (320 members), the Typographical Society (250 members), and the Seamen's Union (210 members). The possibilities of arbitration remained the council's major preoccupation. Amplifying the Typographical Society's original suggestion, the council determined in November 1874 to press for 'an act ... to legalise a Court of Arbitration for settlement of disputes between employers and employees'.[161] Although responding 'favourably' to a council deputation, the Kerferd ministry sought the opinion of individual trades, and despite favourable response from the painters, tailors, typographical, tinsmiths and saddlers societies, this initiative subsequently lapsed.

---

[161] MTLC minutes, November 1874.

In contrast to the Trades Hall Committee, the MTLC did not proscribe involvement in industrial action. Another principal council ambition had been the establishment of a central fund capable of providing grants-in-aid to unions on strike. While such an initiative attracted the interest of a number of unions, within 18 months of its establishment the council had been overwhelmed by strike action. By August 1874 the Tailors' Society had approached the council for support from the Agricultural Implement Makers Association. In October of the same year the council agreed to support the claim by tanners for an eight-hour day, a claim that led to strike action in Melbourne and Castlemaine, and the subsequent jailing of a number of Castlemaine tanners under the Master and Servants Act.

The council saw no contradiction between support for both strike action and arbitration. In recognising the tenuous industrial position of most unions, the council sought to supplement union resources to undertake strike action while also pursuing the resolution of strikes through the adoption of arbitration committees. In each of the disputes previously mentioned, societies were counselled to approach their adversaries to seek settlement by means of arbitration, but little success appears to have accompanied such efforts. Nor did union-sponsored arbitration proposals succeed in resolving the 1875 Melbourne *Herald* dispute. Trouble had been simmering between the Typographical Society and the *Herald* for some months, while the union sought to enforce a wages agreement upon the newspaper's proprietors. The *Herald*'s refusal to accept the society's proposed overtime rates and to reduce its employment of juvenile labour led to the Typographical Society striking in January 1875. Despite financial support from the council and an attempt to implement a boycott of the paper, the *Herald* continued to appear. This protracted strike strained the council's own limited resources beyond breaking point. With all available finance devoted to the Typographers' strike, other affiliates were increasingly left to deal with their own industrial affairs and a number of unions resigned from the council between June and October 1875, including the carpenters and joiners, sailmakers and saddlers.

On 7 October 1875 the council suspended operations for three months due to 'the present unsettled state of things'. Following one further meeting in February 1876 the council was dissolved. The Trades Hall Committee did not lament the passing of the council. Although the council met at the Trades Hall throughout its existence and union affiliation overlapped sufficiently for the council's voice to be heard in the committee, it never felt sufficient need to assist or encourage its erstwhile competitor. In fact, the

Trades Hall Committee twice rejected union appeals for the council to be leased a room at a preferential rate.

Despite its collapse the Trades and Labour Council had opened up new perspectives for Melbourne unionism. Issues such as industrial cooperation, arbitration, strike funds and coordinated strike action did not disappear with the council, but instead acted as points of reference around which unionism would reorganise and expand after 1879. One delegate upon whom the lessons of 1874–75 had not been lost was William Emmett Murphy. Born in Dublin in 1841, the son of a nationalist publican, Murphy had emigrated to Melbourne from Liverpool in 1865, becoming active in both the Cabinet Makers' Society and the Society of Carpenters and Joiners. He represented the latter as a delegate to both the Trades Hall Committee and the Trades and Labour Council. Convinced of his own destiny in colonial society, as much as of trade unionism's, Murphy went on to become a prominent figure in nineteenth-century Victorian unionism. The collapse of the council cleared the way for Murphy to concentrate his efforts within the Trades Hall Committee. A delegate during the 1870s, he became committee secretary in 1877. He occupied this office with a few intermissions until 1886, when he was removed as secretary following charges of financial misappropriation, charges that were neither pursued nor proved by his traducers.

During his decade of leadership, Murphy oversaw the transformation of the Trades Hall Committee. Its insularity had never appealed to him. Outspoken in his support for an extension of the committee's role in industrial affairs, he caused consternation among delegates convinced that the committee's obligation extended no further than the boundaries of the Trades Hall Crown Grant. As secretary, Murphy publicly supported union industrial campaigns and political demands. He succeeded in committing the Trades Hall Committee to support the Victorian Salesmen's Union shorter hour's campaign of 1881 and to coordinate the 1882–83 tailoresses' strike, a strike in which trade regulation and factory reform were major issues. This represented a significant victory for Murphy and his allies, as well as a vindication of his belief that the Trades Hall Committee should be the most influential voice of Victorian unionism.

Three years later in 1885, the now-renamed Trades Hall Council (the new title itself echoes the name of its short-lived rival) opened negotiations with the Victorian Employers Union to establish a Board of Conciliation. Initially, the Trades Hall Council (THC) sought a conciliation system independent of government jurisdiction. Only the bitter experiences of 1891–94 would finally convince the THC to campaign for a state-sponsored scheme, incorporating the essential points of the Trades and Labour Council's 1874 proposal.

From its earliest days the Trades and Labour Council acknowledged that political activity was a logical consequence of its industrial objectives. This provided another point of disagreement with the Trades Hall Committee that, as late as 1881, would be told that the further the committee dealt in politics the less successful it would be. The extent to which the THC should be involved in politics represented the final confrontation between the original eight-hour unions (based upon the building trades unions and providing a majority of Trades Hall Trustees) and the growing number of more recently established unions for whom political involvement was a logical extension of their industrial activity.

This confrontation took the form of an acrimonious debate over the relative powers of the THC and of the appointed Trustees of the Trades Hall building itself. The council's increasing emphasis upon parliamentary politics (Murphy stood for North Melbourne in 1886 as a 'bone fide working man'), upon early closing campaigns and consumer boycotts, upon immigration control and tariff reform proved unacceptable to Trades Hall Trustees. They saw their role as protecting the original union vision of the 1850s, and sought to frustrate the council's now obvious tendency towards political affairs and inter-colonial cooperation. Trustees, they argued, managed the Trades Hall and controlled the affairs of its council: other affiliates were restricted to 'a voice in the management'. Such a differentiation in the rights of union affiliates might have carried weight 10 years earlier, but by 1886 it proved irrelevant. State government intervention decisively supported Murphy and his principal allies Tom Trenwith, secretary of the Boot Trades Union, and Fred Bromley, of the Tinsmiths. Prominent among the new regulations gazetted in 1888 was the council's power 'to consider and make orders upon any matters remitted to it by trade societies and others'. With the adoption of such powers, the transition from building manager to coordinator of a state union movement was virtually complete. It was a transition in which the Trades and Labour Council had played an important initiatory role.

The final vindication of the Melbourne Trades and Labour Council took place a decade after its collapse. The ultimate sanction of the politically minded unions during their dispute with the Trades Hall Trustees in 1886–87 was their threat to quit the Trades Hall and establish an alternative Trades and Labour Council under democratic union control. With their ultimate victory, a union movement that is recognisable today had begun to emerge.

* * *

The minutes of the Melbourne Trades and Labour Council survive only in manuscript form in the AMWU, Victorian Branch collection at the University of Melbourne Archives. These minutes are reproduced below.

Minutes of the Melbourne Trades and Labour Council

List of organisations participating with the names of delegates. (This list is included in the minute book prior to the minutes of the foundation meeting.)

Agricultural Implement Makers – Messrs. Sutherland and Morrison.

Bakers' Society –

Coachmakers Society – Messrs. Gale, Holman and Kennedy.

Carpenters and Joiners Society – Messrs. R Miller, R Symons, G Fox, N Dixon.

Cabmens Union –

Brickmakers Society –

Grocer Society –

Hatters Society – Messrs. Clarke and Rooke.

Painters and Paperhangers – Messrs. Elliott and Meredith.

Saddlers Society – Mr Pearce.

Typographical Society – Messrs. Towson, Dickason, Marr and Hall.

Tailors Trade Protection Society – Messrs. Livingstone, Bolger and Downie.

Tanners Society – Messrs. Alloway, Evans and Jemmeson.

Tinplate and Iron Workers Society – J Miller and JE Reddick

Millsawyers Society – Messrs. Tracey.

Sailmakers Society – Messrs Rankin.

Minutes of Meeting of delegates held at the Trades Hall, Lygon Street, Saturday 13 June 1874. Mr. J Towson, President of the Melbourne Typographical Society in the chair who read the following statement which was prepared by the Society he represented to lay before the meeting for the purpose of forming an amalgamated Trades Union.

... the Typographical Society having for some time felt that desirability of forming a union of trades for mutual benefit and viewing with great pleasure the success attending the congress of trades' unions recently held at Sheffield, have taken upon themselves the duty of inviting the other trades to assist in the furtherance of this object. They did not feel justified in laying down any definite plan of action, but content themselves with placing before you a rough outline, containing a few principles connected with such a beneficial scheme. The scheme will not deprive trades of privileges they already possess, but would lighten the burdens of those who are oppressed, and would strengthen the remedies already obtained. In forming an Amalgamated Trades' Union, the intention is to follow in the wake of a similar union so successfully operating in England. One of two principles must be the basis of such union, either a combination of trade interests on a financial basis – that is by stated contributions so as to assist trades in dispute – or simply on a system of mutual interest by moral influence and support, and voluntary contributions in time of need. The Union to be of a defensive not aggressive character. Another principle is clearly shown – the settlement of disputes by arbitration. This feature will abolish the cause and effect of strike.

As a union we would feel ourselves bound to abide the decision of a fairly appointed arbitration committee. Should employers refuse to accept such decision, then the power and influence of the union must be brought to bear upon the objections in such manner as may be deemed advisable. It would be desirable to have an arbitration committee legalised by Act of Parliament. It is a question whether there should be a regular contribution from all trades, according to members, for carrying out the objects of an Amalgamated Trades' Union, or whether an admission fee should alone be charged, and voluntary contributions or levies made when a case arises to demand such assistance. It is needless to enter into particulars as to what those cases may be for all present, and those whom they represent are fully aware what is alluded to. No case will be sent to an arbitration committee until it has previously brought before the committee of this union and by them recommended to arbitration. The *Times* speaking on this subjects says 'the minds of the working men were thoroughly imbued with the principle of arbitration, and that there were 300,000 men governed by it, who sat down with their employers and arranged with them for the rate of wages which should prevail in their separate branches of industry'. There should be a better understanding between capital and labour. Each is mutually dependent upon the other; though the general opinion prevails that labour has always been worsted in a contest for rights, amply from want of union. The Typographical Society, having initiated the movement, would now urge …

Mr. Taylor of the Masons Society.

… said the promoters had not taken into consideration a subject which he considered of much greater importance than arbitration, in case of disputes, he thought it would be more profitable to endeavour to secure for those trades who have not already got it, the eight hours system. Those trades, who have already attained the boon, should lend every assistance to obtain it for others. The masons for some time past have viewed the efforts that are being made by the Early Closing Association and consider that the results have not been commensurate with the labours.

He moved that 'the extension of the eight-hour system be deemed the primary object in connection with the amalgamated union'.

Mr. Hall (Secretary) pointed out that the Union was not yet formed and suggested that the first steps should be to establish the Union and afterwards to discuss the objects.

The motion was subsequently withdrawn and Mr Jones moved the following resolution.

'That this meeting, representing a very large majority of the most influential trades of Melbourne and suburbs, considers the present an opportune time to form a union of all trades for mutual support had therefore resolves that an Amalgamated Trades' Union be formed on a basis hereafter to be determined.' In moving it he stated that those who had drawn up that resolution had no idea of dictating as to the form, or means by which the union should be brought about, or the basis on which it should be established. We have different ideas on the subject. One man believes its principal object should be to gain the eight hours' system, but as has been said by our acting secretary, it is necessary for us first to amalgamate and to remember that within ourselves we must get the intelligence that will conduct us in the effort with regard to the

Saturday ... holiday movement ... strong should look after the weak, for if they worked for the weak they were bound to work for the strong.'

Mr. Symons (Carpenters Society) seconded the resolution, remarking that his trade believed it would be for the benefit of the united trades to amalgamate into a Union.

Mr. Sutherland (Agricultural Implement Makers Association) supported the resolution.

Some delegates stated that they were there only to report progress and that these delegates would have to know something of the details before they could pledge themselves to the Union.

Mr. Hall remarked that nothing would be binding on the societies till approved of by them, – that the delegates would simply carry such resolutions as they considered beneficial and then get the societies to confirm them.

The chairman then put the resolution which was carried unanimously.

Mr. Elliott moved the next resolution as follows –

'The one delegate from each trade represented be appointed a committee to form the basis of this Union and submit the same to their respective societies previous to being decided on by a general meeting of delegates.'

Mr. Mackay (Cabmen's Union) seconded the resolution which was carried:-

The following gentlemen were appointed as the committee to draw up the basis on which the union should be formed, in accordance with the foregoing resolution. Namely Messrs. Townson (Typographical Society), Boyd (shipwright), Clark (hatter), Hilton (Grocer), O'Byrne (cabmen), Sutherland (agricultural implement maker), Dixon (carpenter), O'Neil (boilermaker), Kennan (baker), Thomas (bricklayer), Elliott (painter), M'Kean (mason), Downie (tailor), Traoy (millwright), Gibbon (seamen), Reilly (labourer), Evans (tanner) and Pritchard (saddler).

Mr. Elliott moved, 'that this meeting adjourn to such time and place as shall be decided on by the sub-committee, the same to be advertised in the daily papers'.

Mr. Boyd (shipwright) seconded the motion, which was carried.

Mr. Symons moved, and Mr. M'Intosh seconded, that Mr. Hall be appointed secretary, pro tem, which was carried.

Mr. Ryan moved, and Mr. Dixon seconded a vote of thanks to the chairman, which ...

A vote of thanks was passed o the Melbourne Typographical Society for the action they had taken in bringing the subject of amalgamation forward.

Estimated number of members represented 3645.

A meeting of the sub-committee was held on the following Thursday at the Trades Hall to draw up the basis of the Union.

Mr. Marr (Chair).

A second sub-committee meeting was held to consider new rules which were ordered to be printed and circulated to the societies. It was decided to hold the next general delegate meeting on Friday 24 July.

Mr. Clark (Chair).

MINUTES OF DELEGATE MEETING HELD IN THE TRADES HALL,

FRIDAY 24 JULY – MR. RYAN IN THE CHAIR

The following trades were represented:-

Shipwrights, Hatters, Cabmen's Union, Bakers, Typographical Society, Agricultural Implement Makers, Saddlers, Painters and Paperhangers, Tailors, Seamen's Union, Brickmakers, Tanners, Sailmakers, and Coachmakers.

Minutes of previous meeting read and confirmed.

Letters read from the Bricklayers and Masons withdrawing.

From Basketmakers and Ironmoulders, declining to join at present.

From Hatters, approving of rules. From Sailmakers wishing to join.

The rules were again discussed, and treated as follows:-

Rules I & II passed. In rule III, on the motion of Mr. Elliott, it was resolved that the word representative be substituted for delegate, and financial placed before member in third line. Rule then passed. Rules 4, 5, 6 & 7, passed without alteration.

Rule 8, Propd, by Mr. Grimwood and seconded by Mr. Kernan 'that the extent of levy be reduced to 6 d. carried. Rule 9 made 'six months' instead of 'three months' in last line. Rules 10, 11 & 12 passed without alteration.

Rule 13 – Add Treasurer's name to signature for cheques.

Rule 14 & 15 – Add remuneration of Secretary and Treasurer to be decided by the Executive.

Rule 16 – Societies to appoint – auditors in rotation.

Rules 17, 18 & 19 passed.

Proposed by Mr. Clark, and seconded by Mr. Holman 'That the amended rules be now adopted, and become the rules of this Council and that the first quarterly contribution are now due.' Carried.

The Secretary was instructed to have 300 copies of rules printed. Resolved that the next meeting of delegates be held on Wednesday 5th August, 8pm.

A vote of thanks to the chairman, and meeting closed.

MINUTES OF DELEGATE MEETING HELD AT THE TRADES HALL,

WEDNESDAY 5 AUGUST, 1874 – MR. TOWNSON IN THE CHAIR

Trades represented – Agricultural Implement Makers, Coachmakers, Hatters, Painters & Paperhangers, Saddlers, Seamen's Union, Typographical Society, Tailors' Trade Protection Society, and Tanners.

Minutes of previous meeting read and confirmed.

ELECTION OF OFFICERS – Mr. Holman proposed and Mr. Elliott seconded 'That Mr. Hall be elected Secretary.

Carried.

PRESIDENT – Messrs. Towson, Elliott and Holman were nominated. The first gentleman declined on account of being engaged on night work. On show of hands being taken, Mr JS Elliott was elected.

VICE-PRESIDENT – Mr. R Holman (C) was elected.

TREASURER – Mr. Downie (T.T.P.S) elected.

TRUSTEES – Messrs. Towson, Sutherland and Kennedy.

A letter was received from the Carpenter and Joiners' Society signifying their intention of joining and naming representatives.

ACCOUNTS: The following accounts were passed for payment –

Trades Hall Committee 18/6, Secretary, Postage/Stationery 9/6, Tribune Advs 8/-, Armstrong Advs 24/-, Walker & May printing rules 24/-.

EXECUTIVE COMMITTEE: Mr. Sutherland (Agricultural Implement Makers), Mr. Clarke (Hatters), Mr. Meredith (Painters & Paperhangers), Mr. Pearce (Saddlers), Mr. Ryan (Seamen's Union), Mr. J Marr (Typographical Society), Mr. Livingstone (Tailors' Trade Protection Society), Mr. Alloway (Tanners' Society).

It was decided that the funds of the Council should be deposited in the Post Office Savings Banks.

It was also resolved that all meetings should be advertised in the daily papers and to be held in the Trades Hall.

First meeting of Executive to take place on Thursday 13th inst.

The following payments were then received from the societies present, with number of financial members:-

Agricultural Implement Makers with 150 members – one pound five shillings,

Coachmakers Society with 102 members – seventeen shillings,

Hatters' Society 45 members – seven shillings and sixpence,

Painters' and Paperhangers 54 members – nine shillings,

Seamen's Union 210 members – one pound fifteen shillings,

Saddlers' Society with 55 members – nine shillings and tuppence,

Typographical Society with 250 members – two pounds, one shilling and eight pence,

Tailors' Trade Protection Society 300 members – two pounds ten shillings,

Tanners' Society 144 members – one pound four shillings.

Total number of financial members 1310. Cash received Ten Pounds eighteen shillings and four pence.

Meeting adjourned

J.S ELLIOTT

MEETING OF EXECUTIVE COMMITTEE,

HELD THURSDAY 13 AUGUST, 1874

PRESENT: Messrs. Elliott, Clarke, Hall, Sutherland, Downie, Livingstone, Alloway, Ryan, Pearce, Meredith.

The Secretary was instructed to write to Trades Hall Committee for room for executive and general meetings. The general meetings to be held on second Thursday in each quarter.

It was decided that for Secretary's services he shall receive ten percent on quarterly contributions received.

Propd. by Mr. Sutherland and secd. Mr. Alloway 'That consideration of amount of guarantee from Secretary and Treasurer be left over till next meeting'.

Carried.

Propd. by Mr. Sutherland, seconded by Mr. Clarke, that Treasurer's salary be at the rate of one pound per annum.

Carried.

Letter received from Tin-plate Workers' Society asking particulars, previous to joining.

Secretary was ordered to procure two receipt books, 200 circulars, 1000 notehead papers, Minute Book, Ledger, and Treasurer's Book. The subject of the strike at Buckley and Nunn's was introduced and – Mr. Hall proposed – 'That this meeting sympathise with the members of the Tailors' Trade Protection Society, disapproving of the recent action of Buckley & Nunn in reference to their workmen'.

Seconded by Mr Pearce and carried.

J.S. ELLIOTT

EXECUTIVE MEETING

HELD THURSDAY 3 SEPTEMBER, 1874

AT THE TRADES HALL

Mr Elliott in the chair.

PRESENT: Messrs Clarke, Marr, Holman, Downie, Sutherland, Gale, Meredith, Pearce, Reddick, Tracey, Kennedy, Livingstone Rankin, Alloway, Miller and Hall.

Minutes of previous meeting read and confirmed.

The following accounts were passed for payment:- Secretary for books etc. 13/-, Walker & May, Printing one pound, eighteen shillings and sixpence.

Correspondence read and received from Victorian Tin-plate workers, and Millsawyers Society, agreeing to join the Council and naming delegates.

From Agricultural Implement Makers' Association instructing their delegates to lay the business in connection with their recent strike before the council.

After some explanation and discussion, it was proposed by Mr Clarke, and seconded by Mr Marr, 'That in the opinion of this Council the Agricultural Implement Makers' are justified in their demand for an increase of wages.'

Carried.

Mr Sutherland stated that the Association merely wanted the advice of the Executive as to the best steps to be taken in the present crisis.

Mr Marr proposed and Mr Holman seconded, – 'that this Executive recommend the Agricultural Implement Makers to endeavour to obtain sanction of their employers to a settlement of the dispute by arbitration.'

Carried.

Cash received – Victorian Tinplate & Ironworkers – 62 members 10/4d.
Sailmakers' Society – 25 members 4/2d,
Millsawyers' Society – 60 members 10/-

J.S. ELLIOTT

EXECUTIVE MEETING,

HELD THURSDAY 1 OCTOBER, 1874

PRESENT: Messrs Elliott (Chair) Marr, Downie, Alloway
            Clarke, Kelligan, Meredith, Tracey, Murphy,
            Miller and Hall.

Minutes read and confirmed.

Letters received from Carpenters and Joiners' Society, also from Tanners' Society, referring to the strike in their trade and asking for sympathy.

After the cause of the strike and had been explained, and progress reported, Mr Marr proposed, and Mr Miller seconded 'that in the opinion of this Council the members of the Tanners' Association are justified in their demand for eight hours and that this Council promises to give its sympathy and support, also recommend that the dispute should be submitted to arbitration.'

Carried.

Secretary's account for commission on twelve pounds, amounting to one pound four shillings, passed for payment.

Notice of motion by Mr Hall – 'That at general meeting next Thursday the subject be considered of forming deputation to wait upon the Attorney-General for the purpose of having an Act prepared to legalise a Court of Arbitration for settlement of disputes between employers and employees.'

Notice of motion by Mr Murphy – 'That it is desirable that a public meeting of all trades should be called at an early date, to consider the action of the Agricultural Society in appointing a deputation to urge upon the Government the advisability of re-establishing the system of assisted immigration.'

J.S ELLIOTT

GENERAL DELEGATE MEETING

HELD THURSDAY 8 OCTOBER, 1874

Mr Elliott in the chair.

The following trades were represented:- Carpenters and Joiners' Union, Coachmakers, Hatters, Millsawyers, Painters, Saddlers, Sailmakers, Typographical, Tailors, Tinsmiths and Tanners.

Minutes of previous meeting read and confirmed.

Delegates from the Tanners' Society reported progress of strike, also handed in a letter received from the Castlemaine tanners, giving full particulars of the strike in that locality.

In accordance with notice, Mr Hall proposed 'that a deputation from this Council be formed to wait upon the Attorney-General for the purpose of having an Act prepared to legalise a Court of Arbitration for settlement of disputes between employers and employees.' Seconded by Mr Tracey.

Propd. by Mr Clark and seconded by Mr Marr – 'that a special meeting be called this day month for the purpose of fully considering the motion.'

Carried.

Mr J.S Elliott proposed

2. That this meeting views with regret the unsatisfactory state of the Master and Servants' Act, and would urge upon the Legislature to make some amendment in order that justice may be done t both parties.

* Seconded by Mr Fox.

H.BENT, M.L.A proposed

3. That this meeting considered it will be to the benefit of the community for the Government to prepare an Act as early as possible, giving power to Courts of Arbitration to settle trade disputes; and, further, it is our opinion that this is the only preventive to strikes.

* Seconded by G.W Hall.

MR CLARK M.L.A proposed

4. That a copy of the two foregoing resolutions be forwarded to the Attorney-General and his attention drawn to the decision given by magistrates of

Castlemaine in the recent case of imprisonment of a number of operative tanners.

* Seconded by Mr Miller.

MINUTES OF SPECIAL GENERAL MEETING

HELD THURSDAY 12 NOVEMBER, 1874

Mr Elliott in the chair.

Minutes of previous meeting read and confirmed. Correspondence read from Trades Hall Committee in reference to quarterly payments. Cheque from Mr J Curtain for two pounds two shillings, on behalf of Tanners.

From Mr Langridge, one pound one shilling for Tanners.

Delegates from Tanners' Society reported upon progress of the strike, and stated that some of the Castlemaine men had come to Melbourne, and had gone to work in the Collingwood wards on 10 hours. Many employers had given in, but a few still held out and there were about sixty men locked out. A movement had been set afoot to start a cooperative tannery.

The adjourned motion by Mr Hall, on the subject of Courts of Arbitration was then discussed, and carried by a majority of 12 to 3.

Mr Gair proposed and Mr Simmonds seconded 'that a deputation of three wait upon the Attorney-General in reference to the resolution, and urge upon him the necessity for immediate action.'

Carried.

The following gentlemen were appointed to form the deputation –

Messrs Elliott, Downie and Hall.

In accordance with previous notice, Mr Murphy moved 'that it is desirable a public meeting of all trades should be called at an early date to consider the action of the Agricultural Society in appointing a deputation to urge upon the Government the desirability of re-establishing the system of assisted immigration.'

Seconded by Mr Carter.

The Chairman pointed out that he scarcely thought such a subject came within the province of the Council.

An amendment was proposed by Mr Marr that we proceed to next business. Seconded by Mr Rankin.

Carried.

Account on 10/- for advertising (Armstrong) was passed for payment.

In reference to the subject of the Tanners' strike, Mr Hall proposed that Mr Tracey seconded 'that a public meeting be called of all trades to consider the subject.'

Carried.

On the Motion of Mr Murphy, seconded by Mr Clark, – it was resolved – 'that the President, Secretary and Mr Fox be a committee for said meeting.'

Carried.

Proposed by Mr Murphy and seconded by Mr Marr, 'that the Secretary request compliers of almanacs to notice 21 April as the anniversary of the eight hours movements.'

Carried.

Notice of motion by Mr T.A Reddick for addition to rules: 'that any society connected with this Council resolving to come out on strike, shall first lay full particulars of their case before the Council for their consideration; failing to do this the members of such society shall not be entitled to receive monetary assistance to aid them in such strike.'

Cash received: Hatters 45 – 7/6d, Tinsmiths 78 – 13/-, Tanners 144 – 24/-, Carpenters 317 – two pounds twelve shillings and ten pence, Tailors – 300 – two pounds ten shillings, Typographical 250 – two pounds one shilling and eight pence.

J.S ELLIOTT

A public meeting of all trades was held on the Old Trades Hall on Thursday 15 October in accordance to resolution of general meeting held on the 8th inst., to take into consideration the Tanners' strike. The chair was taken by J Curtain, esq. M.L.A. and the following resolutions carried unanimously:-

G.D LANGRIDGE M.L.A. proposed

1. That in the opinion of this meeting the tanners of Castlemaine who were imprisoned through the extreme measures taken by their employer, for endeavouring to obtain their rights, deserve our deepest sympathy for the indignity put upon them, and our highest praise for their noble conduct in defending the eight-hours principle; and that this meeting exert itself in supporting the operative tanners of Melbourne and Castlemaine now on strike.

* Seconded by Mr Ryan

Accounts passed for payment – Armstrong advertising two pounds fifteen shillings, Walker & May Printing etc. two pounds and seven shillings.

Receipts – Sailmakers 3/6d, Painters 8/6d, Coachmakers 17/-.

Trades represented – Carpenters, Coachmakers, Hatters, Tailors, Typographical Society, Tanners, Sailmakers, Tinplate-workers.

WILLIAM MURPHY, CHAIRMAN

MINUTES OF EXECUTIVE MEETING,

HELD THURSDAY 3 DECEMBER, 1874

Mr Murphy in the chair.

Trades represented: Carpenters, Coachmakers, Tailors
                       Printers, Sailmakers.

It was decided that the auditors be elected from the Carpenters, Coachmakers and Sailmakers.

The Secretary reported the result of the interview with the Premier, which was very satisfactory. A vote of thanks was passed to the Press, and to the members of Parliament who introduced the deputation.

An account of twenty-two shillings secretary's commission on Eleven Pounds, and post 4/6d, was passed for payment and the meeting adjourned.

J.S ELLIOTT

MINUTES OF EXECUTIVE MEETING,

HELD 7 JANUARY, 1875

Mr J.S Elliott in the chair.

Minutes of previous meeting read and confirmed.

Trades represented: Coachmakers, Painters, Printers
                        Sailmakers and Tailors.

The Secretary reported while at Ballarat lately, he had introduced the establishment of the Council at a meeting and advised that the trades should connect themselves with our body. It was suggested by persons present that if a meeting of trades was called probably a branch council might be started in Ballarat.

The Chairman requested full attendance on the 14th as it was the annual meeting and the night for election of officers.

MINUTES OF ANNUAL MEETING,

HELD THURSDAY 14 JANUARY, 1875

AT THE TRADES HALL

Mr J.S Elliott in the chair.

Trades represented: Carpenters, Coachmakers, Hatters, Printers
                        Painters, Sailmakers, Tailors.

Minutes of pervious meeting read and confirmed.

Election of Officers: President Mr J.S Elliott
                          Vice-President Mr Wolfe
                          Treasurer Mr J Downie
                          Secretary Mr G.W Hall

The Balance-Sheet for the half-year was certified by the auditors, Messrs. Reay, Gale and Rankin, and received. It was afterwards adopted on the motion of Mr Murphy, seconded by Mr Livingstone.

An account from Mr Armstrong for advertising, amounting to 15/- was passed for payment.

Mr Murphy propd. and Mr Dixon seconded 'that the auditors receive the sum of 5/- each for every audit to commence with the present audit.'

An amendment by Mr Hall, seconded by Mr Livingstone, 'that the amount allowed be 2/6d. each.'

Carried.

A letter was read from the Typographical Society in reference to a trade dispute at the Herald Office. Mr M. Thornhill, who was appointed to lay the matter before the Council, stated the nature of the grievance, which was to the effect that the proprietors refused to pay for standing time, which was an infringement of trade practices.

After the matter had been fully explained Mr Murphy moved 'that every assistance this Council can render, monetary and otherwise, be given to the Typographical Society until the dispute is adjusted.' Seconded by Mr Rankin.

Carried.

Proposed by Mr Rankin, seconded by Mr Wolfe 'that the first Thursday in next month be general delegate meeting.'

Carried.

Meeting adjourned

JOHN WOLFE.

MINUTES OF GENERAL DELEGATES MEETING

HELD THURSDAY 4 FEBRUARY, 1875

PRESENT: Messrs J Wolfe (chair) and representatives from the following Societies, Carpenters, Coachmakers, Printers, Sailmakers and Tailors.

Minutes of previous meeting read and confirmed.

The Secretary reported that the Herald dispute, as far as the particular instance mentioned in the minutes was concerned, was settled, but another difficulty had arisen in the shape of boy labour being employed on a daily newspaper, contrary to trade custom.

Mr Thornhill entered fully into the case, and stated that they had all received a week's notice and would leave their employment on Saturday.

Mr Murphy wished to know that assistance would be rendered by the Typographical Society to the men who came out.

In reply it was stated that nothing definite was known as to what would be paid by their Society but that need not influence the action of the Council.

After further discussion, it was unanimously resolved on the motion of Mr Murphy, seconded by Mr Rankin, 'that every assistance this Council can render – monetary or otherwise, be given to the Typographical Society until the dispute at the Herald Office is adjusted.'

Propd. by Mr Dixon and seconded by Mr Simmonds, 'that the Secretary be instructed to procure call-book and note absentees of delegates.'

Carried.

Propd. by Mr Rankin and seconded by Mr Murphy, 'that the next monthly meeting be general delegate meeting.'

Carried.

On the motion of Mr Murphy seconded by Mr Thornhill, it was resolved 'that a deputation from this Council consisting of five members, wait upon the various trades, meeting in this hall, not connected with this body, to impress upon them the necessity of cooperating with us, and to report progress this night month.'

Carried.

Deputation: Messrs, Murphy, Simmonds, Holman, Elliott and Hall-Murphy and Downie.

An account to the amount of one pound for printing was passed for payment.

Receipts: Carpenters two pounds, eleven shillings and eight pence, Typographical Society two pounds, one shillings and eight pence.

WILLIAM MURPHY – CHAIRMAN

MINUTES OF TRADES & LABOUR COUNCIL DELEGATE MEETING,

HELD MONDAY 22 FEBRUARY, 1875

Mr Murphy in the chair.

Present: Delegates from Carpenters, Coachmakers, Printers, Tailors and Saddlers.

A letter was read from Secretary of the Melbourne Typographical Society, appointing Messrs. Wilson, Dummelow, Dow and Hall, as delegates, and furnishing report of the Herald dispute.

The following is the report: (missing, torn out)

Propd. by Mr Dummelow and seconded by Mr. Marshall 'that all delegates to this Council be requested to lay the matter of the Herald dispute before their own Societies, and urge upon them the advisability of discontinuing all support to that paper till the grievance be redressed, and furthermore, that all members of this Council refuse to patronise any public place where the said paper is taken in.'

Carried Unanimously.

Propd. by Mr Holman and seconded by Mr Marshall 'that this meeting be adjourned until Thursday 25 and that the same be advertised and circulars issued to the delegates.'

Carried.

J.S ELLIOTT

MINUTES OF SPECIAL MEETING,

HELD 25 FEBRUARY, 1875

Mr Elliott in the chair.

Trade represented: Coachmakers, Carpenters, Painters, Sailmakers and Tailors.

Minutes of previous meeting read and confirmed.

Further information was reported i.e. the Herald dispute.

Resolved that no proceedings of this meeting be published unless given by Secretary. Propd. by Mr Murphy and seconded by Mr Ferguson 'that a strike committee of three be appointed under sanction of this Council to take what action they may deem desirable in the matter of the Herald dispute.'

Carried.

On the motion of Mr Murphy, seconded by Mr Ferguson, it was decided 'that should the committee meet during working hours, such members shall receive 1/3d per hour.'

Committee appointed Messrs. Elliott, Murphy and Wolfe. Proposed by Mr Dixon seconded by Mr Murphy 'that Herald men receive the sum of 25/- per week while on strike.'

Lost.

Proposed by Mr Wolfe and seconded by Mr Ferguson 'that the sum be fixed at 15/- per man per week.

Carried.

GENERAL DELEGATE MEETING,

4 MARCH.

Mr Elliott in the chair

Trades represented: Carpenters, Coachmakers, Printers, Painters,

Sailmakers, Saddlers, Tin-plate workers, Tailors.

Mr Murphy on behalf of strike committee reported upon action taken in committee.

Mr Ferguson moved and Mr Marshall seconded 'that the report be received.'

Carried.

Secretary reported that police reports in the Herald, also articles were garbled and untrue.

Also that the visiting committee had waited upon various societies not connected with the Council with a view of obtaining their cooperation. The report was favourable.

Proposed by Mr Murphy, seconded by Mr Ferguson 'that any delegate absenting himself from this Council without apology for two consecutive meetings, his Society shall be communicated with.

Carried.

Notice of motion by Mr McDonald 'that any trade society connected with this Council, resolved to come out on strike, shall first lay full particulars of the case before this Council for consideration, and failing to do so, members of such society shall not be entitled to receive monetary assistance to aid them in such strike.

Resolved – that all special meetings be called by circular.

On the motion of Mr Murphy seconded by Mr _____ 'that this meeting at its rising, do adjourn for a month.'

Carried.

Resolved – that next special meeting be called by advertisement as well as circular.

Accounts paid: Auditors 7/6d., Committee's travelling expenses 5/-.

J.WOLFE – CHAIRMAN

MINUTES OF TRADES & LABOUR COUNCIL, GENERAL DELEGATE MEETING,

HELD THURSDAY 1 APRIL, 1875

Mr Wolfe in the chair.

Minutes of previous meeting read and confirmed.

Resolved that Secretary be instructed to forward necessary information to the Press. Mr Fairhurst was present to make some suggestion with reference to land taxation. He also stated that he understood he was appointed delegate for Gas Stokers' Society, but no intimation to that effect had been received by the Society.

A letter was read from the Hatters' Society announcing that men had been called out of an establishment in consequence of more apprentices being employed than their rules authorised.

Proposed by Mr Murphy and seconded by Mr Wilson 'that the consideration of the latter stand over for the present.'

Carried.

Mr Murphy reported that the strike committee were dissatisfied with the laxity of the men on the picket at the Herald. He stated that correspondence had been carried on between the committee and manager of the Herald, which eventually led to a conference, when the representatives of the Herald promised to lay the wishes of the Council before their colleagues.

Secretary reported that Forty-Eight pounds, eighteen shillings, had been received from the trades but many were behind in their payment. The amount paid up to date to Herald men was Fifty-One pounds. The following list was read of the number of men paid; and the weeks during which they received the amounts: 1 week 17 men; 3 weeks 16 men; 2 weeks 11 men, 5 weeks 1 boy at ten shillings; 4 men paid three pounds each, to declare funds, and fifteen shillings per man to come out of Herald Office. Men came out 17 February.

Mr Ferguson moved and Mr Marshall seconded 'that the report be received, and was afterwards adopted on the motion of Mr Murphy.'

Carried.

Proposed by Mr Ferguson and seconded by Mr Howden 'that the Secretary write to societies, enclosing forms and informing them that quarterly contributions were now due.'

Carried.

Mr Hall proposed and Mr McDonald seconded 'that the subject of Hatters' dispute be considered this night week.'

Carried.

Accounts passed for payment: Secretary commission, roll book, postage, etc. – one pound Nineteen shillings and sixpence. Armstrong Advertising – one pound sixteen shillings; expenses of deputation – two pounds eighteen shillings.

Resolved that this meeting stand adjourned till Thursday next.

J.S ELLIOTT – CHAIRMAN

MINUTES OF GENERAL (ADJOURNED) DELEGATE MEETING,

HELD THURSDAY 8 APRIL, 1875

Mr. Elliott in the chair.

Minutes of previous meeting read and confirmed.

Secretary reported on the Herald dispute, and stated that no reply had as yet been received from the proprietors to the proposition of the deputation from the Council, but the manager stated that a meeting would be held on Friday to consider the matter and reply forwarded.

Propd. by Mr Hall and seconded by Mr Wilson 'that the strike committee be empowered to take what action they deem necessary upon receipt of the decision of Herald proprietary.'

Carried.

Letter re-read from Hatters' Society and spoken to by Mr Morgan, who stated that eight men had been called out in consequence of an employer engaging a man per agreement and threatening to employ more apprentices.

After considerable discussion and explanation, it was proposed by Mr Murphy and seconded by Mr Downie 'that the question be adjourned in order to give the delegate of the Hatters' Society an opportunity to refer the matter to his Society' was lost. It was decided that the deputation should be elected by ballot, when Messrs. McDonald and Livingstone were appointed.

Letter read from Hawthorn Branch of Brickmakers and Labourers, with request to joining the Council. Agreed to admit accordingly to rule.

Letter read from Mr Curtis, printer, asking support in establishing a monthly paper, similar to the Workman published in Sydney under the patronage of the Trades & Labour Council of N.S.W.

Received.

Propd. by Mr Holdman and seconded by Mr Hall 'that the matter stand over till next meeting.'

Carried.

According to notice of motion of Mr McDonald proposed 'that any trade society connected with this Council resolved to come out on strike, shall first lay full particulars of the case before this Council for consideration and failing to do so members of such society shall not be entitled to receive monetary assistance to aid them in such strike.' Seconded by Mr Downie.

Carried.

It was decided that next meeting be held on the first Thursday in next month and be a general meeting.

J.S ELLIOTT

GENERAL DELEGATE MEETING,

HELD THURSDAY 6 MAY 1875

Mr Elliott in the chair.

Minutes of previous meeting read and confirmed.

Letters from Geelong Typographical Society asking admission and enclosing 2/- for 12 weeks, quarterly contributions.

Propd. by Mr Livingstone and seconded by Mr McDonald 'that the same be received and the Society admitted.'

Carried.

From Ballarat Typographical Society, asking admission and enclosing 5/8d for 34 members.

Resolved the Society be admitted.

From A.J Curtis in _____ to the intended publication of Tradesman's Journal, and asking patronage of the Council. Propd. by Mr Marshall and seconded by Mr Howden 'that Mr Curtis be requested to forward prospectuses to the various societies and that this Council will endeavour to forward the interests of the proposed journal as far as possible.'

Carried.

From Hatters' Society resigning. On the motion of Mr Ferguson, seconded by Mr Howden, the letter was received.

Propd. by Mr McDonald, seconded by Mr Marshall 'that the Secretary acknowledge receipt of letter and ask specific reason for withdrawing, and reminding them of arrears.'

Carried.

An account of 8/- for advertising, was ordered to be paid.

Mr Murphy reported on Herald strike.

Secretary stated in addition that the proposition in accordance with the wish of the strike committee had been sent to the Herald proprietors, offering to take the paper on contract for a specified sum, but after considerable delay, the final answer had been communicated this morning declining the offer.

Secretary also stated that upon good authority he had been informed two members of the Carpenters' Society had interviewed the Herald manager for information, and circulated reports which were untrue.

Proposed by Mr Murphy and seconded by Mr Marshall 'that the Secretary communicate with Carpenters' Society expressing the unanimous regret of the Trades and Labour Council at the action of a member of the said Society in taking a course calculated to frustrate the interest and influence of the Council in the discharge of its duty with respect to the Herald dispute.

The report was adopted and clause to discontinue of levies agreed to on the motion of Mr Ferguson seconded by Mr Wolfe.

Secretary was instructed to write to the Health Officer, drawing his attention to the state of tailors' workshops in the city.

Notice of motion by Mr Wilson 'that this Council resolve itself into a committee to take best measures in dealing with the Herald question.'

Account of strike committee for eight pounds and fifteen shillings was passed for payment.

J.S ELLIOTT

MINUTES OF DELEGATE MEETING,

HELD THURSDAY 3 JUNE, 1875

Mr J.S Elliott in the chair.

Present: Messrs. Elliott, Downie, Wolfe, Livingstone,

Wilson, Meredith, Kermode and Basedale.

Minutes of previous meeting read and confirmed. Correspondence read from Hatters' Society giving reasons for withdrawing from Council.

Resolved – that the Hatters' Society be asked for five weeks more levy towards the Herald dispute this morning considering that they acquiesced in incurring the expenditures, and therefore are morally bound to discharge their share of the remaining liability.

Letter from the Carpenters' Society, announcing intention to withdraw from the Council.

Resolved that a deputation consisting of Messrs. Elliott, Wilson and Hall, wait upon the Carpenters' Society for explanation.

The following report from the Secretary was read:

'Since our last meeting I received an intimation that my presence would be required at the Treasury to wait upon His Excellency the Acting Governor in reference to the subject of arbitration, anent which you will remember a deputation was appointed to interview the Premier some months since. Messrs, Curtin and Munro, M.L.A's, accompanied me on the 19 May and we found His Excellency desirous of receiving any information available on the subject before introducing the matter into Parliament. Various suggestions were made, including those discussed at our meetings and ultimately it was considered that the practice prevailing in England of arbitration by agreement on entering into service would be the most practicable at present. His Excellency said he felt a deep interest in the matter and would see some measure was introduced to carry the same into effect. You will have perceived by the Governor's speech at the opening of Parliament that measures are to be laid before the house for the settlement of trade disputes and this step I trust, will place the operatives in such a position that they may never have to resort to strikes.'

It was decided that the delegates should bring the subject of arbitration before their various societies and submit opinion to the Council, also that a deputation consisting of Messrs. Elliott, Wilson and Kermode, wait upon other societies for views on the same.

Resolved: That the delegates pledge themselves to use their best endeavours with their societies to refuse all patronage to the Herald.

Secretary's account for One pound thirteen shillings passed for payment.

JOHN WOLFE, CHAIRMAN

*****

Mr Downie moved and Mr Allen seconded 'that the Secretary inform the above Societies that on account of considering the advisability of revising rules during the next three months, it would better to let the matter of new Societies joining the Council stand over for that time.'

Carried.

Accounts passed – Armstrong ads. 12/-, Secretary's account 20/-.

Contributions from Brickmakers' Society for past quarter 10/4d, 62 members.

Resolved that in the event of a change of Ministry or dissolution in Parliament the members of the Council support candidates favourable to the adoption of an arbitration Bill for settlement of trade disputes.

Mr Basedahl was elected president, on the motion of Mr Hall, seconded by Mr Downie.

Proposed by Mr Downie and seconded by Mr Allen, 'that considering the present unsettled state of things and the shelving of the Arbitration Bill it is deemed desirable to suspend operations to allow time for altering rules, if advisable and the next meeting to be held in three months from this date or earlier if requisite, and called by the societies now connected with this Council.'

Carried unanimously.

JOHN DOWNIE

GENERAL DELEGATE MEETING, TRADES HALL, LYGON STREET,

THURSDAY 3 FEBRUARY, 1876

An apology was received from the President Mr Basedahl, and Mr J Downie was voted to the chair.

Minutes of the previous meeting were read and confirmed. Mr Hall proposed alterations in rules to the following effect:-

Strike our after the word 'dispute' in Rule 1.

To insert in Rule 2 after word 'of' – 'and entrance fee of'

And strike our after words 'per member'. Also strike out Rules 8, 9 and 10.

Seconded by Mr Lillie and carried unanimously.

The balance sheet was received and adopted.

Accounts passed – Armstrong Advertising 12/-, Secretary 5/- on the motion of Mr McIntosh.

Meeting adjourned till Thursday 2 March. Confirmed.

C. McINTOSH

MINUTES OF HALF-YEARLY MEETING,

HELD 1 JULY

Mr Wolfe in the chair.

Present: Messrs. Livingstone, Downie, Meredith, Hall

Usher, Brusch and Kermode.

Minutes of previous meeting read and confirmed. The balance sheet was read, received and adopted.

Letter read from Tailors' Society, approving arbitration. Reports from Printers, Saddlers, Tinsmiths and Painters, also approving.

Letters from Sailmakers, in reference to withdrawal.

Accounts from Curtis, printing balance sheets 25/-, and auditors' 5/- passed for payment.

In consequence of the illness of Mr Elliott, Mr Wolfe was elected on the deputation, to wait upon the carpenters.

JOHN WOLFE, CHAIRMAN

MEETING OF TRADES & LABOUR COUNCIL, HELD THURSDAY 5 AUGUST, 1875

Mr Wolfe presiding. Minutes of previous meeting read and confirmed.

Apologies were received from Mr Elliott, and the delegate from the Brickmakers' Society.

Letter from Amalgamated Miners' Association, Clunes, asking attendance of delegates at a meeting held on 27 July, in reference to 'Trades Union Bill'. In consequence of the letter only just being received, the Council regretted their inability to be present at the conference.

Accounts passed – Armstrong Advertising 16/-.

PETER BASEDAHL

MINUTES OF TRADE & LABOUR COUNCIL, HELD THURSDAY 7 OCTOBER, 1875

Trades Hall – Mr P Basedahl in the chair.

Present: Messrs. Downie, Basedahl, Allen and Hall.

Minutes read and confirmed.

Letter was read from Mr Elliott, President, resigning on account of illness. Accepted with regret.

Letter from Saddlers' Society withdrawing. Received.

From Carpenters' Society, Geelong and Miners' Association, Ballarat, requesting to join the Council, and asking information.

(The minutes end here.)

This article previously appeared in abbreviated form in the Recorder, number 171, February 1992, pp. 5–10, published by the Melbourne branch of the Australian Society for the Study of Labour History under the title, 'A History of the Trades Hall Council: A Rift in the Seventies – Which Way?' This version has been updated and now includes the surviving minutes of the Melbourne Trades and Labour Council as well.

Chapter 7

Australia Reconstructed

Andrew Scott

Australia Reconstructed was a major publication of the Australian trade union movement in 1987. Its contents have been widely discussed.[162] This chapter summarises the results of interviews with crucial participants, and of international archival research, to pinpoint how and why the Amalgamated Metal Workers Union (referred to in this chapter as the AMWU) developed and led the interest in Sweden, and other northern European nations, which came to be expressed in that prominent report.[163]

The AMWU developed close links with the Swedish Metal Workers' Union from the 1970s. This interest in Sweden intensified during the 1980s, as the union's leaders sought new ways forward from the tradition of organising under non-Labor governments during a long period of prosperity that had ended in the 1970s.

Leading AMWU official, Laurie Carmichael, made his first visit to Sweden in 1971, to attend the Stockholm Conference on the Vietnam War. The AMWU had actively opposed US involvement in Vietnam from the beginning of Australia's involvement in 1964. Sweden's Social Democratic Party government under Olof Palme was also opposed to the Vietnam War. Palme was more critical of US involvement in Vietnam than any other government in the Western world. Carmichael was a dynamic, militant and effective national union leader who had represented workers in

---

[162] See, for example, 'Australia Reconstructed: 10 Years On', *Journal of Australian Political Economy*, no. 39, 1997.

[163] Further details can be found in my two earlier articles: 'Looking to Sweden in Order to Reconstruct Australia', *Scandinavian Journal of History*, vol. 34, no. 3, September 2009, pp. 330–352 (see http://www.tandfonline.com/doi/abs/10.1080/03468750903134756); and 'Social Democracy in Northern Europe: Its Relevance for Australia', *Australian Review of Public Affairs journal*, vol. 7, no. 1, October 2006, pp. 1–17, which is available online at: http://www.australianreview.net/journal/v7/n1/scott.html).

the car industry for many years. This led him to explore issues about work organisation in a Marxist framework. Laurie had a longstanding passion to create more opportunities for workers to advance their skills. He also had a strong interest in the implications of new technology.

Carmichael's growing disaffection with official communism, especially after the Soviet suppression of the Prague Spring in 1968, led him to look towards alternative political approaches from that time, which led gradually to an interest in industrial democracy. His search became more urgent in the early 1980s following his own ambivalence about the success of the recent campaign that he and the Victorian AMWU State Secretary, John Halfpenny, had spearheaded for higher wages and shorter working hours in the Australian manufacturing industry. Carmichael later considered that this campaign may have been better directed at gaining paid study leave, as the Scandinavian metal unions had done.

Laurie Carmichael had extensive international contacts, including those with Italian communist unions, and he was familiar with the political debates around 'Eurocommunism', as was another AMWU officer with whom he worked, Max Ogden. In 1983 Carmichael continued to support the political analysis of the British left's Stuart Holland. However, following the devastating electoral defeat of British Labour in the 1983 election and Thatcher's dominance there, all elements of the Australian labour movement turned away from Britain as a model. Sweden would then, for a time, replace various earlier international influences on the Australian left.

This occurred largely because of the fact that by 1985 Laurie Carmichael, after a further visit to Sweden, became so enthused by trade union achievements there that he acted on the basis of them to shape the direction of Australian industrial relations differently than otherwise would have been the case. Carmichael and many colleagues found inspiration in the achievements of Swedish trade unions and social democracy, as they tried to transform and transcend a defensive local labourism and push for alternative, more ambitious political strategies than the dominant neo-liberalised Labor Right in Australia would consider.

That shift was part of an international trend of increased left interest in Sweden from the late 1970s, prompted by the Swedish unions' radical wage-earner funds campaign. Carmichael, as a result of his international visits, was well aware of the strong employer opposition in Sweden to the wage-earner funds, and this contributed towards his increased political interest in Sweden by the mid 1980s. The Palme government's introduction in 1983 of wage-earner funds was less radical than the original concept developed by the Swedish trade union movement in the 1970s, but it was still impressive to overseas visitors.

Carmichael nominally 'retired' in late 1984 when he stood down from the elected position of AMWU Assistant National Secretary for health reasons, and moved to a position as a national research officer of the union. This gave him greater 'critical distance' to read and reflect. He held the AMWU research officer role until he was elected Assistant Secretary of the ACTU in July 1987. In the period 1984–1987 Carmichael helped maintain the left unions' support for the Accord while at the same time lobbying inside the ACTU for policy change. He also made occasional, strong public criticism of the Labor government's failure to honour central commitments of the Accord.

Ted Wilshire was a former metalworker who studied political economy at Sydney University where he undertook research on rank-and-file metalworkers' attitudes to union activities. He was then appointed in 1976 at Laurie Carmichael's initiative as an AMWU researcher. The AMWU had links with the Sydney-based political economy movement in its phase of exposing and criticising the growing power of transnational corporations. Wilshire's energetic education campaigns in the AMWU were positively reported in one of that movement's publications.[164]

Winton Higgins was a Communist Party member fluent in the Swedish language and knowledgeable about the achievements of the Swedish trade union movement, whose ideas concerning Sweden, from his position as an academic at Sydney's Macquarie University, came to have a marked influence on Carmichael by the mid 1980s.

In 1981 Wilshire took leave from the AMWU to work for Lionel Bowen, deputy ALP leader. When the Hawke Labor government was elected in 1983, Wilshire became executive director of a unit later named the Trade Development Council, inside the Department of Trade for which Bowen was the new minister, thus creating a research vacancy in the union.

Nixon Apple then went to the AMWU in 1984, filling the research officer vacancy created by Wilshire's secondment to the Labor government, and he began to work closely with Laurie Carmichael. His transfer in 1984 from postgraduate academic study at Macquarie University with Winton Higgins, into working in the AMWU's national research centre with Laurie Carmichael, directly connected Winton Higgins' scholarly analysis of the Swedish labour movement's achievements with Carmichael's quest for a new political vision.

---

[164] Crough, G and Wheelwright, T 1982, *Australia: A Client State*, Penguin, Melbourne, p. 210.

Winton Higgins published an academic journal article in August 1985[165] that was reprinted in a way which increased its circulation and impact. This article emphasised how 'the Swedish labour-market reforms of the 1970s ... substantially increased the powers ... of union workplace organizations', and identified 'recessions ... [and] longer term investment behaviour that winds down industrial activity' as 'attacks on working and living conditions ... which ... cannot be turned back by the strike weapon'. He argued strongly against elements in the left, the 'corporatist' theorists, who simplistically dismissed Accord-type arrangements, and who 'interpret ... any union concern for antirecessionary politics ... as class collaboration'. Higgins contended that 'a developing political unionism ... must develop central ... co-ordinating ... leaderships, which in turn must arm themselves with an ever-expanding body of knowledge ... to match the resources and discipline of their adversaries'.

Higgins went on, as 'the union movement ... projects itself into more and more policy areas, its social monitoring and constant policy initiatives necessitate permanent in-house research establishments'. He also outlined the great political achievements that Swedish unions (led by the Metal Workers) had made through their industry-wide bargaining, including that for the lowest paid; and the Swedish labour movement's longstanding recognition that 'wage levels ... depend ultimately on industrial performance, which now must become a union concern'.

He contended therefore that 'the movement's 'production policy', though 'often ... cited as evidence of Swedish unionism's deep commitment to class collaboration ... [actually] had its immediate theoretical antecedents in the party theoretician Ernst Wigforss' critique from 1919 of capitalism's ... chronic disorganisation... as inseparably linked to its perverse distribution of income and mass unemployment'. Higgins also emphasised that Sweden's 'Rehn-Meidner model ... gives the union movement a central role in policy formation'. Whereas earlier Australian observers had interpreted scarcity of strikes in Sweden as a sign of enlightened management, Higgins argued that they were actually the *product* of the unions' strategic *strength*.[166]

In July 1985 Winton Higgins visited the Trade Union Training Authority's Clyde Cameron College at Wodonga as part of the AMWU's national education program. This program had just been reinvigorated by Carmichael

---

[165] Higgins, W 1985, 'Political Unionism and the Corporatist Thesis', *Economic and Industrial Democracy*, vol. 6, no. 3, pp. 349–381.

[166] Higgins, W 1985, 'Political Unionism and the Corporatist Thesis', pp. 355, 356–357, 354, 359, 360–361, 367, 369, 363.

following the low priority given to it after 1979. It had taken a backseat to the priority that the union leadership had placed on its campaign for higher wages and shorter working hours. Carmichael wrote a cover note to the course materials, explaining the need for the program, and stated that: 'major changes ... are occurring in the economic, industrial, social and political arenas and it is essential to deepen an understanding of the issues and underlying processes involved and to try to calculate future developments in the short and medium term'.[167]

Winton Higgins spoke on the first day of a week-long event on 'broad strategy options' and 'interventionist, Accord solutions'.[168] Carmichael also spoke that day along with Nixon Apple on 'the rise and fall of full employment capitalism 1947-72'. Ted Wilshire spoke the following day on trade trends, wealth creation, balance of payments and currency exchange values; Carmichael then spoke about elements of a program to change the direction of industry development. Carmichael returned on later days to talk about responding to new technology and associated new work organisation. On the last day he gave an overall summary of discussions.

Then, from 13 to 25 October 1985, a high-level five-person delegation from the Swedish Metal Workers' Union led by Union President Leif Blomberg visited Australia at the AMWU's invitation.[169] In preparation for this visit the Australian union arranged for its officials to attend a one-day seminar on the role of unions in management and economic planning.[170] More than 30 pages of briefing notes were compiled in the AMWU for this delegation's visit, drawing on materials sent by their Swedish counterparts, including information about Sweden's export-orientated growth, provision of paid leave for unionists when on union business, the fact that at the just-held elections of 15 September 1985 the Swedish Social Democratic Party and allied parties had been returned to government for a further three years, and renewal funds (see below).[171]

---

[167] Letter formally signed by Greg Harrison Assistant National Secretary, to state secretaries, 7 June 1985: AMWU records in the Australian National University's Noel Butlin Archives Centre (hereafter NBAC), Deposit Z102, Box 650 ('Education Committee 1984–1986').

[168] Document titled 'AMWU National Education Programme', NBAC, Box 650.

[169] Telex of 28 March 1985 from Leif Blomberg, President, Swedish Metal Workers' Union to RT (Dick) Scott, AMWU National President: NBAC, Box 562 ('International ... Sweden 1975–1986').

[170] Letter of 30 May 1985 from RT Scott to L Blomberg, in NBAC, Box 562 ('International ... Sweden 1975–1986').

[171] NBAC, Box 562 ('International ... Sweden 1975–1986'). This file also includes pamphlets on 'The Swedish Act on Co-Determination at Work' issued by the Ministry of Labour

The seminar coincided with an AMWU National Council meeting. The AMWU newspaper later featured the visiting Swedish delegation, and reported on cooperation between unions and government in Sweden, declaring that 'Sweden's strong economic recovery and low unemployment rate … was largely due to the accord the unions had with the social democratic (Labour) government'. Particular emphasis was placed on the role of informal channels of contact with the government.

Direct comparisons were made in the newspaper article with Australia; especially between the Australian Prices and Incomes Accord and successful Swedish attempts 'to improve economic growth while reining in inflation and unemployment, and consolidating its welfare system and public sector – the reverse of the policies implemented by the right-wing Reagan administration in the US and Thatcher government in Britain'. The article also mentioned the role of the unions in introducing new technology, and the adoption of legislation requiring companies with certain levels of profits to devote resources to 'renewal funds' for this purpose. The article concluded that 'joint government–union cooperation on formulating long-term industry policy was a major aspect of the Swedish accord'.[172]

Immediately after this seminar Carmichael prepared to go to Sweden himself. He represented the ACTU at an ILO conference held at Örenas in south-west Sweden, and then made an intensive visit to Stockholm from 28 to 30 October 1985. Leif Blomberg had telexed his union from Australia on 15 October 1985, indicating that 'Brother … Carmichael … desires discussions [on] current laws and position re pensions … laws and operation of special funds, such as employment, training and industry development … degree of regulation and deregulation of capital and currency markets … latest developments re industrial democracy … union education … [H]e is representing ACTU … [so] should also talk to LO and with National Bank representative on capital and currency regulations'.[173]

The visit clearly made a major impact upon Carmichael. He expressed his profound gratitude to his Swedish hosts and commented that the Australian labour movement was:

---

in January 1985, and English-language brochures on the LO and the Swedish Metal Workers' Union.

[172] 'Accord is Essential', *The Metal Worker*, November 1985.

[173] 1985 correspondence file for Australia in the records of the Swedish Metal Workers' Union (IF Metall), in that union's offices, Stockholm.

heading in the direction of policies and strategies that your organisation has already established and largely implemented. Of course they have to be applied in the concrete Australian circumstances. Nevertheless, we have very much to learn from you, which we must explore fully in as short a space of time as possible.[174]

Carmichael's 14-page private 'Report to ACTU Officers' uniquely expresses the image of Sweden he formed then. He found that the Swedish unions were 'socialist oriented', and that this conditioned their attitude to wages, profits and inflation. Their 'wages solidarity policy' was 'the foundation stone of their policy development'. He commended their efforts for study leave, which 'raises productivity' and 'challenges and changes power relations on the job'. Moreover,

They constantly stress the importance of the political dimension of their work and the use of legislative power to magnify their industrial organisation. They have highly developed ... connections into ... political processes starting from their remarkable community discussion groups apparatus up to fortnightly government-trade union consultations.

He warned that, '[t]his does not mean that the ... unions ... achieve all they set out to achieve at any given time. Sometimes the results are less ... than they believe they should be ... but it is clearly apparent that their position is always continuously developing with perspective about it'. Carmichael also reported on the co-determination legislation and its provisions for union representatives on company boards, supported by appropriate education, and on the establishment of wage-earner and renewal funds, the use of which was to be determined by negotiations between unions and management. 'The significance to me of these renewal funds', he wrote, 'is that they ... promot[e] ... industrial democracy ... education, skill, responsibility and cultural capacity in industry'. But, this did

not mean that there is no contest or that unions simply join the industry relationship without working-class purpose. On the contrary, each step in legislation or negotiation has had to be intensively argued against employer opposition and in some cases with industrial action.

---

[174] Letter from Laurie Carmichael, AMWU National Research Officer, to Håkan Arnelid, 9 December 1985, in ibid.

... [T]he industrial democracy movement starting along with other democratic explosions of development from the mid-[19]60s [occurred] to challenge the denial of working people from having a say in decision-making and in particular the most vicious form of this denial in the work process itself.

Carmichael suggested that current industrial trends 'create ... a big ... opportunity to negotiate better working conditions and work practices', and that the Swedish unions, in their attitude to this opportunity, had placed themselves 'in the forefront of the world's working class movements'. Volvo provided a 'dramatic example' for Carmichael, in particular the new plant under way at Uddevalla to replace the former shipyards, in which 'groups of up to thirty workers with ... high ... levels of skills, with thirty minute planned work cycles and not more than 50 per cent of anybody's time on routine assembly, will be involved'. To sum up, he stated that:

> I believe there is so much to learn from their experience. Particularly in relation to Labor being in government and what expectations the ... unions should have ... Of all the countries I have had the chance to visit, Sweden emerges as being the most valuable to learn from in relation to a Labor government being in office ... it leads me to *express a view as strongly as I can that a small representative ... delegation from the ACTU ... should seek to visit Sweden* to undertake a more detailed study of the matters I have only had the opportunity to explore in general terms and to study matters about which I did not have the time to examine.[175]

Thus in this short visit in 1985, Carmichael became very enthusiastic about the political possibilities that Sweden showed. His enthusiasm increased in the following year when he was a member of the delegation for which he lobbied, which would produce the publication *Australia Reconstructed*. This influenced him into renewed support for and perseverance with the Accord, despite its shortcomings, in an attempt to achieve the kind of things that the Swedish unions had through their 'political unionism'.

Public disputes between left unions and the government over its failure to implement important elements of the Accord continued in Australia, and Carmichael continued to participate in them, up to a point. However, in the end he emphasised that: 'it is ... up to the labour movement to revive

---

175 Carmichael, L (National Research Officer, AMWU) nd *c* late 1985/early 1986, 'Report to ACTU Officers', NBAC, Box 555 ('Industrial Democracy 1985–1986'). Emphasis in original.

the Accord to save the government ... the union movement cannot simply be critical. There must be effective campaigning to change [the] course of the government's self-destructive policies'.[176] The *Australia Reconstructed* mission became a central part of the campaigning effort that Carmichael and colleagues would make.

The influence of Sweden had become important enough by August 1986 that a leading academic in the political economy movement, Frank Stilwell, began to raise concern about 'Carmichael's ... view which builds on notions of "political unionism" developed particularly in Sweden and discussed in the Australian context in various writings by Winton Higgins ... [whereby] the Accord could have ... the potential not only for generating absolute and relative gains in the material living standards of the working class but also for opening up hitherto unprecedented access to political power'.

Stilwell reiterated earlier left scepticism about social democratic 'collaboration', stating that, 'the "Swedish road to socialism" remained a hotly contested issue' and that the Carmichael 'perspective of the Accord is simply optimism ... that, because an agreement such as the Accord opens up avenues for unions to be involved in the formulation of government policy, this can lead to benefits for the working class, broadly defined, in the short term and/or conditions more conducive to a socialist transition in the longer term'.[177]

The point, however, is the picture that Carmichael had formed of Sweden gave him reasons for optimism. In 1986, as a result of the AMWU's initiatives, the ACTU sent a delegation to Sweden, Norway, West Germany, Austria and Britain to seek new policy options for Australia. The delegation's report, *Australia Reconstructed*, was published in 1987. The report particularly praised and sought to emulate Sweden because of the overriding priority which that country placed on full employment and wage solidarity, while maintaining a strong economic performance.[178]

The commitment, enthusiasm and resources of the unions' partner in this mission, the Trade Development Council, helped to make *Australia Reconstructed* a major publication. It emerged as an A4-sized official-looking volume 235 pages thick. In those pre-PowerPoint days, the report featured more than 100 colour charts to illustrate statistical trends, policy concepts and organisational arrangements; it made 72 substantial policy recommendations; and it had a bibliography with more than 300 references.

---

[176] *The Metal Worker*, vol. 7, no. 4, May 1986.

[177] Stilwell, F 1986, *The Accord – and Beyond*, Pluto Press Australia, Sydney, p. 28.

[178] ACTU & TDC 1987.

Australia Reconstructed remains the most comprehensive policy manifesto ever published by the mainstream left in Australia. It continued the concern about Australia's excessive economic reliance on extracting and shipping out resources rather than adding value to products, which had been expressed in a series of pamphlets published from the second half of the 1970s by the AMWU. Following those publications, which had criticised Australia's policy direction in the Fraser government years (1975–1983), the union delegation put forward positive policy solutions in *Australia Reconstructed* for the Hawke Labor government, elected in 1983, to pursue.

Although the 1986 mission to Europe was partly sponsored by – and its report published with the official imprimatur of – the Labor government, it contained much criticism of that government's policies. The authors emphasised the achievements of Sweden's model of pursuing full employment by reducing market wage differentials, ensuring an adequate social wage, and improving the mobility and skills of the labour force through comprehensive, active labour-market programs. They argued that this approach had succeeded in Sweden from the 1950s because unions had rejected 'the notion that wage restraint was the only solution, and instead [had] urged the Social Democratic government to adopt an alternative strategy involving the whole policy mix'.[179]

Australia Reconstructed represented the most ambitious attempt towards economic interventionism in the Hawke–Keating years (1983–1996). It sought to develop the original logic, new institutions and progressive aspects of the Prices and Incomes Accord signed by the ALP and the ACTU in February 1983, which had envisaged a regulated economy and a high priority for industry development. In particular, *Australia Reconstructed* sought to counter the federal government's contrary moves to financial deregulation and away from industry policy in the years following the signing of the Accord. Among its policy proposals was a call for restraint of prices and executive salaries instead of just wages, which were still subject to strict control under the auspices of the Australian Industrial Relations Commission. It advocated the development of manufacturing by using new superannuation funds to promote productive investment, among other measures. It called for better formation of vocational skills. It also endorsed the reorganisation of work along more democratic lines.

The year in which the report appeared, 1987, preceded the waves of privatisations, further tariff reductions, and the shifts away from centralised

---

[179] ACTU & TDC 1987, p. 5.

wage fixing that came later in the Hawke–Keating years. As such, *Australia Reconstructed* remains an important reference point for an alternative and more interventionist Labor political and economic approach that came to dominate the period 1983–1996. The relevance to Australia that the delegation then saw in the policy achievements of trade unionist and social democrats in northern Europe remains valid now.

Australia Reconstructed was, of course, criticised at the time by employers. The Business Council of Australia sent its own mission to Sweden, the month after the union delegates returned, to paint a contrary picture. Leading 'Dries' suggested that the ACTU was engaging in Nordic hero worship; and one suggested that proposals to involve trade unions more broadly in national policymaking would inevitably make Australia akin to Fascist Italy under Mussolini.[180] The person who made this second accusation apparently failed to appreciate the distinction between the capricious actions of an Italian dictator before the Second World War, and *social democratic* corporatism as it had gradually and successfully evolved in northern European nations in the decades after the war.

Another repeated complaint about *Australia Reconstructed*, made by the leader of the largest employer organisation of the time, was that it was too hard to read.[181]

Not all criticism came from the employer side, however. Community welfare activists criticised the report for not placing nearly enough emphasis on the role that public sector provision had played in Sweden's success, and also for viewing the social wage too narrowly.[182] The report outlined in detail the laws and programs that Sweden introduced to combat labour-market segmentation and to promote equal wages and conditions for women. It also strongly recommended similar moves in Australia. However, its focus on manufacturing meant that it did not adequately analyse the services sector where most women were actually employed; nor did its recommendations

---

[180] See Hyde, J 1987, 'ACTU Corporatism was a Failure in Mussolini's Italy', *The Australian*, 28 August.

[181] Williams, P 1987, 'ACTU Report Branded as Dangerous by CAI Head', *Financial Review*, 17 September, quoting Bryan Noakes, then Director General of the Confederation of Australian Industry; Confederation of Australian Industry 1987, *Employer Perspectives on the ACTU/TDC Report* 'Australia Reconstructed', Confederation of Australian Industry, Melbourne, 1987.

[182] Council of Social Service of New South Wales 1988, *Australia Reconstructed*: What's in It for the Community Services Industry?, Council of Social Service of New South Wales, Sydney.

reflect women's need for childcare.[183] The document was also criticised by conservationists for purporting to 'encompass the major debates of our time' while essentially ignoring environmental questions.[184]

Nevertheless, *Australia Reconstructed* was generally acknowledged as a sophisticated and somewhat surprising challenge to conventional economic policy thinking in Australia. Debate over the report was prominent in the national media from the time of its launch on 29 July 1987. A series of visiting government ministers and other officials from Sweden and Norway helped to keep Scandinavian nations' alternative economic and industrial policy approach before the Australian public for some months.

On 19 October 1987 the stock market crash shifted attention away from *Australia Reconstructed* – although the collapse of the overvalued speculative activity was one of the very things the union delegation had been foreshadowing. The report had expressed concern at 'the impact ... the recent wave of takeovers ... is having on the level and composition of investment undertaken by the real production and value-adding sectors of the economy', and recommended that the Australian government follow the lead of the Scandinavian governments, which were acting to remedy this problem by 'supplementing private sector activities through collective capital formation ... [for] investment in ... infrastructure, education ... training and capital works'.[185]

Australia Reconstructed had observed that:

> people threatened by adjustments which may force them to accept unemployment, job transfers or lower wages, will obviously oppose change. People with financial security are far better able to see changes as positive opportunities. The Swedes ... see a need to protect workers forced out of declining industries. In consequence, they have developed ... generous unemployment insurance, social welfare, early warning of retrenchments and incentives to retrain, enhance skills and relocate. Rapid structural change can then become an avenue to increased career opportunities rather than a threat.[186]

---

183 Ranald, P 1988, 'Unions Unreconstructed?', *Australian Left Review*, no. 105, pp. 10–11.

184 Toyne, P 1991, 'Trade Unions and the Environment', in *Labour Movement Strategies for the 21st Century*, Evatt Foundation, Sydney, p. 27.

185 ACTU & TDC 1987, pp. 14, 19–20.

186 ACTU & TDC 1987, p. 105.

An initial overview report of the Mission was issued soon after the delegation's return, in October 1986. When Carmichael arrived back, in a detailed oral report to the AMWU National Council, he emphasised that Sweden's 'unions had not been "absorbed" into the system. A Swedish strike in the early [19]80s resulted in a lockout of 750,000 workers'.[187] Days after his return from Stockholm, and eight months before the publication of *Australia Reconstructed*, Carmichael was publicly spelling out his enthusiasm about the Swedish unions, the level of resources they enjoyed and their emphasis on education. His attendance of the Swedish LO congress had demonstrated to him 'the degree of commitment that the ... union movement has to a sophisticated view of the economy'. He reported that:

> one-third of the congress was given over to discussing problems of production. Now in our ... union movement, the amount of discussion of production would be lucky if it was two or three per cent of the period of congress. You would have a discussion about the economy, but it would be largely about what we would expect the government to do about it and very little about what we expect the ... union movement to do.[188]

At an AMWU National School held from 6 to 10 October 1986 at Clyde Cameron College, the entire afternoon of the first day was allocated to Carmichael's report on the ACTU overseas mission.[189] He related how in Sweden:

> Labour market policy ... is a major cornerstone of the ... unions' work ... unions are told of intended plant closures and their main effort is directed not at redundancy deals, but at retraining workers and restructuring industry ... [and] there is expanded power of the shop stewards to intervene in production and investment.[190]

In the nine-month interval before the publication of the full *Australia Reconstructed* report in July 1987, the delegation's researchers followed up their findings.[191]

---

[187] 'European Example is Path to Follow, says Carmichael', *The Metal Worker*, November 1986.

[188] 'Carmichael's Swedish Message to Unions', *Australian Financial Review*, 6 October 1986.

[189] NBAC, Box 669 ('AMWU Education Committee Minutes 1986–1987').

[190] 'European Example is Path to Follow'.

[191] 'European Example is Path to Follow'.

Ted Wilshire and other members of a team of researchers worked intensively through these nine months in a suite of the Department of Trade offices in central Sydney to write up the many features of Sweden that the unions had come to admire as the main theme of the 235 pages of words and charts that made up *Australia Reconstructed*.

As the publication was being edited, Wilshire enlisted Winton Higgins to help. *Australia Reconstructed* was printed prior to, but not released until after, Australia's 1987 national election, at which the Labor government was re-elected for a third term.

There was a major public debate in Australia about the document from July to October 1987. Laurie Carmichael led the case for its policy recommendations. He had regularly to rebut accusations that it was seeking the 'Swedenisation' of Australia.

Carmichael held the position of ACTU assistant secretary until September 1991, during and after which he continued his campaign for the skills training components of the *Australia Reconstructed* manifesto. The favourable impression of Sweden he had formed in 1985 and 1986 sustained him throughout these efforts.

Swedish arrangements in some modest ways came to influence Australia's agenda for training reform, known as 'award restructuring'. Several further, smaller scale visits by Australian unionists and researchers in the late 1980s contributed to detailed debate on issues including skills reclassification – but their policy ambition was nowhere near as great as that manifested in *Australia Reconstructed*. They were like sequels to a blockbuster.

However, during the same period employers (and a few trade union representatives) were developing an interest in Japanese management approaches. These developments attracted criticism from a group of AMWU researchers who had been supportive of the first Accord in 1983 (because of its potential for left interventions). They saw the political achievements of Scandinavian unions and of the goal of 'humanising' the workplace through enhanced training opportunities as positive. By the early 1990s they broke away from the AMWU, feeling that the ACTU and the Labor government were no longer pursuing these goals because of an overwhelming, and contrary, employer-driven agenda for enterprise-level bargaining.[192]

---

[192] Ewer, P, Hampson, I, Lloyd, C, Rainford, J, Rix, S & Smith, M 1991, *Politics and the Accord*, Pluto Press Australia, Sydney, pp. 111–117 and passim.

Winton Higgins shared these critics' concerns.[193] He considers that the 'Swedish model' 'lost a lot in translation' to Australia in the late 1980s, although for this he does not criticise Laurie Carmichael. Rather, he sees Carmichael as trying to achieve what was possible in a political context that rapidly became very adverse and dominated by neoliberal economics.

Australia was not reconstructed in accordance with the image of Sweden formed by the Australian unionists who went there in 1986. It was unfortunate timing that in the very period that the characteristics of the Swedish policy approach most admired by the unionists were highlighted to the Australian public, these were changing somewhat within Sweden. The unionists paid insufficient attention to this but some critics from the right strongly emphasised it in their reaction to *Australia Reconstructed*.

The prominent discussion of the 'Swedish model' receded in Australia, especially following the economic setbacks of the early 1990s amid an inaccurate perception that 'the Swedish model' had collapsed. There has remained, however, a careful but consistent argument for the continuing important differences between national industrial relations approaches even in the age of 'globalisation'[194] and a still hopeful outlook on the possibilities for, and benefits of, industrial democracy;[195] with the Nordic nations in each case still being seen as leading exemplars.

The AMWU's interest during the 1980s in Sweden and northern European policy approaches was forward-looking and visionary. It continues to help the prospects for interest today by a wide range of progressive and egalitarian Australians in lessons that we can continue to learn from Nordic countries, in many vital policy areas.

---

[193] See, for example, Higgins, W 1991, 'Missing the Boat: Labor and Industry in the Eighties', in Galligan, B and Singleton, G (eds), *Business and Government Under Labor*, Longman Cheshire, Melbourne, pp. 102–117.

[194] See Bamber, GJ, Lansbury, RD and Wailes, N (eds) 2004, *International and Comparative Employment Relations: Globalisation and the Developed Market Economies*, Allen & Unwin, Sydney, 4th revised edition.

[195] See Lansbury, RD and Wailes, N 2003, 'The Meaning of Industrial Democracy in an Era of Neo-Liberalism', in Paul J Gollan and Glenn Patmore (eds), *Partnership at Work: The Challenge of Employee Democracy*, Pluto Press Australia, Sydney, pp. 37–46.

Chapter 8

Celebration of a Union

The Banners and Iconography of the AMWU

Andrew Reeves

The Australian Manufacturing Workers Union (AMWU) has a complex and involved history that extends back to the formation of the first Australian branch of the Amalgamated Society of Engineers (ASE) in Sydney in 1852. However, it potentially goes further back, to the first printer's union chapels established in Sydney in the late 1840s. So it is hardly surprising that over this period the various unions that now make up the AMWU have left a rich legacy of artefacts and other cultural material that reflect their role in the celebration of the achievements of the Australian labour movement. The most significant objects that survive from earlier years of union organisation are the banners that unions commissioned across Australia after the 1850s (or in a relatively few cases imported from Britain), but any list of the material culture of Australian unionism is necessarily long: banners, certificates and sashes, membership cards and scrolls, Eight-Hour ribbons, badges, photographs and film, paintings, prints and sculpture, pamphlets and posters. Unlike today, with our disregard of formality, unionists of the nineteenth and early twentieth centuries had no problem with inventing their own rituals and regalia. This culture, and its artefacts, is the focus of this chapter.

Banners have been an important part of trade union practice and culture in many countries for at least 150 years, but their specific purpose and aesthetic significance was not seriously considered until the publication, in 1972, of John Gorman's classic study, *Banner Bright*.[196] Appropriately for a chapter on the AMWU, John was a printer – his firm printed posters for the Royal Shakespeare Company, and Australian artist Sydney Nolan experimented with theories of print production in John's workshop during the 1960s. As an active unionist, committed socialist, graphic artist and printer of note,

---

[196] Gorman, J 1974, *Banner Bright*, Allen Lane, London.

Gorman effectively defined the means of analysing banners, emphasising the process of banner production, the art of banner making, the symbolism and language of banners, and their place in labour's struggles and celebrations.

In part this approach derived from the need to validate the worth of the banners themselves. By the 1960s, they were seen (if they were recognised at all) as dinosaurs of another age, cumbersome, difficult to store and often decaying. In Victoria, at least, no museum was interested in them as historical documents, although the Powerhouse Museum in Sydney adopted a far more enlightened attitude. As a result, much of the early research concentrated on banner design, on the processes of banner making, and the negotiations between artists and union members on matters of style and content for any new banner. And in Australia, above all, the organic link between banners and the celebration of the eight-hour day served to define both use and purpose.

This research rescued Australian union banners from decay and often destruction. However, many had already been lost, often deliberately burned. It emphasised the artistic value of surviving banners and the interpretation of them as artefacts that provided a unique insight into Australia's first popular festival, Eight-Hour Day. Research from the 1970s and 1980s provided banners with a place within interpretation of the history of the labour movement that had previously relied exclusively on archival sources, to the exclusion of artefacts and material culture. The price of acceptance for these new forms of interpretation was an interpretation of banners as cultural works, with less emphasis on their political use, and a further concentration on their artistic merit.

Such an interpretation relies on defining Eight-Hour Day as essentially a celebration, and banners as prominent and attractive elements of that celebration. It is easy to understand why this interpretation proved attractive. In the late nineteenth and early twentieth centuries, Eight-Hour Day processions moved through the streets of cities across the continent, enthralling thousands of spectators and providing a common language and a unifying celebration for an emerging national labour movement. This image still remains valid today. The tradition of making and carrying banners in Australia reflected one of the most potent influences on our labour movement: the generational renewal of politics, ideology and culture by successive generations of migrants, especially those from Britain, to this country. Banners are an obvious and attractive example.

Today, decades removed from the publication of *Banner Bright* and the initial analysis of Australian banners by local historians, it is evident that such interpretation is incomplete. There can be no disputing the significance of banners as works of art or craft, or the relationship between banners and labour celebration – in Australia the Eight-Hour Day especially – but it remains the case that much of this analysis relied on interpreting the form and celebratory nature of the event sometimes at the expense of digging deeper into its political significance.

A more complete argument would develop an interpretation of the use of banners and the significance of Eight-Hour Day within a wider political context. This requires scratching below the celebratory surface to consider in greater detail the use and purpose of Australian banners. So this depends on what the act of celebration, particularly Eight-Hour Day celebration, means and what values or objectives such celebration is designed to represent. It is an argument that acknowledges the utility of banners for purposes such as celebrations of past campaigns, union survival or more complex issues such as dignity and social worth, but seeks to move beyond them.

During the decade and a half following the mid 1870s, Australian unionism took the first steps to becoming a national movement. Catastrophic industrial defeat in the early 1890s confirmed this trend, and as unionism slowly recovered from the twin evils of industrial defeat and depression its national character was unmistakable. Just as the previously exclusive Melbourne Trades Hall Committee began morphing after 1880 into the industrially militant and politically savvy Melbourne Trades Hall Council, so the Eight-Hour Day underwent something of a transformation as well. Prior to the 1890s, many trade unions appeared to attach more importance to *how* their eight-hour day had been achieved than in systematically seeking its extension to other trades and industries, relying instead on some undefined, innate process within individual trades to produce the pressure necessary for acceptance of an eight-hour day for their employees. As a correspondent of the Melbourne *Age* noted in relation to the 1887 Melbourne procession:

> It is impossible to shut our eyes to the fact that a very large number of men and women who belong to the ranks of labour, quite as much as the mechanics and artisans that will take part in it, are excluded from it.[197]

The experiences of the 1890s have often been argued as a catalyst for change – for political labour and the Labor Party, which emerged in this period. However, these years were no less influential for industrial labour. Recovery after the turn of the century, accompanied by the growing apparatus of conciliation, and ultimately arbitration, nurtured a matured

---

[197] *The Age*, 26 April 1887.

union movement that not only sought to rapidly recover lost ground, but to expand into new territories. The mass mobilisation of unskilled and semi-skilled workers effectively dates from this period. It is no coincidence that the years of the Eight-Hour Day's greatest popularity, and impact, also date from this period. These were the years when banners grew in size, to a scale unmatched elsewhere in the world, painted by a generation of artists who, even if they could not all call themselves full-time banner painters, could call on a reservoir of skills and experience that combined artistic effect with clear, coherent industrial and political messages.

If trade unionism had changed, so had the Eight-Hour Day as a largely symbolic or ceremonial event. By this time, the political content of the Day, needs to be considered in the context of both Australian and global society. In particular, the increasing importance of the Eight-Hour Day needs to be re-interpreted in light of the rise of competing industrial economies and the exponential growth of metropolitan centres in Western countries and their colonies in the late nineteenth century. These were societies inventing mass production and mass markets, together with the advertising and communications campaigns required to service them.

This was the world of Australia's increasingly large trade union banners, and in this respect size mattered. Even today, they are recognisable as instruments of union advertising and promotion, seeking, in a competitive, complex and often hostile market, to promote labour priorities such as recruitment, union formation and the mobilisation of unionism's emerging working-class base. In this respect, the Eight-Hour Day and the mass deployment of banners served as a form of political branding. They reinforced not only the collective interests of the labour movement, but also emphasised to others the possible benefits accruing from a partnership with labour. To do so they needed to be appropriate to the scale of their natural terrain: the streets of Australia's cities and towns. These were years of urban rebuilding, of higher and higher buildings and ornate facades, of unregulated advertising on every unoccupied hoarding, shop front and building wall. It is no coincidence, for example, that the Ballarat Trades Hall was contacted at this time by the Ballarat Advertising and Bill-Posting Company, extolling its 22 strategic sites around the city and drawing attention to its removal of old fences and the construction of 'costly erections, towering above the adjoining buildings [that] have taken their place'.[198] And unions

---

[198] Circular, Ballarat Advertising and Bill-Posting Company, nd (late nineteenth century), private collection.

responded to this changed environment: banners increased in size, and many were now mounted and drawn on drays or, later, truck beds, raising them that critical metre or two above the crowds that lined the streets, giving even those at the back a view of the banners and their messages.

Yet in this new environment, not everything had to change. The classical architecture of union banners proved eminently adaptable. Drawing heavily on British practice and precedent, Australian banners mostly conformed to a well-established pattern. Banners were generally two-sided: one side would be highly ornate, decorated with a rich symbolism carried by slogans, classical or, less often, medieval stories and myths, intricate decoration and the imagery of labour and the Eight-Hour Day – clasped hands or the entwined 'three eights', for example; all surmounted with the full title of the union claiming the banner. The reverse side, by the early twentieth century, invariably carried, along with a recapitulation of the union's name, a precise and large-scale illustration of workshops, worksites, machinery or infrastructure relevant to the particular industry. These images could take up virtually the entire face of a banner, such was their scale and detail.

Each made a considerable impression as the eight-hour procession moved slowly through the streets. Each could easily be read: the leading image of work or workplace established the skills of the union, the reverse side told its story of lineage and social responsibility, while the trade float that often accompanied the banner could be used for more immediate political issues – in both Sydney and Brisbane in 1887 Chinese immigration was a target, while less contentiously Fremantle members of the Engineers Union in 1903 campaigned for increased local manufacture. The pace at which the procession moved, with each banner separated by marching members and bands, enabled the messages on both sides of each banner to be easily read and assimilated.

Eight-Hour processions attracted huge crowds. At the height of their popularity, during the period of rapid union expansion in the decade prior to the First World War, tens of thousands would line the streets of the city centre. In Melbourne, for instance, the balconies of Bourke Street or Collins Street (depending on the route chosen each year) would be crowded with spectators seeking the best view. The procession would move east along Bourke Street (or Collins Street), having travelled from the Trades Hall precinct, down to the post office at the corner of Bourke and Elizabeth streets. At Spring Street, the procession swung right past the Parliament House steps and then northward to the Exhibition Gardens. The 'salute' was taken from Parliament steps, or the Old Treasury building, and the make-up of the official party demonstrated the political impact and potential of the massed union marchers.

Figure 8.1 (top) Melbourne 1906.

Figure 8.2 Eight Hour procession travelling up Bourke Street.

Monday 17th April 1914: Melbourne's Eight Hour Day procession travelling east along Bourke Street, approaching Spring Street, with the United Carters and Drivers in the van.

State Library of Victoria.

At the 1891 procession, deep in the time of industrial turmoil that marked the onset of depression, the Melbourne *Leader* reported that 'at the top of Collins Street the attendance was smaller than usual, although at the

Treasury the spectators included the figures of (governor) Lord Hopetoun and a large Government House party'.[199] Depending on the political climate and the presumed influence of the union movement, premiers, cabinet ministers, parliamentarians and other politicians rubbed shoulders or sat down to dine with the vice-regal party and a bevy of union officials. In Victoria at least, this represented the power of the political accommodation struck between liberal politicians and the labour movement in the nineteenth century, and later the growing power of the Labor Party.

The unfurling, or commissioning, of a new banner provided yet another event at which the political character of banners and their use could be exploited by unions. Such an event became an important political ritual in its own right, as a 1914 report from the Victorian Printers Operatives Union demonstrates: 'to celebrate the occasion of the unfurling [of their first banner] a Smoke Social was held at the Old Trades Hall where a most enjoyable evening was spent by a large number of members and their friends, including parliamentary representatives from both federal and state parliaments, and also representatives from the Trades Hall Council and Allied Trades'.[200] The ASE was among the first Australian unions to recognise the potential of parliamentary representation, even if the union did maintain its position of formally keeping the union out of politics. A member, DC Dagliesh, was elected to the NSW Legislative Council in 1860 with union support while another member, J Garrard successfully stood for the seat of Balmain in 1880. Later a minister in a Liberal administration, Garrard was instrumental in having the 1885 Eight-Hour Day proclaimed a public holiday. In South Australia, a foundation member of the Adelaide ASE branch, Laurence Grayson, was elected to Parliament with ASE support, although he soon drifted away from the labour movement. In Victoria, leading ASE member David Bennet held a position on the Trades Hall Parliamentary Committee from 1884, where the following year he supported 'the necessity of having direct representation of labour in Parliament'.[201]

The means by which banners were used to organise and deliver information were also applied in different ways and under different circumstances. In Brisbane, for example, banner imagery went indoors.

---

[199] *The Leader*, 25 April 1891.

[200] Victorian Printers Operatives Union Half Yearly Report, November 1913 – April 1914.

[201] For a longer summary of early ASE political activity, see Buckley, K. 1970, *The Amalgamated Engineers in Australia, 1852–1920*, ANU Press, Canberra, pp. 95–102.

Figure 8.3 Interior of a hall in Brisbane, c.1908–10, showing the highly decorative advertising wall.

Private collection

A remarkable photograph from the first decade of the twentieth century illustrates the interior of a public hall, possibly a union hall, but more likely a hall managed by an organisation such as the Australian Natives Association or the Temperance Society. The photo illustrates a clear example of the dynamic relationship that emerged in the late nineteenth century between the decorative arts trades, advertising and the union movement.

The wealth of imagery and the effective use of space and design reflect the influence of decorative tradesmen, while the sense of order and structure stems directly from union banner design, an influence especially evident in the banner-style advertisements that occupy the central position on the wall. In this respect, this wall of advertising echoes the formal structures of union banners rather than street scenes from the same period, where advertisements of all shapes, sizes and messages compete with each other in grand chaos.

The advertisement for the Queensland Boot Trade Union Cooperative Society is the only one with explicit links to the union movement, but the order and style of the entire wall of advertisements takes its order and style from the principles of banner construction refined across Australia during the preceding three decades. The advertisements in this hall are arranged around an allegorical centrepiece; by the early twentieth century, such a template had become virtually universal for Australian banners. Its imagery is also similar – Fertility or Bounty in classical form stands on a pedestal, receiving the homage of productive workingmen, in this case a miner and a shearer. The pedestal is supported by a heavy wheat sheaf (and an advertisement for 'Silverwood Butter') and accompanied by the necessary motto or slogan; in this instance, 'The Dawn: Australian Unity'.

An advertisement for 'Ada Driver, Photo Artist' serves to bind the 'banner' together, and as a decorative edging defining the 'banner' it is further decorated with an Australian coat of arms and the slogan 'Advance Australia'. The scrolled advertisement for 'C Le Broco, Jeweller, Queen St' occupies the place where a union's title would normally be placed, while six smaller cameos replace the usual images of industry or union benefit funds with advertising messages. Decorative design and allusions to floral emblems complete the banner-like effect while, in the style of union banners, the name and details of the artist or decorator appear in the lower right corner.

This extraordinary wall of advertisements stands in stark contrast to the severe functionality and utilitarian design of the rest of the hall. The wall is designed to catch the eye of anyone entering, and from its scale, design and evident colour succeeded in doing so. A deliberate emphasis on design, decoration and aesthetics is central to its impact. In common with contemporary union banners, it is a carefully manufactured tableau, even if the agency and location are different.

This, then, was the public world in which Australian union banners flourished between the 1870s and the economic depression of the 1930s. And so, to the banners of the AMWU.

Considering their size and fragility, a substantial number of banners commissioned by unions now incorporated within the AMWU survive. Eighteen pre-1950 banners are known to survive, as well as two Metal Trades Federation banners held in the custody of the union. It is to be hoped that this number will increase. Eight are banners of the ASE/AEU, two are Boilermakers Society banners, and there survives a single banner from each of the Coachbuilders Society, the Agricultural Implement Makers, the Shipwrights Union, the Blacksmiths Society, the Federated Moulders Union, the Sheet Metal Workers Union, the Amalgamated Printing Trades Union and the NSW Stove-makers Union. Many date from the nineteenth century, the most recent from the 1940s. Three were made by Tutills in London, the rest were made in Australia. Of the 18, nine come from NSW unions or branches, five from South Australia, three from Western Australia and one from Victoria.

Plates 1 and 2. Gawler Agricultural Implement Union banner.

Above: Plate 3. Banner of Ballarat's Amalgamated Society of Engineers.

University of Melbourne Archives

Facing page: Plates 4 and 5. Amalgamated Engineering Union (Western Australia).

AMWU National Office

AMALGAMATED ENGINEERING UNION

Top: Plate 6. Amalgamated Society of Engineers, Sydney District.

Bottom: Plate 7. Amalgamated Society of Engineers, Sydney District, Banner of Pride.

This chapter will concentrate on four of these surviving banners:

1. The Ballarat banner of the ASE, Blacksmiths, Fitters, Patternmakers, Turners and Machinists, dating from the first years of the twentieth century.
2. The Sydney District banner of the ASE, Machinists, Millwrights, Smiths and Pattern Makers, dating from 1892.
3. The Gawler (SA) banner of the Federated Agricultural Implements Association, dating from shortly prior to the First World War.
4. The Coastal Districts (WA) banner of the Amalgamated Engineering Union, dating from 1938.

Each comes from a different state or region, one was manufactured overseas, and they range in date from the early 1890s through to 1938. Each draws, to a greater or lesser degree, upon the British tradition of banner making that has proved so influential within the Australian labour movement, but each has its own distinctive characteristics. These are not simply artefacts produced to a standard blueprint, although they do, ultimately, reflect their common origin. Each serves to publicly promote the union, but each does so in different ways, reflecting changes in union ideology, the nature of industry and the workforce, and changing labour priorities.

The Ballarat ASE Banner

The Ballarat branch of the ASE was only the third branch formed in Australia, following branches in Sydney and Melbourne. It first met in March 1861, with 22 foundation members employed in the foundries and light engineering workshops that serviced the dozens of mines working the rich reefs and the deep leads of the Ballarat district.

Although an early branch of the union in Australia, it apparently lacked a banner for more than 40 years. Not even an event as significant as the 1891 Inter-colonial Trades Union Congress, held at the Ballarat Trades Hall, convinced the ASE to commission a banner, although other local unions did. Instead, the Ballarat branch waited another decade, until the worst of the depression of the 1890s had passed and union strength was again rising, to commission a banner from local sign-writing and painting firm Kift & Smith, who had earlier painted a banner for the Amalgamated Miners Association. The branch paid for the banner by issuing five shilling debentures, redeemable at the discretion of the branch's Banner Fund Committee.

It is the least complicated of the four banners described here. It is single sided, painted on canvas with only a rudimentary fringe of tassels at its foot. In artistic terms it can best be described as *naïve*. At first glance it casts an innocent eye, its images painted in at-times awkward ways (look at the unconvincing curve of the railway line in front of the train) with the banner as a whole structured in the simplest of ways: union name at the top, slogan below that with three images painted against what seems to be a Scottish Highland scene occupying the bottom half of the banner. Although it lacks much of the complicated imagery of other contemporary banners, it still conveys a clear message of influence, permanence and, in a number of ways, power. The railway engine might be only a few generations removed from Stephenson's Rocket, but the reciprocating engine – the power plant of many a factory or mine site – is more modern. Yet it is the central cameo that really catches the eye. Here we see the flags of Britain, the US and Australia (or at least a version of each). Whether this is the banner of a small or a large branch, whether it is to be found in the Black Country, New England, in the US, or on a regional Australian goldfield, it establishes a valid claim to membership of a powerful international union, drawing its strength not just from its members' influence on job sites, but from the collective influence and power of 100,000 members. Hence the banner's well-known slogan.

We know from contemporary press reports that it made a strong local impression. And so it should: this is a banner that conveys both a local and international story, in classic, simple and direct ways. The banner was funded by direct contribution from members. It is equally clear that it reflects the priorities and wishes of the local membership as well.

The Sydney District ASE Banner

This is an entirely different banner in so many ways. Where the Ballarat banner is simple and one-sided, this banner is complex, with intricate design and imagery on both sides. It is made of silk, not canvas, and it is British-made. Like the ASE banners both from Fremantle and Kalgoorlie (as well as a number of Australian coal miners' banners) this is a Tutill's banner. Tutill made banners for the world; it was the pre-eminent banner maker of the nineteenth and early twentieth century. For an Australian union to commission such a banner was to make a number of public statements – the union wanted the best and could afford it; the union members acknowledged and were proud of their British origins, allegiance and training; that the banners carried in Britain could also be carried in Australian streets. However, there is also a more fundamental message – such a banner lends a union a sense of permanence, sophistication and influence. Australian unions were familiar with Tutill's fine works, for in the 1880s they had carried their own banners at the opening ceremonies of the international exhibitions in both Melbourne and Sydney, where Tutill's products won accolades and gold medals for quality.

The front of this banner is the archetypal British banner design from the nineteenth century. It is based on the emblems of the ASE membership certificate – found in thousands of members' homes – and designed by the artist James Sharples, himself an ASE member. With heavy use of Victorian allegory, this imagery aptly reflects the union's determination to impose its own influence on the trades in which it organised while also participating in, and improving, the society in which its members lived, all aptly summed up in the banner's slogan 'Be United and Industrious'. The ASE accepted a social status quo, albeit one that could be improved.

This is a banner of Britain's high imperial age, and the central panel from the banner's reverse side achieves a remarkable balance between the symbolism and messages of Imperial Britain and the imagery and objectives of the ASE. Three elements predominate: an Australian coat of arms at the top of the arrangement, balanced by a spray of waratahs at the foot of the image to lend it a NSW ambience; a globe of the world, highlighting British possessions, particularly in Africa and Australasia, supported by the national or chivalric flags of countries, colonies and possessions in which the ASE had members. Befitting a true international union, there are flags of 10 such countries or colonies (excluding the Australasian colonies), including England, Scotland, Ireland, France, the US, Malta and Gibraltar. The entire collage is bound together by a series of clasped hands (a classic union symbol), 10 in all, each balancing one of the national flags. Entwined through these handclasps of solidarity is a cable – the overall effect of the hands and cable is that of a lifebuoy, a guarantee of safety, security and the effectiveness of the union. Finally, to emphasise the power of the union, its current total of members internationally is displayed for all to see: 71,221 members. This banner contains British messages, adapted for Australia. It is a banner that is best read as one celebrates the achievements and dignity of the labour movement (and the ASE in particular), but its parallel emphasis on the size and reach of the union conveys an unmistakable message to potential recruits and members.

The Gawler Agricultural Implement Banner

If the Ballarat and Sydney banners, in their own ways, applied traditional rules of banner work to achieve their purpose, the Gawler banner sets out to test them. It is immediately recognisable as a union banner, but it is also an anomaly among banners made in Australia prior to the First World War. Its size and broad format are familiar, but the design, colours used and, in particular, structure of the banner are not.

This is an extraordinary Australian banner, a banner well ahead of its time. It abandons the complex relationship between image, words and decoration established in the late nineteenth century in favour of an almost total reliance on imagery, and imagery removed from trade union concerns at that. It is almost as economical with words as Harald Vike's Perth banner nearly 30 years later (painted in a very different time and place), but even more spectacular in impact is the way in which this banner ignores traditional banner forms and style, and instead embraces the theatre. The journeymen painters and decorators of Australia's cities were necessarily flexible, working on advertisements, on theatre sets and backdrops, and the interior decoration of villas and mansions as well as on banners. However, only this banner seems to have taken this versatility to its logical conclusion and embraced the theatre – or the stage – as the basis for its structure. The other notable anomaly is that this banner virtually ignores the tools of trade or the products of member's labour – these are not highlighted as in other metalworker's banners, but rather appear, in diminutive form, within an overwhelming landscape on the reverse of the banner.

Yet it is the theatricality of this banner that makes sure that it caught the eye of watchers of South Australian Eight-Hours processions. The leading side of the banner is painted as a theatre set, replete with curtains, with a long, curving beach scene serving as a backdrop to the union's name. That really is all that side of the banner is. What could be simpler? It is painted with a limited palate of colours – essentially black, yellow and dull red, while the stylised lettering of the union's name is large, too large perhaps for the size of the banner. However, no one could miss the message – this union belongs to the life of its members, at work and at leisure as well. The reverse of the banner develops this theme. It is no longer a stage set but something equally novel for a union banner – a visiting card, or *carte de visite*, common in polite society during the nineteenth century – this time without words or a photograph, but containing another, agricultural, sweeping vista. This side has no words at all. Contained within a heavy, dark brown border is a bucolic scene of productive wheat fields, backed by what appear to be the tops of the northern Mount Lofty Ranges. Human figures are an important element of most banners, but here they are little more than stick figures, admiring the agricultural improvements of the wheat fields, but in reality dwarfed by the landscape, while the mechanical reaper, the only real reference to the work of the union's members, is similarly dwarfed by its context.

There are no known journalistic references to this banner, but the superficial simplicity of the banner belies the compelling message it conveyed to all who saw it carried in the Adelaide's labour celebrations: 'This is a land that we are changing for the better. Life is good. Come and join us.'

The WA Coastal District AEU Banner

When a correspondent to the *Western Engineer* wrote in 1938 'gone is the old-style flourished and ornamental design of other days, replaced by a new concept of what engineering and trades unionism means today' they were telling the literal truth.[202] The banner's artist, active communist and member of Perth's Workers Art Guild, Harald Vike, was clearly happy in breaking nearly all the rules that had dictated the construction of union banners in Australia for decades.

Vike abandoned the tightly structured format previously adopted by most banner makers and, instead, took his cue from modernism and from the stylistic models of Soviet art. Most significantly, the banner carries just three words – Amalgamated Engineering Union. There is no identification of branch or district, no slogans or verses from past times. Instead, the banner totally relies for effect on the use of Spartan imagery. Massive powerhouses, radio masts and a monoplane look to the future, not the past, and although there is continuity with older banners reflected through a common faith in technological innovation as progress, Vike's images conjure up a vision of a very different society. It is as close to a recruitment poster as any Australian banner has ever got: a conscious appeal to workers to join not only their union, but to join a social revolution. As watchers in the street at Perth Labour Day or May Day processions in the late 1930s watched this AEU banner move away from them, this message of social revolution was reinforced by the stark portrait on the reverse side of the banner. The proletarian figure that dominates (interestingly, Vike adopted an old British

---

[202] Quoted in Layman, L & Goddard, J 1988, *Organise!*, Trades and Labour Council of Western Australia, Perth, p. 19.

union tradition in using a real person, in this case Jack Newman, President of the AEU Coastal District, as the model for this heroic figure) stands in glorious isolation among a rubble of broken weapons while he measures up a globe of the world with a pair of dividers as a prelude to its social reconstruction. Significantly, that area of the globe, rendered as a blueprint, on which the figure concentrates is largely occupied by the Soviet Union.

Funded by a one and sixpence levy on all members, this new AEU banner won first prize in the 1938 Perth Labour Day parade, while in the same year it attracted considerable attention as it accompanied AEU tableaus depicting 'various anti-fascist themes' at Perth's May Day.[203] In Vike's banners, the public purpose of the banner had subtly shifted. It no longer celebrated past success, but future political and industrial gains, while (as suggested above) the banner's function as an instrument of recruitment no longer focused purely on union membership, but also on participation in wider political campaigns and, by implication, political parties.

Most of the banners commissioned by unions now incorporated within the AMWU between 1860 and 1940 have now been lost. Many survive only as photographic images; however, the four discussed here are, I believe, sufficient not only to give a sense of the sweep and diversity of AMWU banners, but also to provide an insight into the many purposes – political, industrial and celebratory – that these banners fulfilled.

---

[203] Quoted by Stephen, A in Stephen, A. & Reeves, A 1984, *Badges of Labour, Banners of Pride*, Allen & Unwin, Sydney, p. 83.

PART 2
AMWU PEOPLE

Chapter 9

The Struggle Continues

Laurie Carmichael Talks with Andrew Dettmer

Laurie Carmichael is in his 88th year. As a former shop steward, state secretary, assistant national secretary and research officer, Laurie has pretty much done it all in our union.

As related elsewhere, Laurie has been active since first joining the AMWU at the age of 18 in 1943. While the years are catching up with him, Laurie still takes an active interest in the union, as evidenced by his speech to the function celebrating the fortieth anniversary of the formation of the AMWU.

Laurie was the first ever recipient of Life Membership of the Australian Manufacturing Workers Union, and a more fitting recipient of this unique honour would be hard to find.

Laurie was interviewed by National President Andrew Dettmer on 11 January 2013.

AD – Andrew Dettmer

LC – Laurie Carmichael

LC: I was born in Coburg (Victoria) in 1925. I started my education at the Merlynston State School, which at the time was across a number of paddocks. That was because if you lived north of Gaffney Street you had to go to Merlynston School and if you lived south of Gaffney Street you went to the Bell Street State School. At first I was in Mercier Street, which was north of Gaffney Street and then we shifted just south of Gaffney Street and I had to go the Coburg State School.

At Merlynston I was just a little bit early for a five-year-old, but they allowed me to go. I liked the Merlynston School because I could go over the paddocks to get there. To go to Coburg School I had to go down all kinds of streets.

I finished primary school at Year 6, and left that to go to the Brunswick Technical School in Dawson Street, Brunswick, and commenced my apprenticeship a little bit earlier than 15.

I was apprenticed to the Dominion Can Company, which was in Melbourne, in the city, and that was where I did my training. It was a bit strange really, in that I was at the Dominion Can Company, but I was going to the Brunswick Technical School, which was a lot closer to where I lived. But in those days you had to do all your studies and training as an apprentice beyond the ordinary working days, working hours.

AD: Was that when you became involved in the apprenticeships campaign to have day release? Did you feel that yourself, that [it was an] injustice?

LC: I felt it as injustice, but it was a bit later that the campaign got under way. It was a campaign that we had talked about in the youth movement that I belonged to, the Eureka Youth League as it was called. And that meant learning a few things about politics and making up your mind that you would do something.

AD: So which came first, joining the Amalgamated Engineering Union (AEU) or joining the Eureka Youth League?

LC: I wasn't allowed to join the AEU by a shop steward who said that you can't join until you are 18. As a consequence, I was dwelling on my age 18 coming around so I that could join the union.

AD: And that was a furphy of course, as you would have no doubt found out pretty quickly.

LC: It wasn't a furphy for the shop steward. He had his mind made up. He came from the union movement in Scotland and he had very strict views about what you should do as a unionist.

AD: So you joined the Eureka Youth League after you turned 15. Was this during the period when being a member of the Eureka Youth League and Communist Party of Australia (CPA) was illegal?

LC: No, it was quite legal to be in either of them at that time. The illegal period was a bit earlier [from 1940 to 1942].

AD: Did you continue in your apprenticeship up until the point that you joined the Air Force in 1943?

LC: No. I joined the Air Force because I wanted to do something in the war, to be plain about it. But I couldn't get released because the company where I was apprenticed was making ammunition – namely, dare I say it, landmines – because the company that was Dominion Can Company was brought to manufacture those things.

AD: How were you then able to get out of a reserved occupation and join the Air Force?

LC: Well it took a while. I had a couple of arguments about it. On one occasion I actually tried to join the Navy, and I'm pretty glad that I didn't succeed with that. The Navy wouldn't have a bar of me because I was in this occupation, and the company had a person whose job it was to oversee things for the government. I don't know what his particular role was but he certainly had a role. I was told I wasn't allowed to break my apprenticeship. So I made up my mind I wasn't going to be very active as an apprentice for a while and they got the message and they let me join the Air Force.

AD: You sandbagged them.

LC: Mmm.

AD: Fred Thompson recalled meeting you for the first time during that apprenticeship campaign. He said you must have been 15 or 16.

LC: Yes, that was about the age.

AD: So you were involved in your first AEU campaign, for apprentice day-release, before you were actually a member of the Union?

LC: Yes. The campaign was very interesting in a way, because we got out some leaflets. Leaflets those days were just cyclostyle productions. You wrote something, ran off a duplicator machine and then we distributed them to all the various tech schools around Melbourne and booked the room for 40 people on the corner of Russell Street and Bourke Street. The only trouble was that we couldn't count them. There were about 4000 that turned up ... All we could then do was to march up Russell Street to the quadrangle in the Trades Hall Council Building. And we got a bit of a roasting from Vic Stout who was the Secretary of the Trades Hall at the time.

AD: Good old JV Stout [a prominent anti-communist of the period].

LC: I got on very well with Stout. For a number of years afterwards, too.

But we didn't know who to ask, we just wanted somewhere to go.

AD: Fred's recollection … was that you came with the same approach that you took throughout your experience and activity as a shop steward and as an official, and that this was on display when you were 15 or 16?

LC: All we did was to distribute these pamphlets.

AD: But it was a very successful campaign because day-release, as well as payments for your books, was then negotiated for part of the apprenticeship. You got the books paid for and half a day of your training was during working hours.

LC: Yes.

AD: When were you discharged from the Air Force?

LC: January 1946.

AD: In your Air Force service did you get sent outside Australia?

LC: No, I was debarred from doing that because I'd contracted rheumatic fever at the cricket ground [the MCG]. The cricket ground was taken over by the Air Force during the war and you went there at your peril because the wind whistled around … I contracted rheumatic fever. Those days there was no known cure and so I was confined to hospital for some months for recovery and then told I wouldn't be allowed out of the country.

AD: So you were in Australia only?

LC: That's right. Lots of people went down with illness. And I was one of them. How I survived I don't know because the character next to me in hospital died from rheumatic fever.

I first of all went to the Heidelberg Hospital and from Heidelberg I was taken by plane up to the Murray River … to Tocumwal Hospital. The hospital and the airport were separated. I was in the hospital there for about three months.

AD: It sounds like it was very tough.

LC: Well yes, you just had to take the risk. There was no choice.

AD: And no antibiotics, I suppose.

LC: No antibiotics, they were invented just afterwards.

AD: So you were discharged in 1946. What happened then? Did you resume your apprenticeship?

LC: Yes.

AD: At Dominion Cans?

LC: Yes.

AD: And they took you back or did you have to wait for a position to be made available?

LC: No, that was required of them as much as it was of me.

AD: As a returning serviceman?

LC: Yes, that's right.

AD: So what year of apprenticeship were you in? Was that your third year or fourth year?

LC: It would have been the fourth year because it was a five-year apprenticeship.

AD: When you came out of your time at the end of 1947, did Dominion Cans keep you on?

LC: I searched around for other employment. I wasn't sacked. I just simply looked for other kinds of employment as well as what they had available.

AD: And was that when you started at the dockyard?

LC: No, before then I was at a couple of other enterprises. And then I got married. We were able to get accommodation there. There was a housing shortage and I got housing down in Williamstown. Which was right next to the dockyards. I got work at the dockyards.

AD: So what year was it that you started at the dockyard?

LC: Would have been late 1948.

AD: And how long was it before you became active in the union at the dockyard? Were you active straight away? Because you would have taken your ticket to the shop steward to say, 'I'm an AEU member of good standing', I assume … as that was what you had to do in those days?

LC: Yes. But this was still a period where if an apprentice didn't finish his time or he didn't turn up at work they would send the police out to get them.

AD: Truly?

LC: Truly. That didn't involve me but I do recall others it did ... Not only that, you could be given real punishment if you were caught fornicating, that was the language used, if you were an apprentice.

AD: Was that a restriction that also applied to married apprentices?

LC: I never found that out ...

AD: So you were at Williamstown Dockyard in 1948. What was the dockyard like at the time? Was it still operating on a wartime footing or had it been cut back substantially?

LC: Well it was a bit strange, during the war the ships that were built at the dockyard ... were fat-bellied ships for trade. During the war they didn't build naval vessels, it was after the war we built them. I was there when they were building the first naval vessel, a frigate, the HMAS *ANZAC*. It was an absolutely hilarious piece of work [for reasons explained below]. I started there and I had only been there a short time when there was a stoppage of work – I had nothing whatever to do with it. It was primarily because, working at the dockyard, you did not get the level of annual leave that was available for other Commonwealth enterprises. Dockyard workers received two [weeks leave], but others had three. A lot of others had three.

*   *   *

AD: So how long was it before you came involved as a shop steward at the docks?

LC: Well, we had this fellow by the name of Alex Jeffries who came from the Glasgow shipyards in Scotland. And he could see that I was interested in major things. In about a year's time he convened a meeting of the engineers – the dockyard had 23 unions there. Amalgamation was a long way off. Anyway, he convened a meeting of all the engineers in the engineering shop and said he wanted to retire and he nominated me as the shop steward.

I got on fairly well with him and others; there were a couple there that were smartarses who always tried to bring down kids ... There was one there who had been on the Melbourne District Committee of the engineers. But he was ignored. So I became a shop steward. Never forgotten it.

AD: So was the AEU part of the shop committee at Williamstown Naval Dockyard?

LC: Yes, there were other people there. We even had a virtual Communist Party branch there.

AD: Were there representatives of other unions?

LC: Yes.

AD: As a shop steward at Williamstown Naval Dockyard, what was the process of becoming involved in the District Committee?

LC: As a shop steward, the rules of the union at that stage allowed for one District Committee member for every two branches, and four representing shop stewards. And it was about 1951–52 when I went on to the District Committee.

AD: Was there a specific AEU branch for Williamstown Naval Dockyard?

LC: No, there were no branches, they were all based on districts. Like Williamstown or Newport railway workshops, which had two branches at the time. Williamstown also had its branch, which was connected with what was called the Melbourne Branch Number 4. I think there were eight Melbourne branches. It was a crazy set-up, because there were about 50 odd branches, so that meant there were 20 District Committee members.

[In 1958, Laurie was voted in as the Melbourne District Secretary of the AEU.]

LC: [When I first became the secretary] there was the district secretary and three organisers: John 'Cup' Southwell, Jack Arter and Bill Wight. There was one other who was responsible as an organiser for [non-metropolitan] Victoria and Tasmania.

AD: Fifty-eight … And that was a hard-fought election, I imagine? That's what the records tell me.

LC: The outcome was that another character got elected simply as a stop gap … and then I stood, when the task came around in 1958. One of the other organisers, Bill Wight, he stood for the right wing.

AD: As an organised Grouper [National Civic Council] candidate or just simply as a more conservative candidate.

LC: More conservative, but being backed by the groupers.

AD: What was it like, coming in as district secretary at a pretty young age [33]?

LC: Well, I have to make clear that I was part of a team of magnificent people. There were only four or five full-time officials who were responsible for organising a union of nearly 40,000 members in Victoria alone. People like Neville Hill, Les Smith, Steve Horrigan and others, and we all worked together.

Neville Hill was a steward at Newport Railway Workshops and a member of the CPA. He became a state organiser around 1963. Neville came from a union family – his father was an official of the Sheet Metal Workers Union. It always seemed to me that Neville was endlessly patient, and he put those skills to good use later when he became a trainer and mentor to young trade unionists at the Trade Union Training Authority.

AD: I remember Neville well. He would always take the time to talk with young delegates and organisers like me, and he was also a pretty funny bloke.

LC: He was. There was also Les Smith, who was a steward in a workshop in Oakleigh, and who then became state organiser, operating from Dandenong. But the one who really impressed me was Steve Horrigan. He was selfless. If I needed an organiser for a period of delegation, Steve would often step into the breach. I don't know how he got on with Monsanto [at West Footscray, Victoria], his employer, but he would always respond to my requests to come in for a period of delegation, to fill in if an organiser was absent or if there was campaigning to do. Steve also dealt with computers in the workplace pretty well. Monsanto had introduced a computer engineer's position, and one of our members had done the training and was put into the position. Then the Electrical Trade Union (ETU) came along and claimed it as theirs [in the ETU's area of coverage]. Well, Steve just stood them up. He demanded respect, and he didn't appreciate fools or being taken a lend of.

AD: So how did the AEU office operate during the 1960s?

LC: Well, we had a lot less officials, not like today. Shop stewards looked to fix things themselves.

AD: Freddy Thompson reckoned that it was only when you got the third letter that you needed to get involved.

LC: Well, I don't know about that, but I did have one occasion, at Spotswood I think, when members went on strike because they couldn't get an organiser to come out to the job. I went out there as secretary and asked them what they needed an organiser for. They said they just wanted to see somebody – and I said that if they had a problem that an organiser would be available, but that the problem that they wanted to fix they'd already fixed themselves. I don't see the point of a lot of handholding. Organisers are there to do a job, but stewards and delegates are the people who have to deal with things every day, and they're the ones who have to live with any dispute, and the resolution of any dispute.

AD: Did the office operate collectively, or did you have to deal with situations individually?

LC: Part of the approach that I had was that there always had to be time for discussion. If we were to make a difference to working people then we had to know what we stood for. It didn't just revolve around the workplace; nearly every Friday night after I became state secretary, people would gather at the union office … [two old terrace houses on Victoria Parade in Melbourne] … and discuss left politics, current events, even the latest novels they were reading, over a drink. Well, they had a beer, I had a cup of tea.

One person who often made a contribution to those discussions was Jack Hutson. Jack was a shop steward at Vickers Ruwolt in Richmond. Jack was a bit prickly, but I always got on with him. He came to work for me when the AEU Industrial Officer [and later Arbitration Commissioner] Ted Deverall was off. Jack was brought in on delegation, and he ran a lot of cases in the commission. Jack wrote a lot, too [Jack Hutson was the author of *Penal Colony to Penal Powers* and *Six Wage Concepts*, seminal texts in Industrial Law]. He was a deep thinker, and between him and others I've mentioned, all of us got an education in thinking and looking beyond the next round of bargaining or the next dispute.

* * *

AD: I want to move on and talk about the shorter hours campaign, and your involvement in that, and the Accord. As I understand it, the AEU and then the AMWU's policy was to have a 35-hour week, going back to the 1930s. Was that something that was discussed during your experience when you were the secretary to the AEU?

LC: It didn't go back to the 1930s ... ACTU Congress decisions date from the late 1950s ... It started when National Organiser Jim Baird, who was responsible for organising the metal industry, was defeated by Dusty Miller. That meant we had to have someone else responsible for the metal industries as distinct from the oils industry or pulp industry, paper industry or the whatever, so I laid claim to do the job in the metal industry.

AD: And this was when you were still assistant national secretary in the 1970s?

LC: The last thing we were going to do was to give Dusty Miller the metals industries, so we gave him the car industry. Now I had had the responsibility for the car industry, and I had a real leadership right across the car industry and I knew how to handle the Vehicle Builders Employees Federation (VBEF) Federal Secretary Len Townsend. I was the only one that could handle him, but by the time this Jim Baird thing came along I could feel the advantage of taking on the metals industries.

So we were finalising, or Jim Baird was finalising, some sort of a payment ... That started with the maritime industry. Jim Baird picked it up and ran with it, and I was able to finalise that, get a result.

But I always had the theory in regard to leadership in campaigning – that you laid the foundation for the next task in the course of finalising the current task. That approach goes back quite some years. So I did this and then got a decision from all the mass meetings before finalising that we would start campaigning for a shorter working week in the New Year. That was the year after. Well, that didn't seem to worry too many people, not until we got it going, but it was my step, the next step, that prepared the way.

So I drew up all the stages that we needed to go through, and drew up what we had to do in order to have sufficient unity, so by deliberate intent I made sure that the next ACTU congress reaffirmed its policy on the shorter working week. I made sure that tied in all the other metal unions. They couldn't escape it. It was an ACTU decision. None of this was an accident.

I also made sure that I attended the next meeting of the International Metal Workers Federation dealing with the shorter working week. I got an alliance with unions, such as the English unions. Nobody would do much, but I knew that the German metal unions were wanting to pursue the shorter working week. I was not certain that the Italians would come in, but I worked with them, very carefully, and got them to agree – I wouldn't say with a great deal of enthusiasm, but the Italian unions agreed. The Italian unions are different to the rest of the world, you had one lot of unionists who were different to another lot of unionists who were different to another lot of unionists ... I got three of the most significant; I got their agreement.

I talked to them and I went, too. I took a delegation to Italy, including Association of Draughting, Supervisory and Technical Employees (ADSTE) ... Arthur Greig. I persuaded all kinds of people, internationally, nationally, and then having got all this, I then confronted the Metals Trades Federation in Australia and I said that these are the decisions that have been made. Are we going to do something about it? It was quite deliberate and I'd built it on the way.

And that was quite deliberate too because I'd finished this other one about September–October one year, and I was planning on saying, 'Well, I need to do all the rest of this work now by about April or May next year'.

So we took the decision, but I knew damn well that I'd be facing right-wing opposition, and lo and behold one of the first to condemn us for taking action was Bob Hawke. I had to stop some of our own people from condemning Bob Hawke. Because it was a set-up you know, and I knew those bloody antics; just proceeded on like it didn't matter. No attacks.

But we would go ahead. I did it using the media because I was reasonably able to handle the media – as much as Hawke was. And so we got a decision and I was benefited by the friendship I'd struck up with the secretary of the ETU, Cliff Dolan, who ended up president of the ACTU. I got along quite well with Cliff, and he backed us all the way on the short working week campaign. So that when people like [Federated Iron Workers Association National Secretary] Laurie Short and others tried to undermine everything that we were doing, I had the numbers.

AD: How did Short try and undermine you in that early phase of 1976, 1977?

LC: Well, in the early phase, preparing the way, nobody took much notice. They didn't know what I was up to, but come May, right, I then pulled the first real banger out of the hat, and that was, 'We've made the decision to go for the shorter working week, so I propose that we take a working day off: one a month'. One day a month.

They hadn't seen this coming, you see. And Laurie Short says, 'Ooh, it's a decision', then the second time 'round, 'No we're not going to be in it'. But Hawke came out and supported us, so I knew all these antics, and Short said, 'I thought we were supposed to be carrying out ACTU policy'. And of course I hit the media just as heavily as they did, and I was always given a fairly good run with the media. So we got it going.

AD: And that one day a month lasted for, was it, 12 months?

LC: No, about nine months or so. Then after that we decided we would go on strike once a month. One day a month, go on strike. Then they realised they'd all been manoeuvred into a corner and they couldn't get out of it.

AD: A rostered day off?

LC: Yes. I was pretty proud of that. I think it was the greatest thing I ever did. Not merely that we went for it, but the way [it was] handled … Step by step, internationally as well as nationally. There was no good any union complaining to the International Metal Workers Federation because they had all supported it … So I said to Laurie Short, you better make up your mind if you want to be a part of it, or if you don't. It was a year in developing, carefully step by step, from the time that Jim Baird got defeated to the time we had the thing on the go. It was well and truly embedded.

AD: If I recall those were the days of stagflation and stagnation in industry. There was no investment occurring, and significant inflation around the 10 per cent mark that entire time, and so the real value of wages was declining. We had those battles in the Arbitration Commission, so that was not exactly a great period for campaigning …

LC: The campaigning was based not on that, it was on unemployment. We said that a shorter working week would mean more jobs.

It was simply in the finish … If I'd kept it going, beyond late November, we would not have been able to hold it together the following year, and I was very clear in my mind that we would be hit with a massive recession. And that's what happened. I wrapped that up as the 38-hour week, but I had to do it. Now there were quite a number of industries that had already gone for the 35-hour week: they were working them, and they still are.

AD: The chemical industry, the oil industry …

LC: I had the oil industry wrapped up earlier, that was foreseen. [ACTU Secretary] Kelty knew, he understood that. But some people think they solve it all by getting in the [Arbitration] Commission. I never did that in my life.

AD: You did it the on the job.

LC: As sure as I'm sitting here, that's exactly how it ran … But I couldn't have kept it going into the New Year … because the recession was coming.

AD: It was pretty bad. There was Fraser's 'wage freeze', that sort of stuff. Were you involved in any way, in the negotiations with Fraser? Did they ever want to have discussions with you about it?

LC: No.

AD: So the Liberal government at the time simply kept away?

LC: They kept away, but they made some awful remarks.

AD: In the end were you able to get all of the Metal Trades Federation of Unions together?

LC: Only to get the 38-hour week and to, as I got the agreement. I got an agreement with the employers. They all lined up, [but Laurie] Short, he had the bloody cheek to turn around and say to me, 'Don't let this get handled by those academics'. It was in the Tom Mann Theatre we were having this meeting and [he and I had words]. He was a Cold War warrior.

AD: So at the same time as the shorter hours campaign was going on there was also discussion on the process of evolving what ultimately became the Prices and Incomes Accord of the ALP. When I interviewed Bill Kelty he said what a crucial role you played firstly in creating a dialogue with the Labor Party and the unions, secondly in the process of negotiation and thirdly in getting it approved, in particular by AMWU members. He recalled very clearly the both of you attending the rally for Whitlam after the dismissal in 1975, and you saying to him that when we have reformist governments in power we have got to give them more time. Was that your view about Whitlam, he just didn't have the time?

LC: Whitlam knew that. Whitlam and I got on well.

With the Accord there were a number of factors that led into it. One was that we were having discussions about the Scandinavian situation, particularly with the Swedes, and I was having discussions about the Scandinavian experience in the union. They were running schools, even brought people out from Sweden to talk about what was done in Sweden.

This was offsetting the view that came from some of the left that we ought to follow the Soviet Union – still – at that stage. I was quite convinced that that was a dead loss. I'd been there … I'd been there a number of times and had a gut full of it. So that was step one.

Step two was to ask 'If Hawke wants the Accord' – and there was no stopping him – 'then why can't we turn it into something like a Scandinavian approach?' So I did that in conjunction with a number of other unions. I might tell you, I went to meet with Cliff Dolan from the ETU at home. Cliff lived in one part of Sydney and I lived almost next door. I went and saw Cliff at his home and had a talk. Not too many people knew that. Cliff was a very important factor in what we [were] doing about the shorter hours and so on. There was an amount of preparation to go into backing the Accord.

The third step in that same direction was to pursue something like what the Scandinavian unions were doing. The outcome of that was we would have a particular trade union delegation go to Europe, which we did, and we came back and produced a document called 'Australia Reconstructed', which was an attempt to attach something to the Accord that was of an Australian nature.

AD: How did you as a member of the Communist Party feel that your views were treated, considering you were talking, effectively, about social democratic policy?

LC: Everybody knew that I had differences with the Soviets. So it wasn't like I had to go and beat a drum about it. I got Hayden to invite me to ALP federal caucus. Hayden was the leader at that stage. You know what Hayden did? He made Hawke give the vote of thanks to me for the address I made to the caucus. Bill Hayden and I were very close.

AD: But in terms of the Accord, there was that process of discussion. Kelty said to me that it really started before the 1975 election because of the recognition of people like you that reformist social democratic governments do need more time, and if they do need more time then trade unions effectively have to moderate their demands. Is that your recollection of it?

LC: Yes. I don't think I would put it quite like that. But it's true that I had that view about the Whitlam government demise. I did a lot to try and assist Whitlam, against what the Governor-General had done [sacking Whitlam on 11 November 1975]. And that became well known and so it was my view that if you were going to do something like that, [then] we had to have the opportunity to sit down and argue with what you call the social democratic government, and that's exactly how it occurs in Sweden. So it wasn't as though it had been just dropped on me or something. You've got to allow for the fact that in the latter half of the 1970s I was already building an approach similar to what they were having in Sweden. Not identical, but similar to it. So when it was a question of doing something to Fraser I did that by pulling the shorter working week campaign anyway.

AD: How involved was the National Council of the AMWU in the Accord process? Or was it something that occurred away from the union?

LC: The trouble was, and I suppose I didn't do enough about it myself, Hawke appointed Keating as the treasurer, and therefore Keating had the run on the Accord. That hit everybody on the back of the head. I mean they all thought it was going to be Ralph Willis. [Ralph Willis had been shadow treasurer.]

So Hawke had to bloody get the backing of the Labor right wing in

New South Wales. So it ended up with Keating, and I might say, I've got a lot of time for Keating. But I never knew anything much about him at all, at that stage. All I knew was that some of the elements of the left in the Labor party hated Keating, that's about as much I knew.

AD: Finally I just wanted to ask you, where you see things going at the moment, because we have just been talking about some of those pressures. We have been talking about the nature of capital and how it is changing. How do you see the union has changed over your 70 odd years of membership?

LC: My feeling is that the unions don't want to know. I see the future of the union movement continuing to be in difficulty. I see it as an absolute necessity that there be an education program in the union movement, through the union movement. I've said that time and time again, as you can see from the literature I'm reading.

We need in the AMWU an adequate union education for the top leadership of the union. When I say top leadership, I don't necessarily mean only [full-time] position holders, I'm talking about the people who are capable of leadership. I don't know what else I can do. I just about tear my hair out every time I raise the need for a union education program. Somehow or another it gets waylaid by something that might be important but is not a vital part. The vital part is where we are historically as a human race.

AD: Do we need more and better analytical tools to deal with that, or do we need more of an understanding of how society works before we start using those analytical tools?

LC: My view is that we should just start. Just get started. Let's get people who are capable, who can open up the subject, get a discussion on the subject and have a debate on the subject. And all together so that it can mean something for the future.

But what are we doing about it? We have people in our own union in leading positions who think it's of no concern. For me it's the most critical thing of all – our own adequate union education program that we would have set up. Pull in lecturers, overseas speakers ... whatever is required in an active education program – way beyond what we had in the 1970s.

Naval Intelligence

Laurie is sometimes seen as a very serious soul. And of course he has always been blessed with a fierce intelligence. But lurking underneath is a man with an uproarious sense of humour and sense of the absurd, as the following story shows.

LC: It finally got around to the time when they would launch the HMAS *ANZAC* into the water. That doesn't mean to say it was fully equipped at that stage, just simply the hull and everything else with it would get launched into the water and it would all be fitted out in the dock. Well it finally came to the day and, you had to be in the Navy to believe it, they had built the *ANZAC* on the same slipway as for the trading ships. Only the Navy didn't realise there was a bit of a difference between a naval ship and a trading ship. One was a flat, big-bellied thing, that when it went to the water would just plonk there. With the *ANZAC* when it went in the water it was like sending in a bullet.

The first thing was … the shipwrights had a longstanding right that on the launch of a new ship they would be shouted a barrel of beer. Well the Navy didn't like that. That was all right for a private ship, but not for the Navy. Nobody is going to get a barrel of beer. So the shipwrights decided they wouldn't launch the ship.

So there was hell to pay. The launching date had been fixed. There was going to be a big turnout. The filming was going to take place. So finally the captain of the Navy who was responsible for making the decision was persuaded to allow them to have their barrel of beer.

Well that was all right.

So the shipwrights had the job of knocking what was called the chocks out from underneath the ship's hull. When the chocks went out, gravity would take over.

Come the day and the chocks were knocked out. But there didn't appear to be any movement and they had the wife of the admiral, who had the job of launching the thing, hitting the side of the hull with a bottle of wine or whatever it was. Only she didn't realise that this ship was shaped with a pointed bow, so the bottle never smashed. It just swung backwards and forwards.

The shipwrights had to get a whistle to let all the naval brass up top know to do the launch. Nothing happened, but finally one of the naval ratings came to the rescue of the Admiral's wife and smashed the bottle.

But then the shipwrights couldn't see anything that was happening because of the shape of the hull. So they're down there and the launching is taking place up top. Finally they get the go ahead, and then the ship starts, just slowly. But by the time it hit the water it was going at a hell of a rate.

There had already been a fight with the ship's painters and dockers who had … if you know the ships painters and dockers …

AD: I did.

LC: Some of them were a bit rough.

AD: They were, just a little.

LC: They'd claimed the right to ride the ship into the water. Only, the Navy wanted to do it, so in the finish there were some of each.

All of us were there watching, and it was quite clear that it was going to hit the pier because they didn't allow for a convergence to take place with a ship going like that.

These painters and dockers threw out an anchor. The only trouble was the anchor only had about ten foot of chain on it so the anchor and chain went straight to the bottom. Afterwards, after they got the ship back off the pier and pulled it into the dry dock, they had to send divers down to get the anchor.

I had a wonderful bloody time. My wife and my son, baby son, were all there. And all the workers and their families.

AD: That was sort of your big introduction to Williamstown Naval Dockyard.

LC: Well, I'd only been there about two to three months.

AD: And you thought you must have been recruited by the Keystone Cops? Did it get featured in the press?

LC: It was all swept under the carpet. But what was worse, you had those newsreel cinemas – you would go in them and they would play continuously – my wife and I and our baby were allowed to go in, and we held our breath, because all the statements being made were about our brilliant naval ability, and you could have sworn that nothing had happened. It was a cover-up. Here we were going and watching this and busting our guts laughing. The whole of Williamstown had busted their guts laughing.

Chapter 10

Three Tassie Women and Their Union Experiences

Robyn McQueeney

Angie Williams, a retired AMWU member from McCain's Foods, Claire Glover, an AMWU member from Norske Skog, and Sue Creed, an AMWU member from Simplot, had very different paths into joining their union. Angie was raised in a Labor family, where being a union member was a fundamental part of working life. Claire's dad was a union member, but she had not really thought about joining until her union delegate suggested it. After talking to her teammates, she readily joined. Sue started work in the days of the closed shop and was only offered a job on the condition she joined her union.

Likewise, their involvement in their union is varied: Angie, now retired, was very active in campaigning. Sue is active in the management of her union and is a member of the AMWU National Council. Claire is simply a union member.

The three women, however, have a lot in common. Each of these women started working life in Tasmanian manufacturing for very basic reasons – to earn a living. All women talked about their workplace with passion … they enjoyed working hard and contributing to their workplace. They valued their work colleagues – indeed, for delegates Sue and Angie, their main motivation and satisfaction was to help people they worked alongside. Likewise, all three women greatly enjoyed their lives outside work, recognising, as Claire put it, 'work is work and home is home'.

All three express confidence in women's opportunity to work in manufacturing. Being older, Angie and Sue both commented on the changes they had seen in their workplaces, with their union actively securing equal opportunity in their factories. Angie and Sue spent many years as permanent casuals and Claire had a close call. Angie and Sue clearly articulate the importance of permanent work and the cost paid by casual workers. Angie, Sue and Claire achieved a great deal through training, including secure work (at least until recently for Angie) and improved self-confidence.

Finally, a major similarity between the three women was their willingness to share their stories with me – they were all candid, but also self-effacing about their numerous achievements. So, it feels wrong to try and muscle my story into theirs. Instead I will tell you what I told them when I asked them to participate in this endeavour.

I am very inspired by my mother who as a sole parent raised three children. Mum worked in a number of factories as a production worker (at Silk and Textiles, Cadbury, Fibre Containers and more). She eventually settled into a career as a hospital aide. The lives of ordinary people are really interesting, as opposed to celebrities and high-profile people who fill the glossy magazines, so I wrote this chapter, which is based on interviews with three Tasmanian women talking about work, home, their union and their other interests. It is important to give women a voice.

I also wanted the interviews to be a fun and enjoyable experience. I simply love Angie's advice to would-be campaigners: 'Put on your lippie, have your make-up done, look fantastic and get your face in front of the camera whenever you can to focus on your workplace and your issues'. I enjoyed talking to Claire about her ATV adventures along Tasmania's wild west coast. And Sue's story is inspiring as she tells us about the supervisor who turned a reluctant trade unionist into an extraordinary workplace activist simply to save the company $2.50.

Angie

I'm Angie Williams. I worked for many years at McCain Foods in Smithton before they shut down. I had a couple of stints as a permanent and then I went back as a casual. On and off, I was there for 30 to 35 years and I've seen many changes.

I left school at 15 and worked in the Stanley telephone exchange. I then worked for a short time at the paper pulp in Burnie in the finishing room, filling in time to go nursing. Next I went nursing for 12 months in Launceston. By that time I had met my future husband and that was the end of nursing. After having three children, I was employed as a casual food processor at General Jones on the veggie line. I worked my way up over the years to work quality control in the lab and grading the vegetables. Permanent part-time was not around then – you were just called in when the veggies were in season and laid off when they were out of season.

Figure 10.1 Angie's certificates.

I was always a union member. I was in the canteen one lunch time and one of the union delegates said to me, 'Why don't you sign up to be a union delegate? You are always fighting other people's battles.' I replied 'That sounds pretty good to me' – so I did. I was always in rebellion against management about many things – workers' rights, the way they were treated, pay issues, personal issues, lots and lots of stuff … I loved being in the union and helping people with their problems. The down side of that, of course, was that you are 24/7 – you've got the phone calls on your days off and weekends. I still get that even though I am out of the workforce.

I have been to many fantastic rallies. If there was ever a rally, I wanted to be part of it. I was the first one to front up! I always opened my big mouth. I always advised anyone attending a rally: 'Put on your lippie, have your make-up done, look fantastic and get your face in front of the camera whenever you can to focus on your workplace and your issues'. I remember one particular time I got a bit carried away with our local newspaper and said what I really thought about my workplace and the bosses. I got hauled in on my holidays, into the manager's office and really, really hauled over the coals. He was not happy with me at all. All the things I said there later came to pass and the factory did end up shutting down. I was right the whole time and that is why he was angry with me …

I remember a couple of huge events. One of the biggest ones would be the rally in Hobart for your rights at work [National Day of Community Protest 1 July 2005]. Anne Urquhart said to me, 'You're coming to the rally, aren't you Angie?'

'Yes, you couldn't keep me away!'

'Would you like to say a few words?'

'Yes, yes', I replied – me and my big mouth. I thought: that'll be great, we'll have a beer or two and we'll be standing on the back of a ute in a paddock. I don't know where I got that idea from, but that is what I truly believed. Anyway, the bus left Smithton and we made all these stops on the way. It kept filling up and by the time we got to Hobart it was full to overflowing. There were protesters everywhere.

'Where are we having this rally?' I asked.

'At the Hobart town hall' came the reply.

There were thousands of people so I asked, 'Where am I going to be?'

'Up on the stage!'

I thought, there is only one way you are going survive this, girl! Take a deep breath, ignore absolutely everyone, concentrate on what you want to say and you'll get through it, and that is what I did. But I was so nervous I thought I was going to die. I looked out into the crowd and it was just a sea of people, with much cheering and clapping. They were great!

General Jones started off as a canning factory in Smithton – they would can the vegetables. Then it was taken over by outside interests: McCain was a Canadian family business. Our first employment officer was a lovely lady – she has moved to Hobart now. It was great then, but it changed and became 'us' and 'them'. Before, it was a lovely family atmosphere – the people in management were locals. In a community, people care about each other. When you've got a management, they are trained in the corporate world of big business. You are just a number doing a job. And that is the saddest thing that I have seen in the workplace – the fact that the boss you knew, who knew your brothers and sisters and went to school with you, is a total stranger, almost as if they are from a foreign country and don't speak your language …

'No, no' management said, 'no way will we ever close this factory'. Then, bit by bit, lines were closed down and workers weren't called in, and there was a gradual decrease in the workforce. Eventually they did end up closing the veggie part of it. It was publicised that there were 100 jobs lost. Well, of course that is not the truth – there were 100 permanent jobs lost. They said nothing at all about the 120 casuals that were already gone. And, of course, there are all the associated people with jobs like the farmers and truck drivers … So the closure of the factory – or the veggie part of it – was the biggest blow that has ever happened to me (and to the local community). It was huge and people are still feeling the impact of that. And that was three years ago.

When I first started work, you had men forklift drivers and women process workers. Gradually, with the union getting involved and our workforce being mainly unionised, there was no discrimination. And it was an equal opportunity workforce. So we had as many females as males applying for jobs – and they got them, too.

I thought it would be a good thing to get involved with health and safety because a lot of things weren't taken care of … One thing in particular really upset me when I was only a novice working in the lab. My leading hand was getting the pea line ready by climbing along a pipe that was up near the roof. The roof would have been … maybe 9 metres high and there was no safety ladder, there was no net, there was no access to that pipe apart from how he crawled over a railing and walked along the top of the pipe. I was appalled – I was terrified that whenever he was up there he would fall and be killed, falling on to the concrete floor. I was so concerned that I passed the issue on to the union. They actually printed it on the back of our magazine. I went back into work after the magazine had been around the worktables and my boss asked, 'Was that about me, Angie?'

'Yes it was', I replied.

It was not long after that that there were scaffolding and safety ramps around the pipes. I was the instigator of that. I got things done because I was like a dog with a bone – nagging, nagging, always nagging. I was a very good nagger.

It was like war from the minute you walked into work, because there would be issues – workers who would want you to take up their case with management. A lot of the times they would not go to management. They had plenty to say about the issues that concerned them and the wrongdoing, but they didn't have the gumption to go and front management. I loved doing that – I really loved, relished, going over to management with work issues. I remember one day in particular, going over three times in the same day to help a foreign worker.

I came from a union-oriented family – strong Labor Party people. I would never, even in those days, ever have been in a workplace and not been in a union. I have passed that on to all my family and friends. I cannot understand anyone who is not in a union, because you've got such wonderful backing, especially the AMWU. That's got to be the greatest union in Australia. They were always available – they were only a telephone call away. Personally, if you wanted help they would assist you ... Now, when I am in a workplace, even a shop, people seem to tell me problems. I always say, 'Are you in a union?' and nine times out of 10 they will say, 'No'. I say, 'Right, I will find out which union you should be in and give you a phone number'. Many, many times I have done that for real-estate people, shopkeepers, hotel workers, lots and lots of people. I have always believed every worker should be in a union.

Anne Urquhart is such a magnificent, passionate unionist – she encouraged us. She'd come down for a meeting, and of course she took the meeting. But she'd make all the delegates sit with her or stand behind her, so everyone in the room knew who we were. And then she encouraged us to say our bit so the delegates always had something to say. Nowadays, you would not think twice about saying your bit. She was one of the main instigators of what was our whole workforce. Anne is now a senator and Shane Littler has stepped into that role of union leadership. He's a good man too! When I first became a delegate, I think there were two delegates. When I left we had 15, and they'd delegate responsibility for other tasks. Now with only the French-fry plant operating there might only be two again.

I used to find that people would ring me up at home and say, 'So and so's got a problem and they don't know what to do about it'. I'd reply, 'I'll fix it – do they want to come with me – we will go together'. I remember one day in particular – a girl got into trouble and I heard this supervisor, who'd just been wearing his white coat for a week, say 'I'll give her what for, I'm going to sack her! I'm going to give her a warning!' I got up there and said, 'You bloody well will not sack her, you will not give her a warning! Who do you think you are?' It's a wonder they didn't bail me up. But she did not have a warning. And by the time I finished with him, he was not game, he just stayed right out of my road. But he was just picking on her, like 'I'll fix her'.

I can't remember what she did – she might have been having too long for a smoke – something really trivial.

Life is like that – funny, funny, funny.

Claire

I'm Claire Glover. I was born and raised at Bushy Park. I went to school up there – the same school from playgroup to Grade 10. Then I went to Claremont College for two years, which was a bit hard to get used to after going to the same school for so long. I have never been the type of person to say, 'I am going to be this or I am going to do that when I grow up' – I have never had that type of ambition. So when the time came and I had to get a job, I started filling out my resume, just out of what was in the paper.

I was lucky to get a traineeship at Norske Skog. It was known as ANM then, then Fletcher Challenge and later Norske Skog. It was a paper and process traineeship, which went for three years. I enjoyed the first year because we did parts at TAFE and at Claremont College, and we had a team training bonding week away. We did shiftwork at Boyer (training) and we got to have a look everywhere around Boyer. Then the second year, you pretty much had a job as a reagent attendant. That was all shiftwork. And the third year, you moved down to the machinery room.

I had just finished the third year of my traineeship, and most of the time they'd keep you on as a temp. But I had a few people leave off my crew, so I was lucky to apply for the job and get a permanent position. I've been there 15 years now. I got a process operator position in the machine room. I was pretty lucky there as I still got to stay on the same crew. I was one of the lucky ones – I have been on the same crew the whole time I have been here.

We went down to Koonya – this was in the first year of our traineeship. There were 10 of us – me and the rest of the boys, as it always seems to end up. It was really good – we got to do abseiling, bushwalking, just team-building things: teamwork and problem solving, and things like that.

On shift at the moment there's only two females; I am one of them and the other was on our crew, but she's moved to another crew as she is doing training on the pulp mill. So there's only two of us on shift. There are other women there – on Human Resources and stuff – but we don't really see a lot of them. As we work on a continuous process, you don't really get to go outside your job very often. You are stuck there for your 12 hours most of the time. So you can't leave until your relief gets there. And if your relief doesn't get there, you can be stuck for another four hours after a 12-hour

Figure 10.2 (top) Claire on her ATV.

Figure 10.3 Claire relaxing with her dog.

shift. So, I am the only female down in the machine room. It doesn't worry me – I don't even see it like that half the time. They are really good people to work with.

I work on the paper machine. It is just the general day-to-day running of the paper machine. Most of our work is based on the winder that cuts the jumbos of paper into whatever the customer requires. It can be pretty physical at times, because you are always pushing paper. One of the processors goes down and we have to push the reels and some of the reels weigh, like, 1 ½ tonnes. If there is a machine break (a paper break), then we have to go and help the machine operator sort that out. So we get the machine going back – which has the priority. Then back to the winder to do our normal day-to-day jobs.

Once you are there, you are there – there aren't many people who get off. The average age when I first started was around 20, but it is not that any more – it is probably 30. It is getting a bit harder as they keep cutting jobs. I suppose they have to cut down on money, but when I first started on the machine there were seven of us and now there are five. We don't go any faster because 'Safety First'. When there were seven, everything was done straight away, but now we have to take our time and just do what we can. They are pretty big on safety, and at the moment they have brought in a safety glasses policy. I am not a big fan of it, but what can you do? You have to follow their policies. Where we are it is hot – it is always hot and humid – and the safety glasses always fog up. I wear earmuffs as well. It is a bit of a pain, but it is something we need to get used to.

We have just been granted $84 million to do a conversion project on our machine. So that will give Boyer a future. They will be making light weight coated paper, which is like the glossy catalogue paper. All of that is imported into Australia at the moment. We are getting a new winder, too, which will be pretty good. Everyone will have to be trained up on that. It's early stages, so we don't really know a great deal about it – they are still doing surveys. They will be doing a bit of building soon. The machine will be down for about three months, so most of the training will be done then, I think.

On our second year of our traineeship I was put onto Crew 5 – the crew I am on now – and we had a union rep actually on our crew. He came around and explained what the union does and said, 'You should maybe think about joining the union'. I spoke to some other people who worked there and filled out the form and went from there …

The people are really good – it's the people you work with who make it that bit easier. They are more like a second family – you probably see them more than you do your proper family. One thing I don't really like would be on call – even though we are only on call once every three weeks. And it's only for two days. But it can seem like a nightmare when you've done your own shift and then someone's sick and you have to go in and do another one. We are mainly only on call for a couple of hours in the morning and a couple of hours at night, and if we don't get called in within those hours we are safe, or it turns into double time and you've got a choice. Friday and Saturday nightshifts aren't the best either, but what can you do? ...

We get good holidays – that is one thing. We have leisure leave and annual leave. We get two lots of holidays a year so it mostly works out you get a four-week lot and a six-week lot. But there is one year where you have to wait nine months for your holidays. It is rostered leave – you can't really pick and choose unless you have long service. It is a bit hard to swap your holidays with someone else.

At Boyer, I think being a woman is not an issue. We all get treated pretty much the same. There's no one singled out or told, 'You can't do that because you're a girl'. So it's really good in that sense.

I do feel sorry for the delegates because they do cop a lot of flack. They are only most of the time the messengers of the company saying what they would like and they got shot down a lot of the time. It would be a tough job.

My partner and I've got ATVs – four wheelers. We do a bit of four-wheel driving ...We do camping as well – we've got a caravan now so it's a lot cosier. It's all thanks to Norske Skog. No one really wants to work – it's just something that has to be done so you can have other things in your life. Work's work. It's not as if I don't care about work. When I am there, that is what I care about – there is no point being there if you aren't going to put effort into it. Work's work and home's home. I think you have to try and keep things separate. You need a break.

Sue

I'm Sue Creed. I work at Simplot Australia, which used to be Edgell Birdseye. I have worked there for 25 years. I became a union delegate probably about three years after I started there, and I have been delegate ever since. The reason I took it on was because I used to work on a permanent afternoon shift basis and we had no union representation at all on afternoon shift. The organiser at the time came out to the site one week for a meeting – and he actually held meetings on afternoon shift as well – and he called for volunteers.

One of my so-called friends commented, 'You've got a big mouth, Sue, you're not afraid to say what you think, you do it!'

'No, no', I reacted.

'Yeah go on ...'

A couple of other people joined in and next thing I knew I was a union delegate.

Figure 10.4 (top) Sue at a training session.

Left to Right: Darren Kettle (Scotsdale), Craig Hanson (Ulverstone), Paul Kruska (Scotsdale), Sue Creed (Dev), Jeff Beswick (Ulverstone), Shane Brown (Dev), Jennifer Dowell (Food Div. National Secretary).

Figure 10.5 Sue at a union picnic.

From there, with the help of training from the union (and I've done a lot of that over the years) I've gained a lot more confidence in myself and in my abilities. My first few years at work I basically would not have said boo to a goose. I was only a casual – you didn't dare rock the boat or say anything.

After three years of being there and not saying anything, they annoyed me one night. We had a night shift where we'd start at 6 o'clock and work until 2.30 in the morning, working on the pea belts. At the time, we knew when the bell rang that we had 10 minutes work left on the line – and that was your knock-off time. So the bell went and we knew we had 10 minutes to go. We were on overtime and we knew we had tea money coming to us if we worked an hour and a half overtime.

Instead of allowing us to get (I think it was) $2.50 tea money that night the supervisor came around and moved everyone off the line who was due to get tea money and brought new people up that were not due for tea money. He marched us down to our time clocks, clocked us off and told us to go home, so that they would save paying $2.50. I thought: How dare you do that! So I went to the union office and asked, 'Can they do that? What are my rights?' About two weeks after that the organiser came on-site and I ended up being a delegate. If they hadn't have annoyed me that night, I might not have become a delegate. They've probably regretted it ever since!

I've done a lot of work in the factory – a lot of different jobs – and the union has helped me to progress through the factory, because they put in training and pushed the company to start a course: the advanced diploma in food technology. They called for applications and I put my hand up and said, 'Yes I'd like to do it'. I was, I think, one point off the criteria mark and the company said no. The union went in to bat for me and said, 'Why can't she? She is only one point off.' The organiser went in to bat for me and came out and added, 'Yes, you're allowed to do it, they've changed their minds because you were persistent'. And they allowed me to do the advanced diploma of food technology. There were about 50 of us who started it – there were only about 30 who finished. I was one of the 30. It took us five years of training to get that qualification, and if it had not been for our union going in to bat for me, I would not have been able to do it – I am sure of that.

When I finally did get the qualification, the company turned around and said with negotiations from the union, they would pay us for the level of competency that we were entitled to. And they would pay everybody except me because I was only a person who worked on the shop floor. Everyone else who did the course with me was middle management or above, or were in quality. They were in roles that the company deemed were entitled to the money – so they gave everyone else in the group the pay rise, except me. The union went back in to battle again … it took them about five months of arguing, and me jumping up and down saying it's

Figure 10.6 Sue's dad, a union member, at work.

discrimination. Eventually the company said, 'We'll give it to Sue, but she has to change jobs and do a higher level job'.

My reply: 'I'm quite happy to do that – it gets me off the inspection lines!'

So I trained in the quality roles in the factory, and I was the first person who learned all aspects of the quality role. This experience helps me understand when we have a problem – we don't often have any – but, for example, if we have a high count of listeria somewhere, it allows me to go back through the line. With my training in the advanced certificate in microbiology and the knowledge I've gained, plus my experience on the line, I can identify the problem – where we are picking up the bacteria. By doing swab or sample testing we can concentrate it down to a specific area so that it can be cleaned and we can get rid of the bacteria.

When I started work, it was back when you could have a closed shop. It was on your application form: 'Are you prepared to join a union – yes no'. If you ticked 'no' you did not get in. We were told in no uncertain terms – if you want to work here you have to join the union. So everyone ticked 'yes'. I had never been a union person. I did office work and they treated me fairly well. I did not feel like I needed a union to assist me. I knew they were in existence because my father was in a union. However, it was never something I joined when I was working in the office. There was never any option – it was only me in the office and the boss's wife ...

Childcare is a big problem – I know my daughter will have that problem if she ever wants to go back to work. She's going to have to find childcare facilities. My daughter in law has gone back to work three days – she is in a situation where she can go back to work three days. But at Simplot and other factories you can't say, 'I don't want to work today because I have not got a babysitter set-up'. You can't put your children into childcare for Monday, Tuesday and Wednesday this week and Wednesday, Thursday and Friday the following week – it does not work like that … Especially the casuals, unless they've got friends or family to support them. There aren't a lot of places that start childcare at 7 o'clock in the morning. Eight o'clock is fine, but if you need to be on the job at 7, you've got to have the kids up, fed, dressed and into childcare by 6.30. It just doesn't work that way – you cannot do it …

It is hard, too, to get a house in the current environment and to have a permanent job. You cannot go as a casual and say you want to borrow money for a mortgage because it doesn't happen …

At Simplot we have about 100 permanents and about 150 casuals. They could make some casuals permanent. We are trying at the moment to get more permanents. Personally, I reckon they could put on another 20 permanents without too much trouble as the company is getting more and more customers. But the company don't necessarily agree with me. Devonport has the lowest number of permanents in all the five factories that we own. One of the head office guys actually stated that every plant in Australia would know exactly how many permanent people they could run to optimise their performance and that they would know how many to have. And I said, 'That's funny because every time I ask at Devonport, it's "No, we don't know … we'd have to work it out"'. The reply: 'No, it's every plant would have an optimum number of employees and they would know what that number is'. So from that point on, I went back to the factory and I have had it on the agenda, if not every month, at least every second month: permanent numbers, permanent numbers, permanent numbers …

My union has always given the support I needed. Even childcare, if I were going away – but I did not need to take it up as I had the support of my family. But, yes, for a lot of newer delegates who are women coming into it, the offer of having childcare facilities or support to help them get the time off to come away and do what we have to do … And as much as you say it doesn't take [up] your time – it does. I'd get phone calls here – not so much now, in the past at 7 o'clock at night. I have always said, 'If you need me just ring me'. The company will ask me to come in. I'll say, 'Yes, I'll come in early' or 'I'll stay back late'. I'll pop in for an hour off shift if they need

Figure 10.7 Ovaltine factory

to do something. People need representation. I'd rather do that than have someone there without representation. The union's always given me all the support I needed.

When I started, you could have maternity leave, but God forbid, you would ever get paid for it. When we started campaigning a lot of the women the same age as me said, 'I had to go without having pay to have my kids, why should they get paid?' I'd reply, 'It's not anyone – it's your kids or your kid's partner who are going to be the ones that are going to benefit'. Now we actually have paid maternity leave from the government.

We still don't have superannuation where we need to get it. We've done a lot towards it – it was good to get it to 9 per cent, but we should have pushed it further. I think it needs to go up on a regular basis. It needs to go higher than 12 per cent, especially for the next generation …

In our agreements, we've got a pretty good wicket – we are not hard done by, by any stretch of the imagination. We've got above award payments, which are quite good. Now that the pulp has gone, we are probably one of the highest paid employers in Devonport. I think the union has done a lot for Simplot and the people who work there.

Chapter 11

'Red' Fred – Left in the Right Time and Place

A Political Analysis of Fred Thompson

Cora Trevarthen

'Red' Fred Thompson was the first full-time union official to organise Australia's 'Red North' for the Amalgamated Engineering Union (AEU). Although retiring as a full-time industrial organiser in 1976, Fred's community work continued until his death in Townsville in 2011. He was primarily an activist, and Fred had to deal with the isolation inherent in organising North Queensland and the Northern Territory. However, these challenges finely honed Fred Thompson's strategic, tactical and analytical skills. These capabilities, and a reasoned leadership style, would enable him, often unaided, to play a decisive role in a number of significant events in industrial relations and the Indigenous rights movement in Northern Australia.

Fred Thompson's life as a unionist started in an inner-city Melbourne engineering workshop in 1934 when, aged 14, he observed the treatment dished out to prevent a scab starting work alongside AEU members:

> He scabbed on us in the 1910 strike and we're not going to work with him. I thought 1910; Christ, I wasn't even born then. They went down to the foreman and the bloke never started. The men went to the trouble to explain why they'd done what they done and also I thought, Christ almighty, if a group of men have a viewpoint that lasts for so long, it's not something one ought to be foolish enough to ignore.[204]

To understand Fred Thompson's later work, it is essential to analyse the cradle of his industrial career: the AEU world in Victoria in the early 1930s.

---

[204] Thompson, F 1989, 1920–2011 interviewed by Daniel Connell for the Townsville oral history project [sound recording], NLA, Bib ID 4664906. All following quotes for Thompson are taken from this interview. Hereafter it is referred to as 'Thompson'.

When he entered the ranks of the AEU as a young apprentice, Ballarat's Ted Rowe was rising to prominence. Rowe's career trajectory and the significance of his role as a national leader of the AEU has been analysed by Andrew Reeves:

> Ted Rowe is remembered as 'an ebullient personality and a gifted public speaker', who combined a flair for theatricality in politics with a fundamental commitment to militant rank and file industrial politics.
>
> Rowe cut his teeth at that Ballarat cradle of militant unionism, the North Ballarat Railway Workshops, where he first came to prominence in the early 1930s ...
>
> He organised a combined union shop committee (combining industrial organisation with social benefits such as an employee-managed sick pay scheme), and later took it as a model for a state-wide Combined Council of Shop Committees.
>
> He left Ballarat in 1943 following his election as the first communist to achieve federal office in the AEU. (He was) the pre-eminent militant union official of his generation: in a union finely balanced between left and right, he showed the same capacity to build coalitions while maintaining the integrity of his politics that he had showed in Ballarat.
>
> He could also be a polarising figure – an object of acute hatred from both conservative politicians and the conservative press – and at times his sense of the dramatic probably cost him support, even within his own union.
>
> Time after time, Ted Rowe demonstrated his skills as a strategic thinker and a fine industrial tactician ... he was one of the AEU's two leaders in the prolonged 1946/47 Engineers strike, described by the union's historian as 'the greatest victory ever achieved by the AEU', one in which 'the gains flowed on to benefit nearly every employee in the Commonwealth in a very short time'.
>
> Rowe could be a spell-binding stump orator, he could move mass meetings by his words and ideas; he was a man of 'fire, of vigour, a sense of the dramatic'. He has been fairly described as the 'stormy petrel' of the AEU.[205]

---

[205] Reeves, A. 2012, *Oration for the 125th Anniversary of Ballarat Trades Hall Celebration*, np, 2012.

Reeves' assessment of the pre-eminent militant unionist of his generation – a national leader of Thompson's own union – is revealing in terms of personal leadership style and the political environment within the union and the broader labour movement.

Rowe's trailblazing as a national communist union leader during turbulent times within the movement was undoubtedly influential, as was the international political context for communists. However, as this chapter will show, other factors not evident in the time or place of 1930s Melbourne, particularly the character of Northern Australia, would later influence Thompson's highly individualistic contribution.

Rowe and Thompson were both on the shop floor in metal trades occupations as Australia emerged from the depression. Thompson points out the prevailing conflict in Victorian society: 'Blamey had become Commander of Police in Victoria after the war. Under his direction the police used batons on unemployed marchers, and workers were in constant conflict with landlords, who wanted to evict them.'[206] Thompson experienced living at home with his unemployed engineer stepfather before he joined the Communist Party of Australia (CPA) in 1937. Both supported workers in the Spanish Civil War, and Thompson was involved in violent anti-fascist demonstrations before his union activism began at age 18 in 1938.

It was in that year, Thompson became the prime mover behind a campaign among apprentices to prevent employers from employing 'improvers' – young workers who would be sacked and replaced as soon as they reached 18 and become eligible for adult wages. This led to him to becoming the first secretary of an Amalgamated Engineering Union Youth Committee. As secretary, Thompson made the running for apprenticeships and to introduce training during work hours. And here we witness the development of Thompson's early political skills. Under the watchful eye of older elected officials he initially needed to convince, Thompson devised tactics and converted them to strategic plays as he produced and distributed literature. He was accompanied by older activists to hone his capacity for oratory as he argued the case for young apprentices atop soapboxes at Albert Park and at League of Young Democrats (LYD) events. It was in 1930s Victoria – on the home turf of 'the pre-eminent militant union official of his generation' – that Fred Thompson's political skill set emerged almost fully formed after five years of union life on the shop floor. Thompson's first campaign not only succeeded, it broke new ground. Victorian metal trades apprentices became the first in

---

[206] Thompson.

Australia to enjoy daytime technical training. Like so many conditions later won by the AEU, benefits soon flowed to other unions and industries.

Later in 1938, Thompson was elected president of the Melbourne Eight Branch of the AEU. 'I was 18 at the time and must have been the first teenager elected Branch President. I didn't stand for it; they hung it on me. I think some very wise men decided to drop me in at the deep end and did that. It was a valuable learning experience and then I got elected onto the State Executive and District Committee.'

From his earliest days in the union, Thompson recognised the need to reconcile AEU internal politics in order for industrial progress to be made. Thompson spoke of the need to 'get pressure on the union officials responsible, who were reluctant to do anything about it, mainly because they did not think it had a chance of succeeding'.[207] These officials were no less than Melbourne AEU organiser and militant Nat Roberts and the district secretary, Albert Fair. In his AEU history, T Sheridan described AE Fair as one of several 'ALP men of impeccable credentials'.[208] Here we can see Thompson learning the trade of coalition building that marked the political arrangements at work within the AEU of the time – between militant and mainstream elements of the AEU, apprentices themselves and the LYD – this was the union realpolitik for the AEU's CPA members. They were influential, but not in the majority. Following the success of the AEU Victorian strike a little over half a decade later, Rowe himself attributed that victory to 'the complete unanimity of communist, ALP, Catholic and even normally right-wing delegates on the Melbourne District Committee, but this was in truth a reflection of the unity of the entire membership'.[209] The need to consolidate political alliances and demonstrate substantial public support was learnt early and, as we shall see, never forgotten, by the card-carrying Fred Thompson who had joined the CPA in 1937.

Fred's early life in Victoria extended beyond the AEU, but even his social activities had a political dimension. Dances and camps were run by the LYD, the AEU Youth Committee ran lightning premiership picnics of Australian Rules football, and Fred's CPA membership gave him access to the world of ideas and intellectuals. He described it as 'a permanent study situation. We were always attending classes and I was reading continuously

---

[207] Thompson.

[208] Sheridan, T 1975, *Mindful Militants. The Amalgamated Engineering Union in Australia 1920–1972*, Cambridge University Press, Melbourne, p. 169.

[209] Rowe, EJ 1947, *Communist Review*, June.

... keeping abreast of what you were studying, but also the material that was being published about contemporary events, the small pamphlet ... it focused your attention on the problems and led to a massive public debate about the issues at stake.'[210] He came into close contact with Melbourne communist intellectuals, including future *Overland* editor Ian Turner, prominent Melbourne University Labor Club member Amirah Gust (later Inglis) and party leader Bernie Taft. A 1940 CPA Senate campaign speaking tour brought him into contact with Aboriginal leader Bill Onus in Swan Hill. Thompson's stump speech on the need for a united front against Germany unfortunately coincided with 6 o'clock closing in a conservative town. Onus's intervention saved him from a beer bottle across the back of the head and helped him make a fast getaway from the ensuing melee.

The outbreak of the Second World War saw the focus of Fred's activism shift to the CPA, partially as a result of Prime Minister Menzies banning the CPA on 15 June 1940. According to Fred, the police were ill-equipped to disable the party that continued to operate. In recounting a meeting of the state executive of the CPA that took place while fishing in an open rowboat off Werribee he said, 'we reckon there's no walls, and where there's no walls, there's no ears'.[211] The meeting was only interrupted when Frank Johnston caught a fish. Fred's Army enlistment and subsequent northern postings saw him relieved of his union responsibilities at the Maribyrnong armaments factory. He took up CPA organising while serving in the Atherton Tablelands, New Britain and Jacquinot Bay. Many Australians are unaware of the operations of thousands of CPA members during the Second World War throughout the AIF. Thompson's CPA wartime activity included arranging his entire unit to make payroll deductions to war bonds, running a District Committee while under fire (which convinced his CO to stay out of harm's way), producing party bulletins and running a lending library. The value of Fred's educational activities was recognised by the Army, which transferred him into the Army Education Unit after his service in the South West Pacific, and where he remained until his discharge in 1946.

When Fred was demobbed he was taken back into the AEU at the Ford factory in Geelong, before working as a temporary country organiser in Victoria and Tasmania. When health complications from the dysentery and malaria he suffered during the war arose, on medical advice he moved to the warmth of North Queensland with nurse Loma Ingles whom he married in

---

[210] Thompson.

[211] Thompson.

1950. Working initially as a maintenance engineer on a pineapple farm on Magnetic Island, Fred got a job at the Townsville Railway Workshops in 1951 and moved his union and CPA activity to Townsville.

In Thompson's words, North Queensland was far from a backwater for a left unionist.

> The militant base in Townsville was quite exceptional. It had a long tradition that went back decades. All party members were active in community organisations including the local authority; we had communist members of the local council. It didn't matter which area you turned to, there were active communists in the trade union movement. I just blended into that and became part of a significant decisive influence in the community. That's the way it was in the early 1950s.[212]

In 1952, 'in a result without AEU precedent, the organiser for 25 years J.A. Willett, was overwhelmingly defeated by a communist challenger, F.B. Thompson'.[213] It may have been without precedent, but it should have come as no surprise given the strength of the Townsville CPA at that time. Fred Paterson had only recently left the city to reside in the electorate of Bowen where he was the first and only communist elected to an Australian Parliament. Militants were in control of the Waterside Workers Federation (WWF) and the Meatworkers Union, while also holding prominent positions on the City Council, at Trades Hall and in many community organisation. Thompson's choice of Townsville as his place of recuperation is perhaps as reflective of his political acumen as it was motivated by medical concern for his health.

There were political similarities, but the differences in the context of location were stark. In Melbourne, thanks to his union training ground, Fred was the president of a group of 13 active metropolitan branches of the AEU. In 1952 Townsville had a population under 50,000. It was still getting over war shortages and subject to price controls, and had limited transport, entertainment, education and facilities.

> [It was] just a big sprawling country town. Very brown. There were outdoor dunnies. People used to ride bikes, hundreds and hundreds of

---

[212] Thompson.

[213] Sheridan, T 1975, *Mindful Militants*, p. 219.

bikes about the town. We had no water, we used to have to hook up water from the people behind us.[214]

The differences that came with Fred's massive territory from Rockhampton north and for many years all of the Northern Territory were even more marked.

In the trade union movement, in the way I was operating in NQ [North Queensland], it rested on me, on the individual. There was a measure of your success or lack of it, there all the time as a yardstick. When it came to the question of what tasks to undertake … first was safety, to stay alive, because the industry in NQ was primitive in the extreme. There was also severe exploitation in the wage rates … the working environment was medieval … we live in the brightest part of Australia and I never found a well-lit workshop … there was a constant film of dust in the air. When you start to talk about ablutions, there weren't any. Showers were not known; men had to go home with the filth of the workshop on them. There was no bitumen, except for half a mile north of Townsville and maybe a hundred yards in the main streets of the small towns on the way [to Cairns]. The roads were atrocious; one shower of rain and they were impassable. The isolation was longstanding and communication was difficult. Workers in NQ, if they belonged to a national organisation, were isolated and frustrated. There was a strong culture … that viewed the Queen Street seat warmers with utter contempt. I faced massive problems as a union organiser and as a communist who was hell-bent on establishing unity.[215]

Other political differences related to the seasonal nature of the North Queensland workforce and the dominance of the Australian Workers Union (AWU). The dominant seasonal industries such as sugar saw itinerant wharfies and agricultural workers head north during the crushing season. Meatworkers from Victoria and New Zealand operated in the north while the southern industries were shut. These people, according to Fred, 'represented the best in the traditions of the Australian itinerant work; humorists, walking encyclopaedias, raconteurs, artists … very special people'. Influential for more than half a century, many of these workers returned year after year, bringing new ideas and political maturity with them. These were the

---

[214] Thompson, F, Loma Thompson quoted in Sellars, N 2011, *Fred Thompson: Communist, Union Organizer, Humanist. A Biography.*, self-published, Townsville, p. 143.

[215] Thompson.

workers immortalised in Ray Lawler's *Doll*,[216] and as Fred's workforce they provided 'the most exhilarating period of my life because of the character of the workers and the fact that Queensland was still the last frontier'.[217] The vast majority of unionists in the north were members of the AWU, which was Queensland's political kingmaker.

As an organisation, the AWU viewed a communist AEU organiser with grave concern and often refused to let Fred address meetings. It failed to back industrial action in the lead-up to the sugar dispute. Fred's democratic philosophy saw him develop strategies to overcome AWU intransigence by keeping the AWU's rank-and-file members in the 22 northern mill communities informed about the issues for six weeks prior to bringing on industrial action. 'They were being consulted and were not getting anything second-hand. We also advised them that, if necessary, we'd take strike action and that could affect them. It was as simple as that. We set out to solve the problems created by decades of isolation.'[218] The dispute was to get the margins for skill, which applied in other industries to be extended to sugar workers. Rejected firstly by the Arbitration Commission, the combined unions' delegates[219] then served a log of claims on the Australian Sugar Millers Association that was rejected. The three-week strike that followed saw distribution of leaflets in four languages, consultation with cane farmers and Fred's analysis revealing the still essentially colonial structure of refiner Colonial Sugar Refining Ltd (CSR).

> It was an important political strike; I'd say the first political strike in Queensland … an industrial dispute in which all of the issues were raised about the structure of the industry, the role of the State Government and what needed to be done. We compromised in our settlement terms in the interests of the industry. We knew how far we could take the dispute without it starting to impact on the farmers, whom we regarded as our allies. They were subject to the same problem of exploitation. It was a decisive victory and it was a beacon for the rest of the trade union movement.[220]

---

[216] Lawler, R 1955, *Summer of the Seventeenth Doll*.

[217] Thompson.

[218] Thompson.

[219] From the AEU, FEDFA, ETU and building unions.

[220] Thompson.

It was this breakthrough that finally led to communication between the AWU and the AEU throughout the north. Fred was cautious about what he told officials, knowing much of the information would go back to the government and the Arbitration Commission. Finally, the AWU agreed to participate in joint organisation at the job level. More than 30 years after Ted Rowe achieved this in Victorian railway workshops, Fred pulled it off across 22 sugar mill communities throughout North Queensland in the face of overwhelming opposition from the dominant union.

Another political constant for Fred was holding the industrial groups at bay within the AEU for over 15 years, leading up to and during the 1956–57 split when the Gair Labor government lost office. He survived four court-controlled ballots by applying communications and campaign skills to highlight the real issues and backgrounds of the groupers to AEU members. The alliance Fred forged with parts of the AWU in North Queensland was pivotal in bringing on the split and formation of the Democratic Labor Party. George Pont was the AWU's organiser in Cairns. He and Fred worked together on the question of three weeks annual leave. It was Pont who moved the expulsion resolution at the ALP State Conference in Bundaberg that ousted Gair because of his refusal to support three weeks leave. Fred explains this momentous historical schism for Queensland Labor very simply.

> These were the bread and butter issues that we took up … this indicates where people stand; they do not represent the views and needs of unionists. They did not just lose government, they lost everything. They handed the government over to the National Party on a platter … it was inevitable. If it hadn't been for the three weeks leave question it would have been something else. The Labor organisation was so corrupt that it would have equalled the corruption of the Bjelke-Petersen government at the time of its demise.[221]

The ALP and the AWU were polarised throughout Queensland and the result was devastating at the community level. The ALP's parliamentary representation finished up being decimated and the party remained in the political wilderness for almost 32 years until the election of the Goss government.

---

[221] Thompson.

The maturation of Thompson's AEU career coincided with the rise of the mining industry in North Queensland and the Northern Territory. While his work at the Mary Kathleen uranium mine in the Northern Territory, at Queensland Nickel's smelter in Townsville and on the development of new fields such as the Bowen basin and at Weipa was pivotal in ensuring appropriate safety conditions, and wage levels flowed across the mining and refining industries, it is on a less successful long-term campaign in Mount Isa this chapter will now focus.

Fred's earliest visit in 1952 highlighted the dangerous and primitive conditions in Mount Isa and the parlous state of union organisation. Fred had to retrieve the AEU minute book from the safe of management's industrial officer and set about structuring the operations of the branch as its secretary faded into the background. Management's pre-war approach to industrial relations included fines and suspensions being meted out to workers trying to rectify dangerous or uncomfortable conditions. Again, Fred built bridges with other unions that saw the establishment of a Trades and Labour Council, and in the mid 1950s a series of general meetings further increased union representation and activism. The AWU was opposed to this development, preferring to refer all matters to the Industrial Commission or court, and accepting the judgement regardless of outcome. Members' dues were collected by the company and paid to the union. Locally, members with compensation claims or issues found their way to Fred because they were unable to get advice from their own union.

The well-known 1964–65 Mt Isa strike developed out of two previous disputes in 1959 and 1961. In 1959 the Industrial Commission (IC) put a ceiling on the lead bonus paid to workers based on the price of lead on the London market. The IC ruling was that the bonus could not go any higher, but could be decreased. Mass meetings as part of a broader campaign led to the sacking of Clerk's Union Secretary Ken Morgan, and a campaign spearheaded by Fred and AWU member Pat Mackie was needed to achieve Morgan's reinstatement.

Former Queensland Minister Don Lane – subsequently jailed for fraud – was stationed at Mount Isa as a local detective at the time. His memoir explains the background to the next phase of the unions' dispute with the company in 1961.

> There had been a long history of bonus payments at Mount Isa, as at Broken Hill. At Mount Isa it was set at 8 pounds a week. Before the Industrial Commission could hear an application to raise it to 10

pounds, as it was at nearby Mary Kathleen mine, the Queensland Government introduced special legislation to remove the bonuses from the award and make them a matter for negotiation. This strike lasted for about eight weeks ... led by a very eloquent Secretary of the Local Trades and Labour Council, Kenneth Austin Morgan, supported from Townsville by the northern district organiser of the AEU and a known communist, 'Red Fred' Thompson. There had been mass meetings of miners in a large open area between the mine and the town known as the triangle and Morgan and Thompson addressed them from a truck.[222]

Lane's account concurs with Fred's as far as it goes. Fred relays that broader safety issues were raised at compulsory conferences with the company and the IC. During one such discussion, Fred felt a tap on his shoulder.

I turn around and it's my Branch President. And he says, 'I want to report that our shift fitter on the afternoon shift has just been decapitated.' The fitter had observed all ... (safety) procedures and he's down at the bottom ... his head and shoulders were out into the area near the sump when some (company) official came through, lifted the (safety) tag off, came down the flea (lift) and it decapitated him on the way down. It was one of those incidents that started to give the Mount Isa dispute a graphic and dramatic impact.[223]

What got the miners back to work on 23 November 1961 was a state of emergency under the State Transport Act enacted on 20 November.[224]

In the years that followed, community sentiment hardened against the company as the number of incidents increased. During peak production periods, as many as 13 workers died in a year. Rank-and-file AWU members fed up with no service from Brisbane elected Pat Mackie as their chairman. He raised pay and safety issues. The company's rejection of these led to the men going off the contract system[225] and on to wages that cut production dramatically.

---

222 Lane, D 1993, *Trial and Error*, Boolorong Publications, Brisbane, p. 26.

223 Thompson.

224 Lane, D 1993, *Trial and Error*, p. 27.

225 Contract work enabled the company to allocate 'bad' ground to militants and rich ore bodies to 'sweethearts', and suspend miners for petty breaches.

Figure 11.1 Fred Thompson addressing union members during the Mt Isa dispute, 1964–65.

Reproduced with the kind permission of Loma Thompson

Figure 11.2 Thompson addressing the same rally, Mt Isa, 1964–65.

Reproduced with kind permission of Loma Thompson

This was unacceptable to the company, and following a number of rebel meetings, over which Mackie presided having ousted the AWU, Mackie was dismissed by the company for failing to turn up for a shift. On 10 December 1964, the government declared a State of Emergency, ordering employees to report for work, not refuse contract or piece work, to confer within five days and to bring any disputed issues to the Commission for resolution.[226]

When Pat Mackie was dismissed it was an AWU issue, but when Fred's members were stood down along with all other employees, the AEU became part of the dispute. The AEU moved to ensure all the available state apparatus was mobilised to get the matter to the conference table. These conferences were held in the Buffalo Hall and over 1000 people would assemble outside. Fred reported the hostility towards AWU officials was so bad they were mobbed, and when they emerged their car was overturned. Little wonder then that by the first week in January 1965 at least 70 per cent of the miners had joined the Broken Hill–based Barrier Industrial Council, located 1500 kilometres to the south. They were

---

[226] Lane, D 1993, *Trial and Error*, p. 27.

determined to build a new union! The Queensland Trades and Labour Council (QTLC) organised funds, food and for moratoriums on workers' hire purchase and rate repayments. By mid January the dispute reached a crisis point when the company agreed to all conditions but not to reinstate Pat Mackie. According to Thompson, with the benefit of hindsight:

> It was at this point I reckon I made my greatest mistake of my industrial life. I knew one thing … there's no such thing as a 100% victory for the working class. If they get stuck on a track to a total victory, they get done like a dinner, so I capitulated. Had we returned to work without Mackie's reinstatement, we would have held the new organisation intact and have been able to continue the struggle for Mackie's reinstatement. But because we rejected that action, it then enabled the Queensland Government to bring down repressive legislation, including anti-picketing legislation, and to place a large body of Special Branch police in the Isa.[227]

Don Lane, who was a member of that special branch contingent, describes the government's measures as 'an amazing piece of legislative overkill under the auspices of a premier (Frank Nicklin) who has not suffered the historical backlash of such draconian decisions as did Premier Sir Joh Bjelke-Peterson'. Lane claimed that the QTLC's Jack Egerton[228] was privately anxious to resolve the dispute as the Labour Council had lost control of it to Mackie.[229]

While Thompson expresses the view that Mackie behaved impeccably throughout the dispute and would have accepted a decision to accept the company's offer without his reinstatement, he points out the decision to prolong it had severe ramifications, including a black list of 47 unionists, a total dismantling of the new miners' union and acute divisions within the Mount Isa trade union movement. However, the dispute was undoubtedly of national significance in terms of the downstream gains it did deliver. US parent company ASARCO sold down its holding to a minority position and management of the mine was fully transferred to Australian managers. The IC settlement conferences under Commissioner Harvey resolved almost all of the safety and economic issues of the dispute, and following the most

---

[227] Thompson.

[228] Later disgraced and disowned by the movement for accepting a knighthood from Sir Joh Bjelke-Peterson.

[229] Lane, D 1993, *Trial and Error*, 28–31.

Figure 11.3 "On the track": organising in the Northern Territory, 1960s.

Reproduced with kind permission of Loma Thompson

significant restructure of its history, the company and its workforce enjoyed over 20 years of industrial calm. The AWU put two organisers into the field in Mount Isa and began to work jointly with the AEU there, in Mary Kathleen and other mines.

What is less well known is that the dispute arose against a backdrop of many years of detailed research by Fred. That research involved understanding the union-busting activities of MIM's parent company in other countries, and that through AWU inertia and company greed the workforce was still subject to the ramifications of a wage freeze implemented during the Second World War. As his son Peter recalls:

> One of the great advantages of Freddie's CPA training was that although he left school very early, he had been taught to go and do research. His mentors in the unions in Melbourne said, 'Go to the right

records son, look 'em up. Once you've got the information, you've got the drop on 'em.'[230]

Thus in crafting the restructure and agreements in the aftermath of the Mount Isa dispute we can observe gains won directly as a result of Fred's early training to research and analyse the corporate and industrial backdrop to events in which he was participating. The lead up to this mining dispute demonstrates Fred's strategic responses to information were rolled out over many years as he built necessary power bases through coalitions of unions and community support.

> The thing about Freddie Thompson is that, a long time ago, he decided that you could think your way through life, so he will think about an issue and adopt a philosophical position and stand by that position. He's sometimes changed his mind but by and large he's done a pretty good job of picking the winners.[231]

In the Mount Isa dispute Fred was dispassionate enough to admit a tactical error in its conduct, but it was his underpinning investment in building knowledge and support that delivered a share of company profits to all workers.

It also had a major impact on Fred's health; one that saw his war service injuries flare up in the following year and led to his admission for four months inpatient treatment at the Heidelberg Repatriation Hospital.

It was in Papua New Guinea (PNG) that Fred encountered Indigenous Australians serving in the forces. When he moved to the north his work for the AEU across North Queensland and the Northern Territory saw him routinely confronted with systemic racism. In Queensland, Aboriginal people held 'under the Act' were legally discriminated against with restricted rights of movement, marriage, residence and ownership; they had no voting rights or access to justice; were subject to the arbitrary removal of their children; and were paid low wages or not at all for their work.[232] Fred's response to witnessing a litany of officially sanctioned thefts, murders, assaults and indignities against Indigenous people was to work with others in the trade union movement in Cairns to assist Indigenous leaders like Joe McGuiness and Gladys McShane to establish

---

[230] Walley-Thompson, P, quoted in Sellars, N 2001, *Fred Thompson*, p. 157.

[231] Walley-Thompson, P, quoted in Sellars, N 2001, *Fred Thompson*, p. 162.

[232] *Aborigines Preservation and Protection Act* and the *Torres Strait Islanders Act 1939*.

what was known as the Aboriginal and Torres Strait Islanders Association in 1956.

The Association, with the support of the trade union movement, held a number of conferences in Cairns, Innisfail and Townsville. These were pivotal in the campaign to raise national awareness of the issues that led to the overwhelmingly successful 1967 referendum. Following the referendum, Fred was instrumental in the organisation of a significant conference: 'After the Referendum. What?' Its organisation divided the community in Townsville, particularly within the Roman Catholic and Anglican churches, as it marked the beginning of the campaign for the removal of Queensland's discriminatory legislation and mission systems. Fred was also involved in the emerging Northern Territory land rights movement, having driven Frank Hardy to the strike at Wave Hill Station in 1967 where Hardy helped Vincent Lingiari and others draft the Gurindji petition to the Governor-General.[233] His work for the AEU enabled Fred to play an influential enabling role beyond industrial issues and there is no better example of this than his involvement in Indigenous rights. Fred observed:

> In a fairly short period of a decade, around '57 to '67 the organisation of the Aboriginal and Islanders had grown to the stage where it could and ought to be standing on its own two feet. Those of us who had been members immediately started to withdraw from the organisation. But the backup was always there ... The message for me was, if you can assist you do, but you don't interfere.[234]

To analyse the contribution of Fred Thompson means understanding the linkages between his family life and his community, political and industrial work. People all over North Queensland and the Territory knew Freddie as an organiser and enabler. He was someone to whom others turned for wise counsel and this spilled into his family life:

> I didn't realise until many years later how lucky I was to have been around the likes of Aboriginal activists Pat O'Shane and Eddie Mabo, author Alan Marshall, anthropologist Fred Rose, poet Kath Walker, musicians Geoff Wills, Don Henderson and Margaret

---

[233] Gurindji petition to Lord Casey, Governor-General, 19 April 1967, National Archives of Australia, Darwin.

[234] Thompson.

Kitamura, union leaders like Laurie Carmichael, John Halfpenny, Gerry Hennessey and Pat Mackie.[235]

Family was incredibly important to Fred. 'They were an essential part of me and I just pined for my wife and kids.'[236] So wherever possible, Fred scheduled his travel to ensure he was never away for more than a fortnight. Even so, political activity and discussion were an everyday feature of life at home. Fred's wife Loma says, 'They used to call our house Mecca. There were a lot of people who used to come and stay.'[237] These included CPA and union officials, performers, Indigenous activists, artists, writers and intellectuals. Fred's son Peter Whalley-Thompson describes a backyard social function:

> I got to see Freddie and Loma in amongst their peers and my strongest impression is ... a sort of Godfather-like role. People would come to Freddie and show some deference; they'd ask his opinion but there was no fear, no terrible authority. It was something much warmer than what you get from the connotations of a godfather. He was very much respected as a leader and somebody who was consulted on matters of consequence, so he was a fairly serious person in those settings, not prone to having much to drink, not prone to telling jokes or being the life of the party.[238]

When Fred finally retired from the union in 1976 his protégé Tom Barton was elected to the North Queensland organiser's position. Barton's early training from Fred obviously stood him in good stead, as he took on a state-wide research role and then went on to lead the QTLC before entering the Queensland Parliament prior to a distinguished ministerial career. Fred went on to have what son Peter Whalley-Thompson described as the liberation of his 'third life'. Rather than give up on his politics after the demise of the CPA, Fred's horizons expanded into new fields and he took up new paid employment working in a pottery. He and Loma remained active in the community organising campaigns for local flood mitigation works, fostering the local arts community, through board and society memberships, community health organisations and gardening. Son Roger Thompson

---

[235] Wilson, J. quoted in Sellars, N 2001, *Fred Thompson*, p. 149.

[236] Thompson.

[237] Thompson, L, quoted in Sellars, N 2001, *Fred Thompson*, p. 148.

[238] Walley-Thompson, P, quoted in Sellars, N 2001, *Fred Thompson*, p. 153.

explains, 'They bring their ability to organise to bear on these organisations which are often a loose grouping of people that have a similar complaint but not knowing too much about it or what to do.'[239]

Fred's contact with his union never really ended. The year before his death, he addressed a conference of apprentices at the invitation of the Queensland state secretary, where he spoke at length of his lifelong fight for improved training and conditions for young metalworkers. He told Queensland State Secretary Andrew Dettmer, 'I was incredibly moved when they gave me a standing ovation. You've got gold there. They are rolled gold.'[240] Fred passed away in 2011.

What made Fred such an influential and successful union organiser over such a long period of time? Fred always took a long, strategic view of events and opportunities, and he had a rare capacity to build alliances that transcended his own political and industrial affiliations. As a consequence, Fred had an ability to not only resuscitate his own union in the far north, but to work with broad coalitions to build new, progressive organisations from scratch.

A century before Fred's career, 26 immigrant engineers formed the first Australian branch of the Amalgamated Society of Engineers in Sydney in 1852. Of these, one, John Davies, would later travel to Melbourne to organise a union branch there, while another, George Newton, would leave Sydney following an unsuccessful strike to form a new branch in Newcastle. A third of their number, DC Dagliesh, would in 1860 be elected as the first generally recognised labour member of the NSW Legislative Assembly. Fred's career bears comparison with these: he stands in the great organising traditions of his union.

---

[239] Thompson, R, quoted in Sellars, N 2001, *Fred Thompson*, p. 172.

[240] Dettmer, A, interview with the author, *np*, 20 November 2012.

Chapter 12

Unity Commands Respect

Memories of EZ

Glenys Lindner

My older brother, Leigh, younger sister, Robyn, and I were raised as zinc workers' children. Our family has worked at the Electrolytic Zinc Works for three generations. If we were tradesmen we joined the Amalgamated Metal Workers Union. Otherwise we were members of the Zinc Worker's Union. The zinc works were established by the Electrolytic Zinc Company at Risdon beside the Derwent River, Hobart, in 1916. My family has had a long association with the Electrolytic Zinc Company (EZ). Many of my childhood memories are intrinsically linked with EZ.

My grandfather Maurice 'Dude' McQueeney was born in Queenstown in 1899. Dude was only ever known as Dude to everyone as far as I can tell. Queenstown is a mining town on the rugged west coast of Tasmania. Queenstown has always been a town dependant on mining, as are Zeehan and Rosebery. The zinc processed at the plant in Risdon is mined at Rosebery, a stone's throw from the town Dude was born.

Dude and his mother and siblings moved to Hobart in the early part of the century. He enlisted in the Army as part of the 40th Battalion, an all-Tasmanian battalion, in 1918. After training in Claremont, Tasmania (the site of the present-day Cadbury's Factory), and Fovant, England, Dude was sent to fight in France. He arrived in October 1918. Luckily, Armistice was declared on 11 November 1918. Dude was returned to Australia in 1919, and lived with his mother in North Hobart.

Dude started working at EZ as a general labourer on 19 October 1920. He was laid off on 5 January 1921. It was during this time Dude met my Nan, Gladys Knight. Nan lived with her Grandmother, Eliza Morley, in Argyle St, North Hobart. Nan worked at the Henry Jones Jam Factory at Hunter St in Hobart. Ironically, this factory is now an exclusive hotel, decorated in

Figure 12.1 Maurice 'Dude' McQueeney.

shabby 'jam' chic. Dude and Gladys met at the wharf, Dude walked Nan home every day. The couple quite clearly loved each other deeply, but they were an unusual pair. Dude was from a strong Catholic trade union family, while Gladys, a Methodist, was an aspirational Churchill supporter with a vehement hatred of Catholicism. After a short courtship they married in the front room of the Argyle St house and made their home with Eliza. My Uncle Syd was the first of their children, followed by Aunty Peg and finally, much later, my father Paul.

Luckily, Dude was re-employed for approximately 15 months on the furnaces at EZ around mid 1921. The price of zinc crashed during the

Figure 12.2 Dude McQueeney at work in the Leaching Division.

Great Depression, so securing employment was difficult. Dude was a member of the Zinc Worker's Union, but it was never really discussed. Nan ruled the house with an iron fist, so I imagine she would have put a stop to any of that talk. As a child I was regaled with stories about the lines of men outside the gates at EZ during the Depression. I was told someone from management would come out each day and take the number of men they needed and the rest would go home until everybody lined up again the next day.

Finally, Dude was re-engaged on the 19 November 1922 in the Leaching Division.

In 1951 Dude was promoted as a crane driver in the Leaching Division. Unfortunately, Dude suffered ill health – when he became ill he was given a job as a change room attendant. This was a job given to those workers who were no longer able to work on the floor. Dude was presented his long service award in 1961, retired shortly after and died in 1963. Dude received a beautiful silver tray, inscribed with details of his 40 years of service. One of my jobs as a child was to polish the silver (mainly it was the tray). I'd pour the Silvo, clean the cutlery and finish with the tray. It would then go back into the wall unit.

One of the family stories that encouraged my brother, sister and I to fight injustice was the story of Dude's ill health and early death. I have no idea if it were true or not, but we were raised to believe that Dude's illness was caused by damaged lungs, which everyone refused responsibility for. We were told the War Department refused to support him because it was damage caused by his EZ employment, while EZ blamed his war experience of being gassed during allied troop training.

The first manager of EZ was Herbert Gepp. Gepp ran the plant in a paternalistic style, but encouraged employee contribution in the Cooperative Council. The Cooperative Council ran from 1918 to 1994, and was made up of employee and management representatives. The council provided cheap goods at the community store, accommodation at the 'company village' of Lutana, assistance in buying homes, a health service, and sports and picnics for employees.

I would hear stories of the community store. This seemed like an amazing place. No matter what you wanted it could be 'got' there. I don't know how it was 'got', and thinking about it now, goods were obviously purchased by the community cooperative and sold with minimal mark-ups. I know people who bought socks, electric frying pans, kettles and dinner sets. It didn't seem to matter what you wanted the store could provide it.

The community store was where you were issued your work supplies. You would be issued boots, overalls, safety goggles, helmets and so on. EZ also issued towels. My Nan's house was full of EZ towels. They were white with a 5 cm stripe of dark red running up the length. The words 'Electrolytic Zinc Coy' were emblazoned up the middle of the towel. Every time we had a bath at Nan's out would come the EZ towels. As time went on the towels were used as bath mats. Sometime in the mid to late 1970s the towels were no longer issued and a plain old serviceable stripy towel was issued. They just weren't the same. I feel sure that with a hunt around one of us will still have an old EZ towel somewhere, they were hard to kill.

Blueys were also issued. Blueys were felted blue three-quarter coats. They were heavy and stiff. The coat could stand up in the corner all by its self. We just sent our last remaining one to the opportunity shop. It still looked as new as the day it came into the house.

Figure 12.3 (top) Company Village, Cook Street Lutana.

Figure 12.4 EZ view from the punt.

EZ's community cooperative organised a picnic day each year. The picnic was held at Long Beach, Sandy Bay, just south of Hobart. It was held around the end of February, early March. All the workers and families could attend

Figure 12.5 The Ladies Committee, Nan, Gladys McQueeney and Cousin Jacqueline Carrick, in the back row.

– as EZ is a 24-hour plant, some men were still required to work. My Nan, Aunty Peg and Cousin Jacqueline were active in the Ladies Committee. I think it was their life mission to make sure that picnics went smoothly. Everything depended on it.

We would be scrubbed clean (I mean this in the most literal sense), dressed in our best clothes and made to sit on the couch until everyone was ready. The oldest would be first and work down to the baby. The oldest had to be boss so that Mum could get ready. Sitting quietly on the couch usually ended up in a punch-up and someone would be crying. Isn't every special event like that? We would be getting sick with the excitement. A nudge leads to a push etc., etc. So finally Mum would sort us out and off we would go. Getting to Sandy Bay took ages. When we arrived, there were families as far as the eye could see. Everyone had a blanket and picnic baskets were open. We didn't care what was in the picnic basket, there was stuff to do.

A carousel was always set up and kids had rides. My first picnic memory revolves around trying to get on the carousel. It was necessary to have a ticket to get on the ride and I didn't have one. The line for the carousel was about 40 kids long. It was miles! I couldn't figure out for the life of me how to get a ticket. I couldn't find my brother so he couldn't help. My sister was too little and I wasn't interested in her. Eventually I found my father, he told me to stop being silly and just go ask for a ticket. So I did and went

Figure 12.6 EZ horse stables on Derwent Park Road.

on the ride. The carousel had wooden horses, all painted dappled grey with incredibly coarse manes and tails. They were suspended from the top at front and back, it was possible to really get them swinging and rocking about. The thrill was not only in the ride, but running about like maniacs.

I am fairly sure, but not entirely, that we were given a sav in bread. Mum didn't approve of saveloys so we would have treated them with suspicion. I do remember though, with absolute certainty, we were given an icy pole and a bag of lollies. Races were undertaken all day: sack races, egg and spoon races, three-legged races and wheelbarrow races. Everyone would compete. We weren't the sort of kids who ever won anything, so I don't know if there were prizes or ribbons, or division tallies. Who knows? The day was about fun and sun.

There is a continuing story about how Aunty Peg was diddled out of a trophy at picnic day. The story goes that she won a race, but someone else's name was already engraved on the trophy, so Aunty Peg was given a second place. Aunty Peg was bitter to the day she died. Uncle Ferg carries the story for her.

During the 1920s the plant grew. It employed 1300 employees. The work was often hard manual labour, made harder because of dust and sulphur fumes. The plant operated 24 hours a day, so most workers were on as shift workers. During the early years, horses were used across the plant.

The stables still exist, as does the original cobblestone road from the stables across the hill to the plant.

The company provided hot showers, employment security, Christmas bonuses and training programs with priority for zinc workers' children. Promotions mostly came from within EZ.

Zinc Works 1920

EZ was a secure site until recently, guards were on the gates, no one went in or out without being checked. An EZ story that amused us greatly throughout our childhood involved getting one over the security guards. One smart employee drove out with a shiny, empty trailer. The guards were suspicious of the driver's smug smile, so they searched the trailer all over but could find no evidence of stolen goods or 'foreigners' – items built for personal benefit and use during work time using EZ materials and equipment. The guard reluctantly waved the driver through. Later it was revealed that the cunning man had built his whole trailer, tyres and all, courtesy of EZ.

'Foreigners' were a common feature of every workplace. My husband also tells a trailer story. A fellow had a chit for the personal purchase of a bag of superphosphate. He was permitted to drive in, as the bag was too heavy to carry. He drove up to the front gate, showed the chit to the guards and drove on. He took tyres out of the boot, attached them to a trailer, made at the Casting Workshop. He then hooked up the brand new free trailer and drove out the back gate. When the security guard checked, yes, he was leaving with the one bag of superphosphate. Scant regard was paid to the trailer.

It was possible to get private work undertaken at EZ for a minimal fee. My father, Paul, had a canvas canopy made in the Sewing Room for the trailer. This provided us shelter on our adventures around Tasmania.

In 1923 Dude and Nan received a war service loan and built a home in Peronne Avenue, Moonah. The house was among street after street of war service homes, most built in the modern Californian bungalow style. The new house was close to EZ, within walking distance to lovely shops and the train station. Dude could easily get to work on the EZ train. My Uncle Syd was a bachelor and lived a long and happy life in the Peronne Avenue house his parents built. Uncle Syd was very comfortable in Moonah with his mother – he always warned us about the dangers of living in Lutana, as according to him there was a boiler that could explode, and if it did it would take the whole of Lutana out with it.

Figure 12.7 (top) The trailer canopy Paul had made.

Figure 12.8 Leigh, Glenys and Robyn at the caravan with Uncle Syd. We certainly had a tight grip on our Barbie dolls.

While EZ began as a benevolent employer, this didn't continue. By the mid 1930s barely average wages were paid. In 1936 the Zinc Workers' Union was formed and the union won a 40-hour week and other improvements. My family were all members of the union.

In the late 1930s my Uncle Syd began employment at EZ. He continued on at the Hobart Technical College and received his electrical qualifications. Uncle Syd was the real success story of the family. He was on 'staff', a part of management. He had made it! We were all in awe of the staff privileges at EZ. Uncle Syd was permitted to use a motorcycle from the pool to scoot around the site. As EZ was a secure site I never saw him ride, but I believe it must have been an awesome sight. It was great to be related to someone who had scooting rights. Well worth bragging to the other kids about. No walking for my uncle!

All EZ property was defined by a white post and rail fence, car parks, golf club and private grassed areas. The enormous car park at the EZ front gates also had this post and rail fence. When waiting for someone in the car park, there was nothing else to do but look at the fence. Uncle Syd always had two cars. One he would take to work and the other definitely didn't go to the plant. The methods used in zinc processing created sulphur dioxide, the sulphur dioxide dust would float all over the plant. When it landed on your car it would create little pits and ruin the paintwork. Uncle Syd constantly fretted about the state of his 'duco'. We all knew what would happen and warned everyone of the dangers of leaving a car at the plant.

Uncle Syd's final role at EZ was as an electrical engineer. He retired in the mid 1980s; automation had taken its toll. Uncle Syd decided to retire and allow a younger worker to continue on. We were so fortunate to have Uncle Syd in our lives. He had made it into the big time at EZ, and the company gave a great Christmas party for the staff's children.

This was the one time of the year that we went beyond the guards at the gate. This was serious business, there was to be no mucking about. If we disappointed the grown-ups it would have been 'off with our heads'. We went past the booth and into the plant. Well, sort of into the plant. Actually, we went past the gate, immediately veered to the right and went to the giant orange brick administration building. But it felt like we were inside. In front of the admin building there was a teardrop garden, filled with flowering annuals. Thinking about it, they must have been very hardy annuals. The driveway for the admin building went around the garden, creating a roundabout effect. There were about 10 steps to the front door; it was clearly designed in the late 1940s, early 1950s. It was a multi-storied building, the doors and window frames were made of steel. It was designed to impress and it certainly impressed me.

Once through the front doors we would head off to the ground floor function room. The room was at the back of the building – it was long and thin. You entered the room from the north, there were long picture windows facing east. The site dropped away below the windows so the view was of the river and a geographical site called Bedlam Walls, a sheer

Figures 12.9 and 12.10 Uncle Sydney McQueeney.

sandstone cliff face with caves dotted along it. The cliffs looked like they were almost in the room with you. The floor was polished parquetry. There were serving hatches providing access to a kitchen on the western wall. The serving hatches had stainless steel bench tops; they were incredibly shiny. The whole room was shiny.

Mum wasn't allowed to come; we were accompanied by Nan. We all had Christmas hats snapped into position – you weren't to touch the hat, it was placed on your head and the elastic was snapped hard enough under your chin so that everyone understood who was boss. And that boss was Nan! There was a trestle table set up in the middle of the room, food may have been served, or not. We didn't care about the food. Santa came at the end of the day, we were mystified how he knew we would be there and how he knew our names. The boys all got a boy present and the girls all got a girl present. The gender divide was clear and unbreachable. Still, this was not what we were excited about.

There were three overwhelmingly special features to the Christmas party. The first was an ice cream called a 'Dixie'. It was produced in a little cardboard cup. You would be given a little wooden paddle instead of a spoon. These ice creams were expensive; your parents could never afford one. They were outside of your everyday life. They were LUXURY!

The second was a train ride. The motorised train and little carriages would go around and around the circular garden out the front of the administration building. We could go on it for ages. It wasn't everyday such a treat was available.

But the best ever was seeing John Sidney, a Tasmanian musician and performer. He had his own show on television and he was there to give us a show. John Sidney had something no one else in the world had – he had a ventriloquist doll. The doll's name was Charlie and he was exactly like a real person. We would all be sitting cross-legged on the floor and John Sidney would come on stage. He would sit down and place a suitcase next to him. Then the show would start, out of the suitcase would come Charlie and we would be howling with laughter. Charlie was the best – John Sidney was good, but Charlie was the best. We would get some songs, some jokes and some stories; John Sidney played the piano well. A boy would be picked on, because that was fun then (actually, probably still is). I really loved the show; my brother and my sister loved the show. We went home very happy children.

When John Sidney passed away in 2002 he was buried with Charlie. Charlie was the best.

My Aunty Peg (Evelyn McQueeney) met her future husband, Fergus Carrick, at the wharf in Hobart. Uncle Ferg was serving with the New Zealand Navy and Aunty Peg was visiting his ship with her friend Dorne. He walked her home and Aunty Peg said goodnight at the gate. Evidently, Uncle Ferg thought Aunty Peg was quite nice; he wanted to see her the next day but couldn't remember where she lived. He went to every house on Albert Road, door knocking until someone told him where he should look. They undertook a romance by correspondence; Uncle Ferg married Aunty Peg as soon as she turned 21 (the legal age of marriage). Uncle Ferg started work at EZ in the Leaching Division in the early 1950s. He was issued with cotton leggings and wooden clogs.

My father, Paul McQueeney, was considerably younger than his siblings. He started work at EZ in the early 1960s and also worked in the Leaching Division. Paul and Mum initially lived at Peronne Avenue but moved to Risdon Vale, a new public housing area. Geographically this area was on the opposite bank of the River Derwent to the EZ plant. The Derwent was only served by two bridges: one at Bridgewater and one in town, the Tasman Bridge. You could almost see EZ from our house in Risdon Vale, but to drive from one to another was quite a distance. The tyranny of distance was overcome by the Risdon Punt. The punt traversed the river from the eastern side of the river at Risdon Vale to the western side, almost outside the Leaching Division. Some magical and mystical person would drive us to the punt. I didn't care who, the adventure of the punt was almost overwhelming, and the important thing was getting on. We would wait in the line and when the punt reached the shore, there were bangs and clangs, grinding, growling, while the punt settled down to take us over the river. The yellow 'submarine cable' sign was right in front of us. In my five-year-old mind a submarine cable had to mean submarines were about! About six or eight cars would fit on the punt. The cars went on in single file, but would park two a breast. Hopefully your car would be first on! Just a single chain was placed across the front of the punt. It seemed as though your car would fall clean off, only magic held the car on. We jumped out of the car as soon as the driver permitted. We were quite rambunctious children, so we were probably let out earlier than other children. The water was so close to us, it appeared as though death was imminent. It was SOOO exciting. I kept a vigilant eye out for the submarines, but never saw one. Mum recalls the punt was very inexpensive. It really saved the day during the 1970s – a section of the Tasman Bridge was destroyed when it was hit by the *Lake Illawarra* on 5 January 1975. The punt was used extensively by emergency services when the only crossing available was at Bridgewater, a distance of 30 km each way. The Risdon Punt was closed when a third bridge was built.

As a result of the Menzies government 'credit squeeze' policy, my parents were unable to borrow money. They had to wait until interest rates dropped to be able to purchase their first home. Mum still gets quite cross about being unable to borrow money. They ended up buying in Glenorchy right next door to my Aunty Peg and Uncle Ferg, and on the same side of the river as the EZ.

Zinc Works 1960

Crib is the common name given to mineworkers' meals. As far as I am aware crib is short for cribbage; cribbage is the style of mine construction where overlapping beams provide structural support in corners. Probably men had their meals in places like this, where the cribbage provided the most protection from rock falls. The meal has taken up the name from the meal area. Crib rooms were provided all around the plant. Men would have their crib in the crib rooms. A small stove was provided; these were called choofers, so named because of the choofing noise they made once really heated up. My family would all take their crib in little tin bowls called a dixie. I suppose the dixie is named after the manufacturer, although I really don't know. The tin was circular with a much smaller base than top, a small lid would fit on and be held secure with three clips that were slid around. The tin lid had a Bakelite knob. The tin had a very specific shape and all tins were the same. The dixie was the precursor to modern Tupperware. The dixie would sit on top of the choofer so the meal was heated for crib. Some of the older dirty blackened crib rooms existed at EZ right up to the mid 1980s. Every crib room would have a cribbage board. Every worker learned to play cribbage.

Mum and Paul never quite seemed to have their act together. Crib was a hit or miss affair. Workers usually took their crib with them, but Paul didn't always have his. Mum would pile all the kids in the car and we would be driven like there was no tomorrow to get Paul his crib. A road went right through the plant, cyclone wire fences stretched along either side of it. By entering at the northern end you would go past the abattoirs, the old manager's house and the superphosphate plant. We would stand up at the massive cyclone wire Leach gates. Paul would trundle out and we would throw his crib over the three metre high fence. Mum would throw us all back in the car and off we would speed again, out through the southern end of the plant and on to Risdon Road.

A train service took workers to EZ; the train would enter the northern end of the plant. We went on the train a couple of times to pick Paul up. We never got off, so goodness knows what was outside, where it stopped or what

Figure 12.11 My brother, Leigh McQueeney, and my future husband, Peter Lindner, at the machine shop in 1980.

happened. We would just run up and down the carriages until we got back to Nan's in Moonah.

As an EZ worker's child (and a boy), my brother, Leigh, was offered any apprenticeship he wanted. Us girls were not allowed to be involved in EZ business, except for the social activities. There was never any thought that we might want or need an apprenticeship. As girls, we were also completely shut out of any union talk. I vaguely recall having to wait in the car while adults ran in and out of the Zinc Workers Union office in Moonah. At 15, I started work at the Government Printing Office and was handed a form, which I took home to Mum. When I asked her what it was, her answer was short and simple: 'It is a union form – fill it in'. So, my first union was the Printing and Kindred Industries Union, which later amalgamated into the AMWU. And I have been a union member ever since. The women in the family joke that we have a 'no ticket, no start' policy in the bedroom. Well, some of them are joking.

All Leigh wanted and lived for was to be a motor mechanic, but this was the only apprenticeship that Leigh couldn't get. He started his fitting and turning apprenticeship at EZ in 1979. Although EZ was a closed shop and union membership was compulsory, apprentices could choose whether to join the union. Leigh immediately joined the AMWU. By 1979, a bus service was available. The route was a public bus service route, but it was timed specifically to get zinc workers to and from their shifts. My brother would jump on his 10-speed bike and race the bus to work. He was very well pleased with himself when he beat it. The bonuses paid at Christmas time were phenomenal. I couldn't believe how much money was paid. In 1982 Leigh was given a $1800 bonus.

One day, Leigh brought home a fellow fitting and turning apprentice, Peter Lindner. Peter was a bloody good looking bloke. I thought he was good enough to marry, so I did. Peter was a member of the AMWU, eventually as a delegate at Incat International, a shipyard built on the site of the old abattoir abutting EZ.

The End of a Family History

Uncle Syd died peacefully in the family home at Moonah in 1998. Uncle Ferg is still going strong and has just turned 91 (he is waiting for his second hip replacement). Aunty Peg passed away in 2011, leaving a son, Ian, and a daughter, Jacqueline (whose husband, Denis, worked at the EZ laboratories).

Leigh is now living in Queensland, working as a nurse, and has two children: Joel and Ruth. Peter is now working as a bus driver and we have two children, Rose and Jim, both trade union members. My sister, Robyn, has one daughter, Winona, and is a proud AMWU member.

Our family association with the Electrolytic Zinc Company has finished now. But the childhood memories are fantastic and give us a fundamental link to AMWU. Thanks for the memories, EZ.

Chapter 13

A Self-contained City

Metalworkers and the Midland Railway Workshops, 1904–1994

Ric McCracken

A working relationship/friendship of over 30 years is uncommon in this day and age. My father, Frederick Foreman McCracken, 1915–1965, worked for one employer for his whole working life: Olympic Tyre and Rubber Company. I've worked for 23 different employers, so far, in at least five different careers, and I'm not dead yet.

When you think about metalworkers in the twentieth century, you think about relationships and employers. Employers had a tendency to be big. Relationships were often tight. In smaller workshops, battles were personal and usually short; if you lost you left. In larger workshops, battles could be more constructed and the individual had more chance of survival.

My official introduction to the Midland Railway Workshops, a government workshop in the east of Perth, was hearing a talk by the last timekeeper, a lifelong employee, Kevin Mountain, at an open day in 1999. Kevin said:

> The Workshops, in my opinion, was a self-contained city. Apart from all the core tasks, normal duties and special constructions by a very proficient workforce, you could obtain food from the canteen, ranging from an on-site made pie or pastry to a sit-down one-course meal at the cost of one shilling and six pence. You did have to provide your own eating irons. You could get your hair cut for two bob on Block One. You could hire a dance band – I was aware of three dance bands in the Workshops. You could hire one of five magicians. You could hire a ventriloquist; even a Punch and Judy Show. You could purchase eggs, fruit and vegetables from various workmates. You could have a bet on the races. You could borrow money from the moneylenders.

We also had many State Champions in growing flowers. We had a State Champion orchid grower. We had a State Champion chrysanthemum grower; I believe he is now judging chrysanthemums. We had the State Champion gladiolus and the State Champion cacti and succulents.

We produced many champion athletes in most sports. We had our own football team in the Sunday League competition; they were known as the Right Angles.[241]

This is a very rich description of a workplace and a lifestyle, with not a mention of a union. And yet unions were central to life at the workshops.

At the Midland Railway Workshops [Government Railway Workshops] in Western Australia, 1904 to 1994, we had WA's largest industrial manufacturing and maintenance establishment. The vision was formulated by legendary State Engineer Charles Yelverton O'Connor as a manufacturing and skills development base. A weakness in engineering skills had been identified by O'Connor as a result of the 1893 gold rushes in the Eastern Goldfields: WA's population was expanding rapidly, its industrialisation needs were changing from agrarian output to mineral output, but the speculative miners were not bringing in the manufacturing skills needed. The first railway in WA, constructed from Geraldton to Northampton and opened in 1878, was built to facilitate the export of galena lead from hand-worked mines. All rolling stock and locomotives used were imported. First established at Fremantle in 1893, the government railway workshops were moved to Midland in 1903–04 by O'Connor; he needed more land at Fremantle for his redesigned port, and Midland, at the other end of the suburban line, provided the site. CY O'Connor also achieved fame for the Mundaring to Kalgoorlie water pipeline.

Historian Charlie Fox identifies 10 major trade groupings at the Midland Workshops:

At the beginning the Workshops were organised around 10 trades: car and wagon builders, boilermakers, blacksmiths, turners, fitters, coppersmiths, moulders, patternmakers, electricians and painters, and it added others such as carpenters later.[242]

---

241 McCracken, R 2006, 'The Workforce Cultures' in Bertola, P & Oliver, B *The Workshops: A History of the Midland Government Railway Workshops*, UWA Press, Nedlands, p. 200.

242 Fox, C 'Work Organisation' in Bertola, P & Oliver, B *The Workshops: A History of the Midland Government Railway Workshops*, UWA Press, Nedlands, p. 86.

All trades and professions were unionised, and the Midland Workshops were considered to be a closed shop. The unionised activities at this, a major government workshop, are well documented. Less documented are the ancillary activities run by the blue-collar workforce. The social organisation at the workshops is both a reflection and by-product of the union organisation. If the workforce is not well organised internally, how does it produce events such as annual picnics at Coogee (a popular Perth beach), an annual camp at Busselton (in the south-west of the state), trade-specific picnics at Point Walter (on the Swan River), a welfare committee, a staffed canteen and a provident fund; all recognised by workshop management? Good union organisation breeds good social organisation. Internal organisation at the workshops is the reflection of this.

The Welfare and Canteen Committee is a prime example of worker-initiated organisation that became recognised by management. Attempts to improve the conditions for workers emanated from the shop floor. The Welfare and Canteen Committee had humble beginnings. A canteen committee – comprising C Sinclair (blacksmith), EJ Clay (belt attendant) and G Low (slotter) – was established on 23 July 1923.

> It was their function to strive to get a canteen and dining room erected for the men to have a hot appetising meal in comfortable surroundings as distinct from a cold unappetising meal at their workplaces … [but initially] they kept getting knockbacks from management because of a lack of funds.[243]

Two of these three men were elected to the first welfare committee, which was 'approved' by the Commissioner for Railways in 1925. Industrial Awards negotiated between unions and management through arbitration could not cover every contingency of safety and welfare in such a huge and complex enterprise. While the union shop stewards worked assiduously to improve conditions, management did not necessarily recognise all these issues as being within the province of the unions or arbitration. Thus the object of the Welfare and Canteen Committee was 'to promote the welfare of the staff as a whole in all matters not specifically dealt with by industrial awards'.

The committee comprised one representative from each of the major shops in the workshops. Areas represented included the car and wagon shop, boiler shop, paint shop and yard gang, ways and works, tarpaulin shop, mill

---

[243] McCracken, R 2006, 'Workforce Cultures', p. 201.

and lifters, coppersmiths and patternmakers, fitting shop, machine shop, foundry and electrical shop, and the blacksmiths shop. It is interesting to note that, while the Welfare Committee's role was 'to promote the welfare of the staff as a whole', no representative, or representative work areas for salaried staff appear to have been included until very late in the history of the workshops, when salaried workers were represented in 1992, two years before closure.

Kevin Mountain says that two of the first tasks of the Welfare Committee involved dealing with:

1. nails protruding from the wooden decking of the overhead footbridge from the Midland Junction Station to the workshops

2. motorbikes and sidecars parking illegally in the bike shed and sidecars damaging spokes in the bike wheels, and damage to pedals and cranks on bikes.[244]

Some time in the following 14 years, the Welfare Committee planned and achieved a canteen that opened in 1939, just west of the wood mill. It comprised a corrugated iron building including kitchen and servery. In 1946, the Welfare Committee was re-incorporated as the Welfare and Canteen Committee, a move that acknowledged the new role in managing and staffing the canteen.

The rules of the Midland Junction Western Australian Government Railways (WAGR) Workshops Welfare and Canteen Association Incorporated show that the Association was registered on 10 September 1946 under the *Associations Incorporations Act 1895*, and that the committee would comprise 'one member elected annually from each section of Midland Junction WAGR Workshops'. These sections were: the car and wagon shop, the sawmill and lifters and tarpaulin shop, the boiler shop, the blacksmiths shop, the machine shop and track equipment, the electrical shop and copper shop, the pattern shop, foundry and tool room and the paint shop, trimming and yard gang. All these sections on the Welfare and Canteen Committee represented blue-collar 'wages' employees. The 800 'staff', or white-collar employees, had no representation, hence no voice in the direction of the actions of the committee.

In 1953, a new purpose-built brick canteen building with a stainless steel full kitchen, cool rooms and eating areas, including a 'foreman's dining room', was officially opened by Premier Sir Ross McLarty, a divisive figure

---

[244] Mountain, K 2003, Personal correspondence, 24 July.

who had been vilified and ridiculed during the six-month metalworker's margins dispute and strike in the previous year. The 1942 timber and corrugated iron dining room adjacent was retained, now used as a games room for chess, darts and badminton until its closure in 1994.

Membership of the Welfare Committee was not by nomination or by the prerogative of senior personnel; rather, it was by direct endorsement from the employees of the particular shop. While the formal power to conduct ballots for membership of the Welfare Committee was vested in the Works Manager, under both the constitution of the Welfare Committee and the Workshops Rules, some work groups had other, less formal, more participatory ways to select their delegates.

Dave Moir, a blacksmith, remembers the time when two workmates wanted to nominate for the position of blacksmiths' shop representative on the Welfare Committee. The issue was resolved by way of a footrace around the interior of the blacksmiths shop. The interior of the blacksmiths shop was a very cluttered and dangerous space. In addition to the drop hammers, air hammers, anvils, marking-out tables, tool racks, benches, water tanks and fires, there were raw materials stacked up against the racks and benches, dog spikes stacked in bags, pallets and racks of products, and all the ancillary materials of an active workshop. There was also heat from the furnaces, the smoke and soot. The race was conducted at the appointed time with the supporters of the contestants, amid much cheering and yelling, attempting to impede their opposition by tripping with steel bars and throwing rags and other objects until the race was won. The winner became the blacksmith shop representative on the Welfare Committee.

Peter Carty, boilermaker and delegate, related another footrace between two workers for a place on the Welfare Committee, in this instance to represent the machine shop. One contestant, 'Little' Jimmy, was 'a bad-tempered little bastard', while the other 'had a gammy leg'. The race involved pushing two wheeled barrows along the roadway between the main blocks from the test room at the eastern end of the machine shop to the powerhouse just past the western end. The time was fixed on a Monday morning when all the foremen and sub-foremen went to a meeting in the main office.

So at ten o'clock we left the job, went there, thousands of bloody blokes watched the race. They run like bloody hell down there and this bloke with the gammy leg kept pushing Jimmy over and Jimmy picked something up and threw a brick at him. So, in the end we pulled his bloke aside, and somebody sat on him towards the end and Jimmy won. Well, the little bloke did the best job on the committee.[245]

These comedic nomination methods belie other roles for the Welfare Committee in the membership and purpose of the committee. Wally McManus, a trained chef from England, commenced work as a labourer in the car and wagon shop in 1977. Wally later worked as a yardman in the canteen. Wally also became the voluntary chairman of the Railway Institute [Midland Branch], a director of the Railway Institute Credit Union, and a commissioner for declarations. He was also active on the social committee. Clearly, Wally's employment as a yardman/labourer was not an impediment to important voluntary office. Dennis Day, an active communist, unionist and machinist in the workshops, was asked about the involvement of Premier McLarty in the opening of the new canteen in January 1953. He recalled in a conversation with me that 'the Midland Workshops had a Welfare Committee that took an interest in the social side of the life in the workshops. It was not considered militant.' Militant or not, it reflected the rhythms and patterns of the life of a highly unionised, engaged workforce.

Another of the functions of the Welfare Committee was administering various sickness benefit funds. In the days before sick leave became cumulative, workers received only five paid sick days per year – serious injuries or other family needs when absent from work were hardly recognised. Workers voluntarily paid a contribution each payday, which appears to have increased with pay movements and inflation, but was not a significant sum of money. If an employee was off work for longer than the allotted five days, their wages were paid from the fund. Several workers remember other services that employees rendered when a fellow worker, or family member, was injured or unwell, such as helping with lawn mowing, driving wives to hospital to visit husbands, child-minding, assistance with shopping or cash donations. They attributed some of these services to the Welfare Committee, others to spontaneous actions of support by workmates. Peter Carty acknowledges the role of the various social clubs in the workshops.

> If you got sick and you only had five days a year, so you paid into one in the machine shop, three bob [three shillings, or 30c] a pay. You paid into one in the auto shop, paid into one in the blacksmiths

---

245 McCracken, R 2006, 'Workforce Cultures', p. 203.

shop. So if you were off more than five days, some blokes were off for a month, had a heart attack, or busted toes, kids are sick, or missus is sick, you've got to stay home. You got more than your week's wages staying home, you never paid any tax and somebody would chip in for a weeks' groceries.[246]

The brick and tile 1952 purpose-built canteen was constructed by the WAGR. The souvenir program for the opening of the canteen mentions, but does not define, the canteen as 'being run under license by the Welfare and Canteen Committee' on behalf of WAGR. Employees of the Welfare Committee, that is the canteen staff, were not employees of the government, though there are some ambiguities in this. Kevin Mountain remembers the well-regarded George Brookes, first canteen manager, as being a painter prior to becoming canteen manager in 1939. There are no employment records in WAGR archives for George Brookes. However, Ray Parks, who became manager in 1979, was employed as a moulder from 1962, and his employment record shows him continuously employed as a moulder until he left the railways in the late 1980s.

There are definitely no employment records for the many 'canteen girls' who worked in the canteen from 1939 until closure in 1994. The canteen girls were for many years the only women employed in the workshops. They were invariably young girls from nearby suburbs and often daughters of workshops families, and almost invariably married workshops employees. The girls started work at 5.30 am, peeling vegetables and preparing meals. At 'morning smoko' [8.30 am, later 9.00 am] each escorted a wheeled trolley pushed by a labourer to a designated shop and sold cups of tea at one penny, later rising to threepence. A 1953 photo shows 16 canteen girls, their trolleys and attendants. At lunchtime, the girls served in the canteen and cleaned up afterwards. The Welfare and Canteen Committee was thus a direct employer of labour.

Life within the workshops was governed by a set of regulations, known colloquially as the 'King's Regs', framed, broadsheet-sized copies prominently placed in every workshop. Evidently developed and changed over time, some rules appear concerned with the minutiae of working life within the workshops and their application appears to have been selective, particularly in relation to the 'self-contained city' identified by Kevin Mountain.

---

[246] McCracken, R 2006, 'Workforce Cultures', p. 204.

The buying and selling of produce within the workshops was specifically prohibited by Sub-rule 26 [1]. Sub-rule 63 [2] prohibited money lending. While Sub-rule 27 [2] prohibited the playing of sports and games, there are photographs of a cricket match being played in the yard, and in the early 1990s I counted five basket ball hoops on various exterior walls of different shops. Betting within the workshops was also outlawed, but on the exterior wall of the electrical substation in the machine shop, adjacent to the large marking-out tables, was a painted bookies' 'slate' that showed a punter's name, race, horse number and odds. Betting evidently took place in full view of everyone who walked through.

The best known rule was Sub-rule 57 [1]: 'An employee shall not convert to his own use any material ...' and 57 [2] provided for 'summary dismissal' for breach of 57 [1]. This was intended to regulate the practice of making 'foreigners' – the making of items not covered by a works order.

'We made the tools to make the tools' is a common boast by a most proficient and skilled workshops workforce, which was intended by CY O'Connor to be fully able to do just such a thing. An example of such ability came early in 1942 when it was decided to tool up the workshop for munitions production, specifically 25 pounder shells. At the time, the machine shop was using English manufactured, Dean, Smith & Grace lathes. As more of these lathes were unavailable from Britain, an existing lathe was dismantled, measured, machined and cast with 40 new machining shop-built and equipped lathes completed in three months.

Of course, this diversity of skills and a large workforce meant that 'we made the tools to make the tools' had another aspect – workers could make anything. 'Foreigners' were numerous, very varied, frequently requiring inter-skill cooperation, were illicit and required an ability to be smuggled past the patrol officers on the gate. There was a coppersmith who came to the gate one lunchtime on his motorbike, and received permission to ride down to his shop to do some minor repairs to the spokes. Registration number duly noted and pass given, he rode in. What was not noted when the bike came back out was that it was now equipped with a beautifully finished and painted sidecar. Allegedly, there was a production line in trailers for cars. When yours was ready, you simply went to the salvage yard, paid for a trailer load of firewood, went to the gate with the receipt, got a pass for your car, drove in, hitched up the trailer, collected the firewood and drove out, proceeded to the Midland Police Station to register the trailer. This seems awfully prosaic until you consider the number of skills, the equipment required and the attachments not available from WAGR

Stores Branch, such as taillights, tyres and rims, electrical plugs and the complicity between individuals. The trailers even had false manufacturers' names stencilled on the tailgate.

A 'foreigner' story that can be sourced to both Midland in WA and Ipswich in Queensland involves the making and smuggling out of aluminium dinghies. At the same time as aluminium came into the workshops for bulk wagon production, 12- or 14-foot aluminium dinghies became popular recreational fishing accessories. It was inevitable that the two would meet. In Midland, thousands of 60-ton bulk grain and ore wagons were manufactured to such a high skill level that the Midland Workshops achieved the highly coveted AAA manufacturing classification from Lloyds of London; a classification of such pride that it was used as a key, unsuccessful, argument against the closure of the workshops in 1994.

Sneaking an aluminium dinghy out of the workshop? You can't buy them from the salvage yard, put them on your trailer and front up to the patrol officer with a receipt. The answer is so ingenious and obvious, but it requires a non-railways employee. Bottled gas was brought into the workshops by trucks. Typically, these trucks have a flat bed with metal cages to hold the gas bottles upright and in place; full bottles were brought in and empty bottles taken out. Now, if you have a cooperative driver, the bottles could be arranged in a hollow square on the back of the truck. As the truck drove through the Boiler Shop, where the dinghy had been made, a cooperative crane driver could load a dinghy into the hollow. The truck would leave the workshops and a transaction would take place, after hours, at the Commercial Hotel over the road.

There is no evidence of complicity by the gate-keeping patrol officers. In an unrecorded conversation, a young tradesman told of applying for a transfer to the position of patrol offer, thinking 'it might be a bit of a bludge or a way in to a white-collar job'. Within three months he transferred back to his trade; as a patrol officer he found himself ostracised by his workmates, abused and reviled. The only story involving the complicity of a gatekeeper is one by a homing pigeon fancier who had made a portable pigeon coop in the workshops. Over weeks he had smuggled in a pigeon each day under his shirt and had populated his coop. One day he asked the gatekeeper to release the pigeons at a set time so that his wife could time their arrival back at home. The next day, with the same attendant on duty, he drove in to collect his coop and take it home.

The vast majority of 'foreigners' were much smaller, though, and these could easily be taken out of the workshops in the ubiquitous 'Gladstone' bag. These foreigners can be classified as ceremonial or functional. In the working life of your average worker, in the twentieth century, there were three key milestones: twenty-first birthdays [which usually coincided with the end of the apprenticeship], weddings [which often came soon after] and retirement [which came 44 years later]. Many ceremonial foreigners relate to these milestones.

Twenty-first birthday keys were commonly produced. Frequently, they were chromed metal, about 15 cm × 3 cm, engraved and presented in a felt or silk-lined, carved wooden box. It required five different tradespeople to make the item: a metalworker to cut the key, the electroplaters for the chrome, the engraving [probably done by the locksmith], a woodworker for the box [made in either of the wood mill or the car and wagon shop] and a trimmer for the lining. The physical distance the key needed to travel from inception to completion was close to two kilometres.

Wedding gifts were traditionally a boxed full cutlery set. The manu-facturing team was almost identical to the birthday keys, but obviously involved more participants as more items needed to be made, and it would be too obvious to have one tradesman making so many pieces.

Retirement gifts were frequently quirky and related to individual characteristics. Jim Gillam could turn out a tow ball on request on his lathe in the machine shop in an hour. His retirement gift is a very detailed model of his Dean, Smith & Grace lathe complete with a tow ball in the jaws. 'Lance' was obviously in need of dental work. His gift is a set of cast bronze dentures, mounted on a timber plinth and engraved plaque with the wording 'Lance, the Dentists Delight, 25/6/82'. After 1988, retirement gifts could be covered by a works order upon application to the works manager, and so they ceased to be foreigners. Elaborately carved and polished nests of three occasional tables were a favoured gift. Over decades, functional foreigners were as diverse as the imagination of their makers, frequently being well-crafted items for use in the home. Foreigners as a whole are deserving of greater discussion. A book exploring foreigners at Midland Workshops has been published by Curtin University.[247]

The Midlands Railway workforce, with the advantage of comprising government employees (3500, including 800 apprentices at its peak), provided opportunities for advancement through further study, particularly in engineering. At least two men, Lukas Pitsicas and Darrald McCaskill,

[247] Harris, J (ed.) 2009, *Foreigners: Secret Artefacts of Industralisation*, Black Swan Press, Perth.

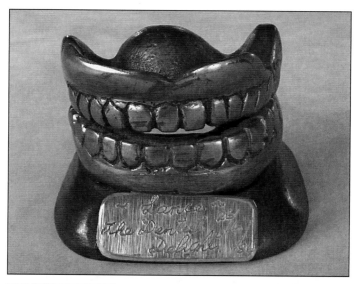

Figures 13.1 and 13.2.

Photos by Gina Pickering

started as junior workers and retired as chief mechanical engineers, an employment life of 51 years each. With such a large and diverse group, coupled with ample, shop floor organised, social events, marriages within workshops families were not uncommon. Mary Sharpe, nee Cox, had married into the Sharpe family. Her sister-in-law had married into the Christie family. Her sister, also a canteen girl, married into the Pendlbury family. Between the Cox, Sharpe and Christie clans there was a total of over 130 years of employment covering the 90 years of the workshop activity. Two other families, the Watsons and the Pendlburys, had at least one male family member at the workshops during the same full 90 years.

A final example of the power of the shop floor and the unions was the free lunchtime concert given by African-American singer Paul Robeson at the Midland Workshops in the early 1960s. In addition to his abilities as a singer and actor, Robeson was a renowned radical peace and human rights activist, and visited Perth at the conclusion of his only Australian concert tour. Earlier in the tour, Robeson had sung for construction workers at the Sydney Opera House site. Colin Hollett, a machinist at the workshop and an AMWU activist and admirer of Robeson, recalled:

> We wanted, or I wanted because I loved Paul Robeson as a person and his politics. I went into Perth where he was staying. I didn't meet Paul, I met Eslanda, his wife, and explained to her that I was the Secretary of the Joint Railways Union Committee and we would have loved to have had Paul come up and sing to us. She said, 'Oh well, he's busy now, but I'll mention it to him later'. So I left and went back home. At 2 o'clock in the morning, I got a phone call from Eslanda saying that Paul would love to go and sing to the railway workers. From then on I rang everyone I could to let them know, and then at nine o'clock I rang the Works Manager and asked if we could use the flagpole [the usual site for stop work meetings] and allow the public in, and he said no. So I had to ring around again and tell them we were having it outside and to let the general public know they did that and the Mayor came over and introduced it and half of Midland came down and there were thousands there. He sang to the workers ... and it was huge success. Thanks to the Works Manager's refusal.[248]

The concert was followed by a mayoral reception in the Midland Town Hall.

There is great difficulty in wrapping up a chapter on a place such as the Midland Workshops. It was a place of dissention and dispute, as well as hard work and cultural activity. Unions exercised considerable influence, but Midland was not all peace and power to the workers. A place such as this can be examined through any plane of a multifaceted prism and all can be seen as accurate. From the misogyny shown to the few women apprentices that came in later years, the brutality and bastardisation rituals,

---

[248] McCracken, R 2006, 'Workforce Cultures', p. 206.

the heavy industrial manufacturing and maintenance workshop, and the fear of the first day apprentice, 'it was like Dante's inferno', the 'old men's camp'. Any of these truths can fit.

You have to wonder what it would have been like to follow my father's example, go into a workplace and stick at it. Like all these folks above.

Chapter 14

The AMWU Queensland Coal Shop Stewards

John Hempseed and Chris Harper

As the Australian Manufacturing Workers Union (AMWU) celebrated its 160th anniversary as a union in 2012, it was an appropriate time to look back and reflect upon the story of the Queensland Coal Shop Stewards (QCSS) as part of the AMWU history.

The original idea of a Coal Industry Committee was brought to the Queensland State Conference and State Council by Brother Hec Hoskins, who had originally come into contact with industry committees during his employment in the steel industry at Newcastle, in New South Wales. Brother Hoskins had gained employment at a mine in Moura, 180 kilometres south-west of Rockhampton in the Dawson Valley (at the southern margin of the Bowen Basin), and saw the need for an organised approach by AMWU members to keep the different coal pits in touch with each other and to organise for better wages and conditions.

The proposed QCSS could draw on a tradition of multi-site union organisations within the AMWU and also in the coal industry. The AMWU, most notably through its predecessor the Amalgamated Engineering Union (AEU), has long relied on district committees – aggregating individual union workplaces in any particular region – as a basis for cooperative union action. Similarly, many of those unions that went on to form the AMWU have led the formation of shop committees – inter-union organisations based on major shops or workplaces: the combined shop stewards committees at railway workshops such as Ipswich (Queensland), Eveleigh (NSW) and Newport (Victoria) are good examples. At the same time, unions in the coal industry had extensive experience in combining resources to meet a variety of industrial challenges, including the consolidation of mines in the hands of fewer, though larger, companies. There was also the influence of British traditions and connections in the coal industry, traditions often transmitted through migration to Australia from British mining regions. This includes the lessons learned from the combine committees in South Wales in the years prior to the first World War, where committees representing different mines and pits owned or operated by a single employer coordinated union responses to employer industrial strategies.

While elements of all these union strategies can be identified in the QCSS, in many respects it remains unique. While its primary purpose is industrial coordination, the QCSS represents members of a single union – it is not an inter-union or combined shop committee. But neither is it a district committee. Its focus is on AMWU members across an entire industry – the coal industry in Queensland. This capacity to draw on a heritage of collective organisation while responding to the specific circumstances of the Queensland coal industry helps explain the resilience and longevity of the QCSS. While the danger of the industry helps explain some of the passion behind the QCSS and its campaigns, Hec Hoskins's original advice still holds true: while employers seem to compete, they organise together, swap information and develop communications strategies together. We, as unionists, need to combat that by sharing our ideas and our experience.

The union's newly appointed Central Queensland organiser, Ron 'Buster' Keating, was given the job of getting this committee together in Blackwater in 1974. From humble beginnings in 1974 when coal industry delegates held unpaid meetings on weekends in Blackwater (and later in Rockhampton), the Queensland Coal Shop Stewards have evolved into one of the longest surviving and successful industry or district committees in Queensland. The model developed in Queensland has now been adopted by members in other states to assist them in setting up their own industry committees.

The coal industry in Queensland in the early 1960s was predominantly based on the West Moreton coalfields around Ipswich in the south-east, with a sprinkling of mines close to government-run power stations around the state. After much coal exploration in the mid 1960s, a massive expansion took place around the Moura, Blackwater and Moranbah areas, resulting in the giant open-cut mines of today. The expansion of these areas coincided with the decline of the old Mount Morgan gold and copper belt. It was from here that a ready-made unionised workforce found employment at these new coalmines, bringing not only many union members but also union values. As the expansion took place, new towns such as Moranbah, Dysart and Middlemount were developed to house the growing workforce, while established communities such as Moura and Blackwater also benefited. Inevitably, all these communities experienced acute growing pains, and these early years were marked by disputes over housing, safety, working conditions, employment conditions and inter-union demarcation, to name a few.

This resulted in the need for a more organised structure to address such issues and for the coal mining unions to work together to get these outcomes, not always an easy task because sometimes when the unions weren't fighting against the mining companies, they were arguing over demarcation and other matters among themselves.

Initially, maintenance employees were represented by the Amalgamated Engineering Union (AEU) and Boilermakers & Blacksmith's Society prior to the amalgamations in 1973, which formed the Amalgamated Metal Workers Union. Production employees were represented by two unions, the Queensland Colliery Employees Union (Miners Federation, Queensland Branch) and the Federated Engine Drivers and Firemen's Association (FEDFA), which subsequently amalgamated, forming the United Mineworkers Federation of Australia, and now the Mining and Energy Division of the Construction, Forestry & Mining Employees Union (CFMEU). The electrical employees were represented by the Electrical Trades Union (ETU).

In 1974, the first Queensland Coal Shop Stewards meeting took place in Blackwater, chaired by Central Queensland organiser Ron Keating, with delegates attending from Goonyella, Peak Downs, Saraji, Thiess South Blackwater, Utah Blackwater, Thiess Callide, and TPM Moura & Kianga Mines. These were volatile years in the coal industry, and Hec's experiences in NSW struck a chord among coal members. The current QCSS chairman, John Hempseed, attended his first QCSS meeting in 1976 and has been a leading activist in the organisation ever since. (At that same meeting, an up-and-coming federal Labor parliamentarian, Paul Keating, 'outlined the ALP's policy in respect to minerals and energy and clarified that policy'.) Significantly, the issues raised by the coal delegates in 1974 are similar to current areas of discussion and activity: safety, apprentices, allowances, accommodation, and terms and conditions of employment. The battle is still far from won.

From 1974, one QCSS meeting was held each year, initially at Blackwater and later in Rockhampton, until 1984 when it was decided to hold two QCSS meetings annually. These meetings were funded through a levy paid by the coal industry AMWU members. These two-day meetings are preceded by a one-day steering committee meeting, funded by the Queensland state branch. At the second QCSS meeting each year, the levy paid by the membership for funding the QCSS is reviewed, and a rate set prior to being sent out to the rank-and-file membership for endorsement. This levy funds the costs of delegates to attend QCSS meetings and has allowed union delegates to attend from Ipswich in the south to Collinsville in the north. This means that there has been representation from both underground and open-cut mines over the years. This one, regional, industry committee covering all the major mining districts, has been a critical element in the success of the QCSS. At different times, QCSS meetings were held in Mackay, although since the late 1990s the AMWU Rockhampton regional office has been the regular venue.

These processes have stood the test of time and form the basis of QCSS meetings today. Along the way a constitution was developed and endorsed by the membership, as were a number of QCSS policies, including industrial issues such as the provision of work clothing, apprentices and overtime, and social issues including nuclear disarmament and support of mining communities and amenities.

A sense of community has been a constant thread in QCSS activities since its first meetings. One of the debates at the first QCSS meeting in 1974 concerned the role of contractors and employment prospects in mining towns. The Winter 2012 issue of *On the Job*, the Queensland AMWU magazine, carries an article on the influence of 'fly in, fly out' policies on mining communities, expressing concern at its impact on community amenities and quality of life.

One significant influence on the development of the QCSS in the early 1970s was the work of the AMWU National Coal Committee. The first meeting of this national committee took place in August 1973, with five delegates from Queensland, three from NSW, as well as state and national officials. Meetings of this national committee took place every two years, and soon expanded to include delegates and officials from WA and Tasmania.

In the 1960s, when the Moura field was first being developed, workers repeatedly agitated against the living conditions that they were forced to endure, such as tents and tin humpies that they had to construct themselves, either adjacent to the mine site or on any other land that they could get hold of. After sustained complaint, Justice Gallagher finally ruled on this dispute, with his determination leading to housing being built for mineworkers, initially by owners of each operation and later on by the Queensland Housing Commission.

The QCSS has always been willing to address issues of social and community significance, as well as more obvious industrial demands. There have been many disputes in the Queensland coal industry that the AMWU has been involved in, either directly or by striking a levy and financially supporting other workers in times of need. The QCSS has always been an active and enthusiastic participant or supporter, whether it be for a national log of claims (at a time when all coal industry workers were tied to the Coal Award), the housing tax dispute of 1980 in which John Howard, as Liberal federal treasurer, figured so prominently, the apprenticeship dispute of the 1980s or the SEQEB strikes in 1985 when AMWU members were active in supporting Queensland power industry workers in their dispute with the Bjelke-Petersen government's draconian industrial legislation. Similarly, the QCSS led its AMWU members into support for all mineworkers involved in the 16-week Curragh Mine dispute in the mid 1990s, the Patricks waterfront lockout in the late 1990s through to the current BHP Billiton – Mitsubishi Alliance (BMA) EBA dispute of 2012. No doubt there will be further disputes in the future that will involve AMWU members in the coal industry, either directly or indirectly.

The Curragh dispute of 1997 emphasised the importance of the QCSS and the significance of community support in industrial disputes. However, it also highlighted the problems of inter-union rivalry in the industry. This dispute began at the Blackwater mine in May 1997 following a breakdown in negotiations between the company, ARCO, and the Single Bargaining Unit (SBU), representing the AMWU, CFMEU and ETU. ARCO's initial insistence on a reduction in manning levels, unfettered use of contractors, as well as issues relating to performance payments, led to union members walking off the job.

The strike lasted 16 weeks. Negotiations resumed on 10 June, but again stalled late in July over issues relating to the use of contractors and other work practices, and the company's rejection of union counteroffers on changes to work practices. From the point of view of the three unions, ARCO was claiming complete and total control over workers, who were legitimately resisting. The company also rejected an SBU suggestion of third-party mediation, responding instead with the introduction of staff to operate equipment and subsequent advice to the SBU that in early September it would withdraw from all agreements with its workforce.

The QCSS played a critical role in this strike. On its initiative, a $20 weekly levy was struck among AMWU members in the coal industry to support the Curragh workforce, a figure later raised to $30. This remained in place for the duration of the strike. Equally importantly, the QCSS led community mobilisation in support of the Curragh strikers. From the first days of the strike, picket lines had been established just outside Blackwater, and these were maintained by union members as well as members of mining communities across the Bowen basin. Such community support proved essential in maintaining the morale of the strikers, particularly after the strike dragged into its third month.

The company and the workers were ordered to resume work by the Australian Industrial Relations Commission (AIRC) in early September, although the company's first instincts had been to pay members without offering work. Employment recommenced after a further two weeks of difficult negotiations, although, even then, in its first pay for three months, the company took out 15 weeks of accumulated deductions, leaving pay packets a bit skinny.

The resumption of negotiations for a new agreement now led to tensions between the unions on-site, particularly between the AMWU and CFMEU. The CFMEU resumed its campaign to recruit AMWU members, both by offering a higher amount of strike pay and at times claiming that the AMWU was selling out members' interests. This tactic failed totally; indeed, a number of non-union members joined the AMWU to the consternation of the CFMEU. However, the increasing tension between the unions reflected different approaches to resolving the dispute. AMWU members did not appreciate the CFMEU acting unilaterally in discussions with the employer either.

The AMWU believed that conciliation was proving ineffective and as a consequence took a decision to reach an agreement at Curragh that took the matter out of the court and back into the workplace, with decent outcomes for members. For the AMWU, the outstanding questions remained the size of a wage increase and the resolution of 'Last On, First Off' (LOFO) provisions, although, because of the large number of expected voluntary redundancies, LOFO was not considered to be a major problem. CFMEU rejection of an interim package negotiated with the company did not help matters. And when AMWU and ETU members did not take part in a 24-hour stoppage called by the CFMEU, collaboration between the unions hit rock bottom. The QCSS maintained a clear strategy designed to maximise the conditions of Curragh workers from the outset. Negotiations with the company resulted in the best possible outcome for its members, while CFMEU efforts proved less successful. With relations between the two unions at a low ebb, many Curragh workers opted to be employed as non-unionists under Australian

Workplace Agreements (AWAs), while for a number of years the AMWU became the biggest union on-site.

Relations between the unions on-site have been rebuilt since 1997. There is now a strong SBU again. The drift to AWAs was halted (and they have now been abolished), while a number of the deficient conditions conceded in the aftermath of the Curragh dispute have been substantially improved.

Nearly two decades previously, in the formative years of the QCSS, another protracted strike had served to define the close links between the industrial militancy and community activism of the QCSS and AMWU members on the Queensland coalfields. The 'tax dispute' of 1980 lasted for 12 weeks and revolved around an attempt by the Fraser government to impose a tax on subsidised housing enjoyed by mineworkers as a result of negotiations with the mining companies a generation earlier. Unionists understood this attempt to tax a 'non-taxable' condition of employment stemmed from the Commonwealth's need to make up tax revenue foregone in 1978 when a reduction in the export coal levy on companies saved them millions of dollars at the expense of public revenue.

Australian Taxation Office figures suggested that housing at Moura, for instance, where miners were paying a subsidised weekly rent of $13.40, was to be taxed at a value of between $40 to $60 weekly, commencing in May 1980. Communities at Blackwater, Gregory, Dysart and Moranbah were also involved. Walkouts stopped all these mines in late June 1980, although essential services were maintained to ensure mine safety. This strike cost both the Commonwealth government and coal companies millions of dollars in revenue, and was ultimately settled by the adoption of a revised formula for establishing tax rates for such housing and an agreement with employers to upgrade housing conditions in exchange for a small rental increase, thereby forestalling any likelihood of a tax on such subsidised housing.

However, the real significance of this strike was the degree of community support and direct involvement that sustained such protracted action and enabled the striking miners to take the attack up to the federal government. In this respect, the level of community organisation and corroboration echoes that of Victoria's Wonthaggi mineworkers throughout their legendary five-month strike in 1934, during the depths of the Great Depression.

With essential services guaranteed, mineworkers formed strike committees that in turn elected an overall strike committee to coordinate union resistance. This group met every Friday at Blackwater (where the QCSS also met), with reports back to all sites the following Monday. Mineworker's families were intimately involved in this strike from the outset. The local Miner's Women's

Auxiliaries provided early funding to set up 'Strike Offices' that operated five days a week, maintaining a flow of information and a support centre for community members, as well as establishing the Moura 'Food barn' and other community centres for the distribution of food and other relief. As one participant recalls in a later conversation:

> Strike committees worked on a points system to establish what each family was entitled to get each week for their food. Lots of donations were coming into the head strike committee ... Each town had their own set up to distribute goods to their people [to receive] extra donations of fruit and vegetables. Meat was donated from local graziers in each area, with one Moura grazier donating a beast per week to be cut up into steaks and mince for the striking miners. One week a goat was donated for mince, but once the word got around, Moura Committee had some excess mince left over to be used the next week.

Women, the wives and partners of the overwhelmingly male workforce, joined striking miners' representatives in touring Australia to address stop-work meetings and explain the implications of the strike for workers in many other industries. Many other wives and partners took advantage of the rules governing unemployment benefits to apply for such a benefit while the strike lasted. As a result, it was later estimated that the federal government was actually paying as much as $20,000 each week to the wives of striking mineworkers, with additional payments for dependent children.

Union advocacy attracted widespread support from other unions and the Labor Party. Unexpectedly, conservative politicians such as Queensland Premier Joh Bjelke-Petersen also supported the campaign. Action by the Queensland Trades and Labour Council led to the suspension of hire purchase repayments for the strike's duration: local organisation provided offices and other facilities rent free. By the end of the strike, cash donations from around Australia had exceeded a million dollars, in addition to the large amounts of food donated locally.

In August, a number of leading federal ministers visited coal communities to address strike leaders and gauge the temper of the miners. At Blackwater, tempers flared and John Howard got a bit roughed up after the meeting had concluded. Strikers were not about to give way, and the escalating cost of the strike drove a compromise solution. Work resumed on 8 September following mass meetings that voted overwhelmingly to accept the solution worked out by the Strike Committee, employers and government representatives. The victory would have been inconceivable without the level of direct community support the mineworkers enjoyed.

Since 1974, there have been many industrial battles fought by AMWU members in the coal industry: for improvement in safety, miners' pensions and superannuation, the provision of work clothing, the 35-hour week, job allowances, increases in sick leave, annual leave and long service provisions. Some of these claims have been pursued site by site, but more often they were fought on an industry basis with the unity provided by members across many sites acting in concert to ensure the delivery of outcomes in most cases over and above industry standards. On many occasions this has put coal industry workers at odds with some state and federal governments who have tried to constrain, or reverse a number of these hard won benefits. On many occasions industrial stoppages have been undertaken, some brief, but many lasting for weeks or even months, to protect our hard won gains.

Coal mining remains a dangerous industry, whether for production or maintenance workers. It is impossible to ignore the impact of the many disasters that have taken place in the Queensland coal industry, with many lives having been lost in the Mount Mulligan disaster, the later Collinsville disaster, the Box Flat explosion at Ipswich in the 1970s, to the many lives lost at Moura with the Kianga (20 September 1975), Number 2 (7 August 1994) and Number 4 Underground (16 July 1986) disasters. While as a result of union action there has been much improvement in the health and safety conditions for mineworkers, it has been achieved at a terrible price for the workers, their families and the mining communities. The Miners' Memorial Day is now held on 19 September each year, since its inception in 2009. This Memorial Day is always held on the anniversary date of the Mt Mulligan disaster that resulted in 75 miners paying the ultimate price for the winning of underground coal.

Safety in coal mining has improved over the years, but still has a long way to go, as workers are still being injured and killed on the job. More challenging work conditions, such as 12-hour shifts and extended rosters, inevitably present new challenges to safe working environments. And safety is not simply an issue on the job. 'Drive in, drive out' employment presents its own challenges, with an increase in mineworker road fatalities on the increase.

Prior to the advent of enterprise bargaining, coal industry workers were covered by the Coal Mining Industry Award, which regulated the pay and conditions of the miners, electrical and engineering tradespeople, and engine drivers and firemen in the industry. The Award's terms, conditions and entitlements was generally in line with national wage case decisions, a number of significant improvements were won after local industrial campaigns involving the QCSS and AMWU coal industry employees. This included the 35-hour week, increases in provisions for annual and sick leave, bonus agreements and work value cases. All of these matters led to improvements to wages and conditions for coal employees.

New winds were blowing in the late 1980s. The Australian Council of Trade Unions (ACTU) was promoting its 'Future Strategies Policy', which would have a dramatic effect on coal industry employees, including AMWU members, especially with regard to 'Principal & Significant Union Status'. This policy introduced the rationalisation and amalgamation of many unions and union membership, as well as new principles guiding the demarcation of union membership, including the 'Principles of Competition', 'Union Membership Moratorium' and 'Greenfield Agreements'. These policies significantly impacted the AMWU membership in the coal industry. At the same time, negotiations for a new industry agreement and award restructuring, under the 'Structural Efficiency Principle', was taking place. All of these developments saw significant movement away from the traditional awards, such as the coal industry award.

With changes to the Industrial Relations Act in 1988, the 'Enterprise Bargaining Principles' and Certified Agreements became the means by which enterprise bargaining started to take shape by 1991. Later in the 1990s, the coal industry award came under further attack from the 'Award Simplification' process put in place by the Liberal government of the day. Through this award simplification process the Coal Industry Production & Engineering Award that covered coal industry workers had a provision inserted that allowed for enterprise bargaining in the black coal industry. This provision, known as Clause 20 agreements, allowed for the substitution and/or trade-off of any matters in the agreement if agreed to by all respondents. This was the start of the deviation away from the award and award conditions, but around the same time, the federal government also imposed a freeze on wage increases in the coal industry award for nearly 10 years. Further bad news occurred in 1995 with the abolition of the Coal Industry Tribunal, which brought the coal industry into the mainstream of the AIRC. This then saw further change with the election of the Rudd Labor government in 2007, when the AIRC underwent change to then become Fair Work Australia, which oversaw the award modernisation process that led to the old Coal Industry Production and Engineering Consolidated Award being changed to the Black Coal Mining Industry Award 2010.

With the move away from the award, the only way terms and conditions could be improved was through enterprise bargaining, which often forced unions into a position of having to trade off some employment conditions in order to gain wage increases or other improvements on the job. Clearly, such a process was to the disadvantage of workers, and the QCSS played a crucial role in protecting the interests of AMWU members. Most importantly, the QCSS served as the collective memory of the workforce, providing a historical perspective on the conditions of employment in the industry. This deliberate process of education emphasised the importance of base wage rates and the 35-hour week, promoting workplace discussions on the primary significance and ways to protect them. Similarly, the QCSS first debated and then confirmed targets for union claims in bargaining, coordinating its work with that of union organisers. Such a strategy resulted in general improvements for employees, such as the introduction of medical redundancies while also negotiating and implementing initiatives at individual sites – the introduction of an insurance scheme at Moura, in addition to workers' compensation, is a good example of this.

As referred to above, the disbanding of the Queensland Coal Board of Reference and the Coal Industry Tribunal in 1995 caused major problems for the industry. While working in concert with the AIRC, these organisations were unique to the coal industry. Their impact over many years cannot be ignored. Neither were creatures of the unions: the QCSS regularly and vigorously disagreed with many decisions. But at least they had an affinity with mineworkers and understood the coal industry. We should acknowledge the impact of Norm Mansini, who was Board of Reference Queensland chairman for many years, Coal Industry Tribunal Chairman David Duncan and AIRC Commissioner Ken Bacon, who held many coal industry hearings over the years as well.

Sometimes they would be convinced by our arguments, sometimes not, but their affinity with the industry ensured a continuing influence. In this respect, many of the determinations of the Coal Industry Tribunal had a particular impact on AMWU members. These include the Huntley decision of 1952 and the AEU and Federated Mine Mechanics decision of 1968, the Fumini decision of 1979 and the Gunnedah dispute of 1984 (all relating to demarcation issues limiting AMWU coverage in the industry). Later CIT decisions, in regard to the South Bulli demarcation dispute in 1990 and a similar decision in the same year relating to the coverage of maintenance tradesmen at the Gordonstone mine in Queensland, served to further confine AMWU coverage.

This encroachment on AMWU coverage in the coal industry came to a head in the early 1990s, the Miners Federation commenced a planned assault on AMWU membership. Their confidence was based both on a series of tribunal decisions that favoured production unions over tradespersons' unions and on the partiality shown to the Miners Federation by senior ACTU officials in identifying a number of mine sites and mine projects as 'greenfield' sites, thereby allowing the United Mineworkers Federation of Australia exclusive coverage.

Since the time of the First World War, the Miners Federation had argued the case for a single union in the mining industry, although this position had never been accepted by unions such as the Engineers Union or the Engine Drivers and Firemen. This time, however, UMFA and its successor, the CFMEU, enjoyed more success. The majority of AMWU membership in NSW was swallowed up by UMFA. AMWU membership was decimated and the union has never really recovered the ground lost in NSW at that time. In the same period, nearly a third of our membership was also lost in Queensland. However, the overwhelming majority of the AMWU membership in Queensland held firm to the view that their interests were best served by the union that has historically represented the mechanical trades: the AMWU. The difference between the course of events in NSW and in Queensland can be largely attributed to the actions of the QCSS, supported by a number of key officials, particularly National Organiser John Royle and Ron Keating, who by then was state president of the union. In particular, the structure of the QCSS and its direct links back into individual mine sites enabled the union's Queensland membership to be continually updated and informed of developments across the industry. Special meetings were also held at Blackwater, Rockhampton, Emerald and Mackay.

The support of key officials, arguments based on the history and the influence of the union in the mining industry, and the impact of well-trained, committed delegates all contributed to the AMWU holding its ground in Queensland. A further attempt to poach AMWU members occurred a few years later, following the amalgamation of the Miners Federation and the FEDFA into the CFMEU (Mining and Energy Division), but resistance again led by the QCSS ensured that the impact in Queensland was muted. Today, some tradespeople in the Queensland coal industry still remain CFMEU members, but the vast majority continue to be with the AMWU. Since the 1990s a significant number of former members have now elected to rejoin the AMWU and our membership on the Queensland coalfields currently stands at nearly 1000, with hundreds more employed by industry contractors. And the relations with the CFMEU are again cordial. However, we work in an environment that is hostile in a number of key respects. As a union, we must ensure that in future we do not face these problems again, and an informed and engaged membership, backed by industry coverage that allows the AMWU to protect its members, is our best guarantee.

The AMWU has a proud history in the Queensland coal industry, stretching back for more than a century. In this history, particularly over the past 38 years, the Queensland Coal Shop Stewards have survived many turbulent periods, industrial disputations, union demarcation fights, the boom and bust of coal mining in Central Queensland, hostile governments, and attempts by employers to marginalise trade union organisation. It remains proud of its achievements in the fields of working conditions, wages, superannuation, health and safety on the job, and the health of the communities that support the coal industry and the AMWU.

The work of the QCSS is not finished: it remains an important instrument in the AMWU's future industrial campaigns. And not only in the future. Current campaigning for the health of coal communities, constraints on the uncontrolled growth of 'fly in, fly out' employment arrangements and negotiations for affordable accommodation in the mining towns and communities of regional Queensland are major social (and industrial) priorities facing both the QCSS and the AMWU. On the industrial front, reclaiming certain conditions of employment from the 'Prohibited Content' deep freeze of the Howard years' Work Choices laws, and addressing the outsourcing of what are legitimately permanent mine jobs to the many contracting companies who have moved into the coal industry, remain priority targets.

Queensland CSS Membership

Over the years there have been many delegates who have represented their respective coal mine branches as AMWU delegates, Queensland Coal Shop Stewards delegates, Queensland Coal Shop Stewards Steering Committee members, National Coal Committee members, State Council and State Conference delegates, and National Conference delegates. There are many names too numerous to mention, apologies if any are missed. We will try and do justice to all of the branches:

> Moura – Hec Hoskings, Reg Woodward, Peter Wetherall, John Hempseed and Maurice Bissell

Callide – Rob Thompson, Peter Lees, Chris Harper

BMA Blackwater – Tom Hall, Max Tanzer, Rocky Daniels, Gary Howard

Curragh – Jeff Hume, Phil Pitt, Jeff Brotchie

BMA Goonyella/Riverside – Jack Kosh, Jeff Bail, Ian Humphreys, Mark Johnstone

Tarong – Tom Reilly

Collinsville – Walter Bulloch

The current four-member Steering Committee has a total of 105 years experience in the Queensland coal industry.

Chris Harper – Member no. 4045719

John Hempseed – Member no. 4017567

Mark Johnstone – Member no. 4070290

Jeff Brotchie – Member no. 4134321.

Acknowledgements

It is important that the contribution the Queensland Coal Shop Stewards and AMWU rank-and-file members in the coal industry be both recognised and remembered.

One of the big strengths of the Coal Shop Stewards has been the amount of committed and skilled delegates who have been nurtured and trained along the way to enable them to organise their own workplaces to a high degree of efficiency. In this respect, they all stand in the great union tradition of committed shop stewards and effective on-the-job organisation.

We have also been privileged to have a number of outstanding state officials who started their tenure as organisers, men such as Ron 'Buster' Keating, Kev Dwyer, Austin 'Aussie' Vaughan, Dave Harrison, Rene Veltmeyer and Peter Lees, who worked their way to executive positions at the AMWU Queensland state branch. We also were privileged to have very outstanding national officials in Harry Gillman, Jack Kidd, Billy Martin, John Royle and Pat Johnstone. Recently, we have had the help and assistance of Callen Parsons, National Industrial Officer.

Along the journey we also have also benefited from the support of State Secretary (now National President) Andrew Dettmer, Howard Smith, Bill

Welch, Jeff Hume at the Rockhampton and Mackay offices; with current officials being Phil Golby, Jason Lund and Assistant State Secretary (now State Secretary) Rohan Webb; and also trainers like Sean Mountford, Brian Devlin and recently Doug Loggie.

It would also be remiss not to mention the work of AMWU Rockhampton Office Secretary Elaine Rasmussen, who has held the office together for over 25 years, and the tireless efforts of Caroline Pryor from the National Office in Sydney who provided many a document for reference from the Coal Industry Archives going back many years.

Notes on Contributors

Nikola Belnave is Senior Lecturer in the Department of Marketing and Management, Faculty of Business and Economics at Macquarie University. Her research since 2005 has focused on consumer cooperatives in Australia and New Zealand. Nikola is president of the Australian Society of Labour History and is Deputy Editor of the society's journal, *Labour History*.

Cathy Brigden is an Associate Professor in the School of Management and Co-ordinator of the Women + Work research cluster in the Centre for Sustainable Organisations and Work at RMIT University. Her recent research has focused on recovering and restoring the historical patterns of women trade unionist's activism through her study of women delegates in the Melbourne Trades Hall Council and her work on the history of the Female Confectioners Union.

Chris Harper is a long-term delegate of the AMWU in the Queensland Coal Industry. Commencing his apprenticeship at Callide Mine in 1980, he joined the union as a second-year apprentice in 1981. At the conclusion of his apprenticeship, Chris went to South Blackwater, retaining his union membership. He then returned to Callide Mine in 1987, when he became an AMWU delegate, a position he has held continuously since. Chris has been an active participant in the AMWU Education Program which has further honed his considerable skills. Chris has been Convenor of the AMWU at Callide Mine and Secretary of the Queensland Coal Shop Stewards since 1996 and AMWU State Councillor & State Conference Delegate for a number of years. Chris is passionate about apprenticeships, and has mentored many apprentices in his workplace as well as encouraging them to become AMWU members and grow the union. Chris and his fellow AMWU members support many community and junior sporting organisations through yearly donations in and around the Biloela community.

John Hempseed joined the Amalgamated Engineering Union as a second year apprentice fitter in 1971, while employed at the Mount Morgan gold mine. When Mount Morgan closed, John shifted to Moura coal mine in 1972. While he has been employed there continuously since, the mine has been owned by Thiess-Peabody-Mitsui, BHP, Dampier Coal, Utah, Peabody, Rio Tinto (Coal and Allied), and now Anglo. John has been a delegate since 1974, and convenor at Moura since 1996. Since 2004 he has been Chair of the QCSS. John is heavily involved in his local community through the fishing club, support for breast cancer research, Moura hospital, and the soccer club, where he is a life member after coaching many teams. Recently retired from work (but not the union), he and his wife Mary have been married since 1973.

Glenys Lindner is a member of the CFMEU and the CPSU. She started work at the Tasmanian Government Printing Office as a fifteen year old in 1980, joining the Printing and Kindred Industries Union, one of the AMWU's antecedents. She later joined the Commonwealth public service. Glenys is a busy mother of two, working full time and studying part time at the University of Tasmania. She gets her greatest enjoyment from being organised.

Ric McCracken is an artist and labour movement activist, with a long history of involvement in community project development. Based in Western Australia he has worked as Arts Officer for the Trades and Labour Council, as CEO of the Community Arts Network and as a project manager at Curtin University. He has been involved in a number of research projects relating to the Midland Railway Workshops, where he coordinated a major oral history recovery project and initiated the Interpretation Centre at the workshop's site.

Robyn McQueeney is an AMWU member in Hobart who has a long, albeit second-hand experience of Tasmania's manufacturing industry. She grew up making Barbie dolls from fabric from her mother's workplace, Silk and Textiles. She built caves from boxes in her mother's workplace, Fibre Containers. Then when her mother worked at Cadbury's, a lifelong chocolate addiction was born. Growing up on the wrong side of the tracks, Robyn's inability to climb a tree, ride a bike or do the drawback resigned her to the fate of being a good girl and she has pretty much stuck to that path, working as a public servant and doting on her daughter, Winona.

Bobbie Oliver is Associate Professor of History and Head of the Department of Social Sciences at Curtin University. She has also taught at universities in Western Australia and the ACT and held research positions at the ANU and the Australian War Memorial. Her recent research activities include contributing to history of the East Perth Power Station and a history of the Locomotive Engine Drivers, Firemen and Cleaners Union in Western Australia. Other publications include: *War and Peace in Western Australia*, and *Unity is Strength: The History of the Australian Labor Party and the Trades and Labour Council in Western Australia, 1899–1999.*

Greg Patmore is Professor of Business and Labour History and Director of the Business and Labour History Group and the Co-operative Research Group in the School of Business, University of Sydney. His main interests are labour history, comparative labour history, Rochdale consumer cooperatives and the comparative impact of industrialisation and deindustrialisation of regional economies.

Dr Keir Reeves is based at the Faculty of Arts at Monash University. He is a senior Monash Research Fellow in the School of Journalism, Australian and Indigenous Studies, where his current research concentrates on cultural heritage and history in Australia and the Asian Pacific regions. His recent work in labour history has concentrated on labour heritage in Australia. In 2013 he is a visiting fellow at Clare Hall, Cambrige.

Dr Andrew Scott is an Associate Professor in Politics at Deakin University. He has been a prominent academic since 2000, before which he worked for the AMWU as a research officer (1986–1990) and research consultant (1999). He is the author of three books and many chapters and article on Australian, British and European politics. He has recently been enquiring into, and advocating, the lessons for Australia from the continuing policy achievements of the nation's of Nordic Europe, including their achievements in reducing child poverty.

Cora Trevarthen is from a third generation Queensland Labor family. Her father was born in Mt Isa and joined the ALP after moving to Brisbane. Her maternal grandfather was an ALP member in Townesville and worked as a prices control officer after World War II. Growing up around the ALP in Queensland, Cora saw at first hand the devastating impact of the Split on the party in that state. Following work as a staffer for the Hawke, Keating, Rudd and Gillard Governments, she now works at Deakin University and is a member of the Alfred Deakin Research Institute.